by Peter Farenden

A John Wiley and Sons, Ltd, Publication

ITIL® For Dummies®

Published by
John Wiley & Sons, Ltd
The Atrium
Southern Gate
Chichester
West Sussex
PO19 8SQ
England
www.wiley.com

For general information on our other products and services, please contact our Customer Care Department within the U.S. at 877-762-2974, outside the U.S. at 317-572-3993, or fax 317-572-4002.

For technical support, please visit www.wiley.com/techsupport.

Wiley publishes in a variety of print and electronic formats and by print-on-demand. Some material included with standard print versions of this book may not be included in e-books or in print-on-demand. If this book refers to media such as a CD or DVD that is not included in the version you purchased, you may download this material at http://booksupport.wiley.com. For more information about Wiley products, visit www.wiley.com.

ITIL® is a Registered Trade Mark of the Cabinet Office
The Swirl logo™ is a trade mark of the Cabinet Office © Crown copyright 2011. All rights reserved. Material is reproduced with the permission of the Cabinet Office under delegated authority from the Controller of HMSO.
PRINCE2® is a Registered Trade Mark of the Cabinet Office
MSP® is a Registered Trade Mark of the Cabinet Office
M_o_R® is a Registered Trade Mark of the Cabinet Office
IT Infrastructure Library® is a Registered Trade Mark of the Cabinet Office
Quoted ITIL text is from *ITIL Service Strategy, ITIL Service Design, ITIL Service Transition, ITIL Service Operation* and *ITIL Continual Service Improvement,* all © Crown copyright 2011. Reproduced under licence from the Cabinet Office.

British Library Cataloguing in Publication Data: A catalogue record for this book is available from the British Library

ISBN: 978-1-119-95013-4 (pbk); 978-1-119-95117-9 (ebk); 978-1-119-95119-3 (ebk); 978-1-119-95118-6 (ebk)

Printed and bound in Great Britain by TJ International, Padstow, Cornwall.

10 9 8 7 6 5 4 3 2 1

WILEY

About the Author

Peter Farenden is the Managing Director of Tanlan Training Limited. He is also one of the four principles and directors of Youplus Education Services Limited. These are companies that specialise in service management training, as well as providing training materials to other organisations.

Peter is an IT service management and business analysis consultant trainer with over 30 years of experience spanning IT management, business analysis and project management.

Originally from an engineering background, Peter has applied his skills across many disciplines culminating in joining the training and consultancy profession in 2001. He has practical experience of implementing and managing all service management disciplines gained through the delivery and support of many IT services.

As an active examiner Peter has written and marked papers for both service management and business analysis qualifications. More recently, Peter has been involved with the creation of the new generation of ITIL® Version 3 examination qualifications as a senior examiner for the APM Group.

Peter has trained and assisted representatives from hundreds of companies to develop their skills and IT processes. He prides himself in delivering training courses in a lively and enthusiastic, interactive and innovative manner whilst communicating the subject matter clearly.

Peter passionately believes that ITIL is not dull and boring! The best feedback he receives is when delegates say that a potentially dry subject was made interesting and relevant. In fact, a delegate once described attending Peter's training course as the most fun he'd had with his clothes on.

Peter is an overgrown teenager and still attends noisy rock concerts with his wife and really should know better. When doing none of the above he can be found at home on a mountain in the depths of rural Wales surrounded by sheep.

www.tanlantraining.co.uk

www.you-plus.co.uk

Dedication

This book is dedicated to Georgie.

It is also dedicated to my Mum and Dad and sisters; my middle name really should be *eventually*.

And lastly Adrian, David and Derek; without whom . . . etc, etc.

Author's Acknowledgments

I have spent the last ten years delivering training courses throughout the UK and beyond. I have enjoyed every minute of it. However, occasionally the pastime of admiring the hotel wallpaper does lose its excitement. There are many friends and colleagues that have provided me with an attractive alternative. This normally involves eating and drinking; however the main source of relaxation is the opportunity to engage in the universal language of consultants everyway; fluent rubbish.

The other important point to make about a long period of delivering training courses is that you forget where you first heard the anecdotes and stories that form parts of the courses. In some cases I no longer know if some things happened to me or to other people. The consequence of this is that many of the stories and examples that appear in this book may well have been stolen from others. To those other people; thank you and sorry!

So bearing in mind all of the above my heartfelt thanks go to: Hairy Dave, Bob (ZBD), Mark M, Conrad, Ed, Lisa, Ellis, Mark H; and to anyone else I have forgotten to mention.

Finally, I would not have been able to write this book without the support, help and guidance of those fine folk from John Wiley & Sons. Special mention goes to Kerry Laundon, Simon Bell, Charlie Wilson, Kim Vernon and Mary White.

Publisher's Acknowledgments

We're proud of this book; please send us your comments at `http://dummies.custhelp.com`. For other comments, please contact our Customer Care Department within the U.S. at 877-762-2974, outside the U.S. at 317-572-3993, or fax 317-572-4002.

Some of the people who helped bring this book to market include the following:

Acquisitions, Editorial, and Vertical Websites

Project Editor: Simon Bell

Commissioning Editor: Kerry Laundon

Assistant Editor: Ben Kemble

Development Editor: Charlie Wilson

Copy Editor: Kim Vernon

Technical Editor: APM Group, Ltd.

Proofreader: Mary White

Production Manager: Daniel Mersey

Publisher: David Palmer

Cover Photos: ©iStock/Jordan McCullough

Cartoons: Rich Tennant (`www.the5thwave.com`)

Composition Services

Project Coordinator: Kristie Rees

Layout and Graphics: Claudia Bell, Carl Byers, Joyce Haughey, Sennett Vaughan Johnson, Mark Pinto, Lavonne Roberts

Proofreader: Lauren Mandelbaum

Indexer: Potomac Indexing, LLC

Publishing and Editorial for Consumer Dummies

Kathleen Nebenhaus, Vice President and Executive Publisher

Kristin Ferguson-Wagstaffe, Product Development Director

Ensley Eikenburg, Associate Publisher, Travel

Kelly Regan, Editorial Director, Travel

Publishing for Technology Dummies

Andy Cummings, Vice President and Publisher

Composition Services

Debbie Stailey, Director of Composition Services

Contents at a Glance

Introduction 1

Part I: How ITIL Can Help You 7

Chapter 1: Managing IT Services: Welcome to the World of ITIL 9

Chapter 2: Using the Building Blocks of ITIL 19

Chapter 3: Outlining the Structure of ITIL 37

Part II: Getting to Grips with the Service Lifecycle and the Processes 61

Chapter 4: Thinking It Through: Service Strategy 63

Chapter 5: Are We All Agreed? Service Design Part 1:
   The Relationship Management Processes 95

Chapter 6: Designing Services to Be Fit for Use: Service Design Part 2:
   The Warranty Processes 117

Chapter 7: Getting Physical: Service Transition 139

Chapter 8: Making Services Work Every Day: Service Operation 167

Chapter 9: Striving to Do Better: Continual Service Improvement 195

Part III: Getting Practical 215

Chapter 10: Implementing ITIL 217

Chapter 11: Getting Carried Away: Using Service
   Management as a Strategic Asset 245

Chapter 12: Going Back to the Drawing Board: Design Projects 265

Chapter 13: Organising the Troops: Transition Projects 281

Part IV: The Part of Tens 301

Chapter 14: Ten Ways to Help ITIL Work for You 303

Chapter 15: Ten Key Bits of ITIL: Some Possible Quick Wins 309

Chapter 16: Ten Places to Go for Help 317

Part V: Appendixes 323

Appendix A: Getting Qualified in ITIL 325

Appendix B: Glossary 333

Appendix C: Cross Referencing Processes 349

Index 355

Table of Contents

Introduction *1*

About This Book 1
Foolish Assumptions..2
How This Book Is Organised 3
    Part I: How ITIL Can Help You...............................3
    Part II: Getting to Grips with the Service
        Lifecycle and the Processes 3
    Part III: Getting Practical................................3
    Part IV: The Part of Tens..................................4
    Part V: Appendixes 4
Icons Used in This Book 4
Where to Go from Here..5

Part 1: How ITIL Can Help You *7*

Chapter 1: Managing IT Services: Welcome to the World of ITIL.....9

Defining Some Basic Terms 10
Equating Service Management with Customer Service 11
    Seeing why IT service users complain 11
    Understanding the IT provider's point of view..............12
    Why can't customers and IT just talk to each other? 12
    Improving IT services.....................................13
Understanding ITIL: Best Practice Guidance 13
Piecing Together the Jigsaw: The Content of ITIL...............15
Debunking Some Common Misconceptions about ITIL................16
    Treating ITIL as training only 16
    Misinterpreting ITIL......................................16
    Thinking ITIL is for the service desk and support staff only..........17
    Believing that processes introduce unnecessary bureaucracy.....17
    Assuming that ITIL uses a lot of time, staff and money 17
Taking the ITIL Qualifications 18

Chapter 2: Using the Building Blocks of ITIL 19

Defining Services 19
Understanding IT Service Management............................21
Understanding Who Provides the IT Services 22

Knowing the IT Service Management Stakeholders 23
    The user 23
    The customer 24
    The supplier 24
Creating Value 25
    Considering utility 25
    Weighing up warranty 26
Having the Right Assets 27
    Resources 27
    Capabilities 28
    Using your assets 29
Exploring Processes, Functions and Roles 30
    Understanding processes 30
    Understanding functions 31
    Understanding roles 32
    Using processes, functions and roles in service management 32
Who Does What? Looking at Some Important Roles 32
    The service owner 33
    The process owner 34
    The process manager 34
    The process practitioner 35
Understanding Governance 35

Chapter 3: Outlining the Structure of ITIL 37

Getting to Know the Service Lifecycle 37
    Introducing service strategy 39
    Considering service design 41
    Looking at service transition 42
    Moving on to service operation 43
    Maintaining success with continual service improvement 44
    Applying the service lifecycle to IT projects 45
So Who Actually Carries Out ITIL Activities?
  Understanding the Functions 46
Dealing with the Users: The Service Desk 49
    Knowing what the service desk does 50
    Choosing a service desk structure 51
    Getting the right service desk staff 53
Managing the Day-to-day Stuff: IT Operations Management 54
    Considering teams and skills 55
    Looking at typical activities 55
Managing the Technology 56
    Considering teams and skills 56
    Looking at typical activities 57
Managing the Applications 58
    Considering teams and skills 59
    Looking at typical activities 59

Part II: Getting to Grips with the Service Lifecycle and the Processes 61

Chapter 4: Thinking It Through: Service Strategy 63
Understanding Strategy 64
Understanding the Purpose of the Service Strategy Stage 65
Understanding Some Basic Principles 66
    The value proposition 66
    Understanding what the customer wants 67
    Service providers 67
Overview of the Service Strategy Processes 68
Knowing Your Services: Service Portfolio Management 69
    Defining some service portfolio management terms 69
    Looking at the activities of service portfolio management 75
Managing Your Finances: Financial Management for IT Services 78
    Creating a cost model 79
    Creating a business case 81
    Looking at the activities of financial management
       for IT services 82
Identifying the Demand: Demand Management 83
    Defining some demand management terms 84
    Looking at the activities of demand management 86
Getting Friendly with Your Customers:
    Business Relationship Management 88
    Explaining the terminology 89
    The activities of business relationship management 90
Using Technology for Service Strategy 92
    Technology to support the service strategy activities 92
    Automation 93

Chapter 5: Are We All Agreed? Service Design Part 1: The Relationship Management Processes 95
Understanding the Purpose of the Service Design Lifecycle Stage 96
Understanding Some Basic Principles 96
    Keeping in mind the four Ps of service design 96
    Knowing the five aspects of service design 97
    Creating a service design package 97
Managing Service Levels: Service Level Management 98
    Defining some service level management terms 98
    Looking at the activities of service level management 103
Keeping Information about the Live Services:
    Service Catalogue Management 107
    Defining the service catalogue 107
    Looking at the activities of service catalogue management 110

Getting Friendly with Third-party Suppliers: Supplier Management 110
Defining some supplier management terms 112
Looking at the activities of supplier management 113
Design Coordination 115
Identifying Service Design Roles 116

Chapter 6: Designing Services to Be Fit for Use: Service Design Part 2: The Warranty Processes 117

Making Sure the Service Is Available: Availability Management 118
Seeing the process in action 119
Defining some availability management terms 120
Improving availability 121
Looking at the activities of availability management 121
Have We Got Enough? Capacity Management 123
Defining some capacity management terms 125
Understanding capacity management sub-processes 126
Looking at the activities of capacity management 127
Being Prepared for Anything: IT Service Continuity Management 128
Defining some IT service continuity management terms 129
Looking at the activities of IT service continuity management ... 130
Ensuring Security: Information Security Management 131
Defining some information security management terms 133
Looking at the activities of information security management ... 136
Identifying Service Design Roles 137

Chapter 7: Getting Physical: Service Transition 139

Understanding the Purpose of the Service Transition Lifecycle Phase ... 139
Looking at an Overview of the Service Transition Processes 140
Controlling Change: Change Management 141
Defining some change management terms 142
Deciding the scope of your change management process 144
Looking at the activities of change management 144
Knowing What You've Got: Service Asset and Configuration
Management 148
Understanding the asset and configuration aspects 148
Defining some service asset and configuration management
terms 149
Looking at the activities of SACM 151
Getting the Release Out There: Release and Deployment
Management 154
Defining some release and deployment management terms 155
Looking at the activities of release and deployment
management 158
Making Better Decisions: Knowledge Management 160
Defining some knowledge management terms 161
Looking at the activities 162
Transition Planning and Support 163
Identifying Service Transition Roles 164

Chapter 8: Making Services Work Every Day: Service Operation . .167

Understanding the Purpose of the Service Operation
  Lifecycle Stage..168
Understanding Some Basic Principles.......................................169
  Getting the balance right 169
  Communicating well 170
Listening to the Technology: Event Management 170
  Defining some event management terminology.....................171
  Looking at the activities of event management 172
Stuff Happens: Incident Management 174
  Balancing incident management and problem management.......174
  Defining some incident management terms 175
  Looking at the activities of incident management.................176
Dealing with Those Strange Things the User Asks for:
  Request Fulfilment 179
  Defining some request fulfilment terms................................181
  Looking at the activities of request fulfilment 182
Allowing the Right People to Use Your Services: Access Management ... 183
  Defining some access management terms...............................183
  Looking at the activities of access management 185
Getting to the Bottom of an Issue: Problem Management 186
  Defining some problem management terms............................186
  Looking at the problem management activities 189
Identifying Service Operation Roles...191
  Service desk roles 192
  Incident management, request fulfilment and access
    management roles..192
  Problem management roles...193
  Event management roles..193

Chapter 9: Striving to Do Better: Continual Service Improvement . .195

Understanding the Purpose of the CSI Lifecycle Stage...........196
Understanding Some Basic Principles.......................................197
  Looking at the activities...197
  Creating a business case for improvement 199
  Identifying baselines...200
  Keeping a register of improvements 201
Knowing Where to Start...201
  The Deming Cycle 201
  The CSI approach..202
Measuring, Measuring, Measuring 204
  Identifying what to measure...204
  Deciding what to measure and how 205
  Working out how to use measurements 206
  Understanding the seven-step improvement process.................207
Linking Governance and CSI..210
Getting to Grips with Risk..210
Identifying CSI Roles..212

Part III: Getting Practical 215

Chapter 10: Implementing ITIL 217

Planning to Implement ITIL 218
    Seeing how projects fit with implementing ITIL 218
    Using the service lifecycle to implement the ITIL processes......219
Creating a Plan for Your Implementation Project 220
    Using the CSI approach 221
    Grouping ITIL processes for implementation 222
    Implementing the service lifecycle 224
    Assessing the maturity of processes 225
    Deciding which processes and in what order 226
Designing Your Processes 227
    Knowing what to adopt and what to adapt 227
    Allocating roles and responsibilities and using the RACI matrix.....228
Following an Example Implementation Project 232
    The scenario 232
    The planning phase 233
    The design phase 234
Dealing with the People Stuff: Organisational Change............241
    Planning to involve people 242
    Identifying stakeholders 243
    Communicating effectively 243

Chapter 11: Getting Carried Away: Using Service Management as a Strategic Asset 245

Defining a Strategic Asset 246
Creating a Strategy for Your Services: Strategy Management
    for IT Services..246
    Carrying out a strategic assessment 247
    Generating strategy 248
    Executing strategy 249
Defining Services 251
    Step 1: Defining the market and identifying customers 251
    Step 2: Understanding the customer 252
    Step 3: Quantifying the outcomes 252
    Step 4: Classifying and visualising the service..............253
    Step 5: Understanding the opportunities (market spaces) 254
    Step 6: Defining services based on outcomes 254
    Step 7: Defining service models 254
    Step 8: Defining service units and packages................255
Working through Examples 255
    Internal provider example 255
    External provider example 257
Using Service Portfolio Management to Implement Your Strategy.......259
    Have you already got a suitable service? 259
    Using the activities of service portfolio management.............260
Getting to Grips with Demand Management 260

Chapter 12: Going Back to the Drawing Board: Design Projects . . .265

Seeing What Happens in a Service Design Project 265
Gathering and analysing requirements 266
Designing solutions 267
Bringing Together ITIL and Service Design Projects 270
Following the design process 270
Coordinating the design processes 272
ITIL and requirements 273
ITIL and design 274
Looking at an Example of a Service Design Project 277

Chapter 13: Organising the Troops: Transition Projects 281

Introducing Service Transition Projects 281
Seeing What Happens in a Service Transition Project 283
Getting started 283
Building services 283
Testing the service 285
Implementing the service 287
Bringing Together ITIL and Service Transition Projects 288
Service validation and testing 288
Change evaluation 290
Linking the service transition processes 291
ITIL and build, test and implement 292
Finishing off the projects: business acceptance and sign-off 295
Looking at an Example of a Service Transition Project 296

Part IV: The Part of Tens 301

Chapter 14: Ten Ways to Help ITIL Work for You 303

Detailing Your Vision for ITIL 303
Having a Plan 304
Doing Your Homework: Building a Good Business Case 304
Involving People 305
Getting the Right People Involved 305
Communicating 306
Documenting 306
Training 307
Being Pragmatic 308
Persevering When Something Doesn't Go as Planned 308

Chapter 15: Ten Key Bits of ITIL: Some Possible Quick Wins 309

Implementing Basic Service Level Management 309
Introducing a Service Level Agreement 310
Creating an Operational Level Agreement 311
Setting Up a Service Desk 312
Cataloguing Services 312

Establishing Some Basic Change Control...313
Knowing the Difference between Incidents and Problems 313
Measuring Your Achievements...314
Gathering Tools 314
Getting Your Staff ITIL Trained...315

Chapter 16: Ten Places to Go for Help **317**
Your Colleagues...317
The Internet..318
Cabinet Office 319
APM Group 319
Examination Institutes 320
ITIL Live 320
IT Service Management Forum (ITSMF) 321
ISO/IEC 20000 321
Complementary Approaches 321
SFIA 322

Part V: Appendixes **323**

Appendix A: Getting Qualified in ITIL. **325**
Looking at the ITIL Qualification Structure...325
Foundation..326
Intermediate 327
Expert 329
Master..330
Examining the Exams 330
Knowing Where to Attend Courses and Sit Exams...............................331

Appendix B: Glossary **333**

Appendix C: Cross Referencing Processes. **349**

Index **355**

Introduction

● ●

*M*aking computers work the way you want them to should be easy – shouldn't it? Information technology (IT) is now everywhere; you can't get away from it. Walking down the road you see people doing the *texting walk:* wandering aimlessly across the pavement because they're either reading or writing a text on their mobile phone. Mobile phones, e-books, tablets, laptops, the Internet, websites – you can't get away from IT. But does IT do what you want it to do? Do the companies that provide the technology know what you want? Do they provide the necessary support to go with the systems? I expect you've spent many a happy hour trying to get through to the right person at a call centre who can resolve your issue. By the time you've waited, listening to recorded messages all the time, at least you know that your call is of *importance* to them. They tell you enough times!

Well, a whole topic out there in the big wide world is dedicated to managing IT systems in such a way that customers – people like you and me – get what they want. I'm talking about *IT service management.*

ITIL® For Dummies is a book about IT service management. In others words, this book's about managing IT services. ITIL, which stands for *Information Technology Infrastructure Library,* is a bunch of books published by the UK Government that describes best practice for service management. The trouble is that these are five quite long books that can appear a bit theoretical and unfriendly. Don't get me wrong, the ITIL books are excellent. But they're a bit much to take in all in one go if you just want a flavour, or overview, of what ITIL is. So that's where this book comes in . . .

ITIL® and IT Infrastructure Library® are Registered Trade Marks of the Cabinet Office.

About This Book

This book describes ITIL as simply as possible, avoiding technical language and explaining in simple terms. You find plenty of examples – some of them very ordinary, day-to-day situations – that help you understand the principles and concepts. The basic principles of ITIL are very straightforward, and I hope to prove that.

For those of you who have experience of working in IT departments and organisations, you may read some of this book and think to yourselves, 'That'll never work in my organisation!' Please remember that ITIL is *guidance*. It's full of good ideas about managing IT systems and services. It's not prescriptive. ITIL describes the things you would like to do if you had the time and money. I like to think of the ideal world of ITIL as the place in which you do things *properly*. In this case, *properly* refers to understanding what customers wants, agreeing it with them, and then providing it. Everyone should aspire to doing things properly.

No substitute exists for the ITIL books themselves. *ITIL For Dummies* isn't a replacement for the ITIL books; it's a simple introduction to the principles and framework of ITIL. So when it comes to applying the information I supply in this book to your organisation, I urge you to pick up the ITIL books for more detail. They're an excellent reference.

Quoted ITIL text is from *ITIL Service Strategy*, *ITIL Service Design*, *ITIL Service Transition*, *ITIL Service Operation* and *ITIL Continual Service Improvement*, all © Crown copyright 2011. Reproduced under licence from the Cabinet Office.

Throughout the text, I have indicated where text is quoted from ITIL publications, and placed it within inverted commas.

Foolish Assumptions

Someone wise once said, 'Never assume anything other than the fact that some idiot will assume something.' Still, in writing the book, I found it necessary to make a few assumptions:

- ✔ You don't know very much about ITIL yet. If you do know a bit, that's a bonus.

- ✔ You know a little bit about IT. You can at least use a computer.

- ✔ You may have seen the ITIL books but found them too big or too theoretical.

- ✔ You work in an organisation that uses IT or even provides IT services to other people. Or you want to get involved in such an organisation.

- ✔ You may be thinking about getting qualified in ITIL. You like the idea of getting ITIL on your CV.

How This Book Is Organised

The book is split into 16 chapters and 3 appendixes. To make life easier I group the chapters into five parts, each of which focuses on a particular theme. The following sections outline the focus of each part to help you navigate your way around the book.

Part 1: How ITIL Can Help You

This part gives you a real grounding in ITIL. The first chapter gives you a clear understanding of what exactly ITIL is and how it helps organisations. The subsequent chapters describe the basic principles, the building blocks, of ITIL – the foundations on which the rest of the book builds. Here you get to know much of the terminology used in other parts of the book, and come to understand the backbone of ITIL: the processes of the service lifecycle.

Part II: Getting to Grips with the Service Lifecycle and the Processes

Having armed yourself with basic principles in Part I, now you're ready to explore each of the ITIL processes. Quite a few processes exist, and this part takes you through each in turn. Each chapter focuses on a different group of processes that follow the service lifecycle, so Chapter 4 looks at service strategy, Chapters 5 and 6 at service design, Chapter 7 at service transition, Chapter 8 at service operation and Chapter 9 at continual service improvement.

Part III: Getting Practical

Sometimes the core ITIL guidance can seem a bit dry. After you have an understanding of the basics of the processes and the lifecycle (which Parts I and II lay down), you can then consider the more practical concerns of how all this ITIL stuff applies to your organisation. Part III takes a practical view of how you can implement and use the service management processes and practices in your organisation. This part really pulls together the theoretical information I provide in Parts I and II.

Part IV: The Part of Tens

Every For Dummies book has this part which provides some handy quick-reference info that consolidates the contents of the book. In this part: I provide some condensed advice on making ITIL work for your organisation; I suggest some elements of ITIL to implement first to see quick, and pleasing, results; and I give you a list of the top ten places to head to when you want some ITIL-related advice.

Part V: Appendixes

This part contains some additional information. First I talk about the ITIL qualification structure, in case you're thinking of adding ITIL to your CV. Then I offer a glossary of key ITIL terms that I use in the book, and a quick reference guide to the service lifecycle processes.

Icons Used in This Book

Scattered through this book you find some funny little icons which help you navigate your way through the book and highlight some of the key points:

This is where I quote ITIL definitions more or less word for word (if you find these tough to understand, don't worry: I always follow a definition with my own explanation). You can find loads of ITIL definitions in the glossary at the back of the book.

Some straight talking to summarise some possibly confusing stuff.

Important things to keep in mind as you think about applying ITIL.

Here you find an example to help illustrate an important point.

This icon indicates the occasional bit of brow-furrowing ITIL detail; useful to know, but not essential.

 A useful point you can apply yourself.

 Occasionally I explain things to avoid. Ignore these points at your peril!

Where to Go from Here

He or she who hesitates is lost, as someone much cleverer than me once said. The point is that now you've read this introduction, get stuck in. Anywhere.

The great thing about For Dummies books is that you don't have to begin at the beginning and end at the end. You can dip in anywhere you like. *ITIL For Dummies* is no exception. Where some of the content relies on you understanding principles that I describe in other parts of the book, I provide cross-references so you can skip over to the relevant chapter. And you'll also find a glossary in the appendixes, so you can check any terms that you're unsure about.

So, knowing that this book helps you really get a handle on the wonderful world of ITIL, feel free to flick to a chapter that interests you. The water's nice – jump in.

Part I
How ITIL Can Help You

The 5th Wave   By Rich Tennant

Say what you want, but some of us miss the old ways of IT management.

In this part . . .

This part delivers the nitty-gritty basics of ITIL. Here you can find a clear understanding of what exactly ITIL is and does, and why organisations need it. The subsequent chapters describe the principles and terminology of ITIL – the foundations on which ITIL itself, and the rest of this book, builds. Perhaps most importantly, this part will help you understand the backbone of ITIL: the processes of the service lifecycle.

Chapter 1

Managing IT Services: Welcome to the World of ITIL

. . . .

In This Chapter

▶ Defining IT services and service management

▶ Understanding what ITIL's about, and who it's for

▶ Getting the gist of the content of ITIL

▶ Clearing up common misunderstandings about ITIL

▶ Seeing how this book fits with the ITIL qualifications

. . . .

Aren't computers wonderful? Well, they are when they work and do what you want them to do. But what about the organisations that provide services using computers, or information technology (IT) as it tends to be known? You have the Internet providers, such as your broadband supplier. You have the companies that allow you to shop on the Internet. What about the place where you work? Who provides the IT stuff that sits on your desk? The answer is, the IT provider. Perhaps you even work for one of these organisations. If so, this book is right up your street.

This book is all about the Information Technology Infrastructure Library (ITIL). Huh? Sounds meaningless, I know. Basically, ITIL is a bunch of books that give advice to service providers about how to manage their IT services in such a way that they meet your expectations.

The focus of this book is service management. Users have great expectations of IT services. You expect IT services to be there when you want them. You expect them to be easy to fix when they break. You expect there to be a nice person on the end of the phone to help you out and give you advice. Well, this book turns the tables and looks at how the companies that provide IT services do what you want them to do.

Defining Some Basic Terms

I'm going to start by ensuring you understand some basic terms:

- ✔ **Service:** Something that provides value and is available to a customer from a provider. For example, take travel agents. They sell you a holiday package and make sure all the individual bits work together. They book the flights, the transfers, the hotels and any excursions. What do you do? Pay the money and turn up. Travel agents save you the effort, cost and risk of doing the individual bits for yourself. They provide a service that is of value to you.

- ✔ **IT service:** A collection of IT bits and bobs along with the people and documents required to provide an IT system which delivers a service that provides value to a customer. Basically, a bunch of techie stuff that allows you to do something useful with your computer.

For example, when you shop using the Internet, you're using an IT service. Your PC, your Internet provider and the company providing the website are all providing IT services for you to use. When you shop online, the service you use consists of many component parts – some of them you own, some of them other people own. You own your PC. Your Internet provider owns your Internet connection and some network stuff. The online store that you're buying from owns the website. But you want it all to work as one seamless system. Wouldn't it be great if regardless of which bit breaks, one person deals with it for you?

- ✔ **Service management:** Brace yourself, this is a tricky term to define. Only joking – service management means managing a service. In a nutshell, the provider is encouraged to identify and agree what the customer needs and then provide it in an ongoing way. The following section elaborates further on service management.

- ✔ **IT service provider:** An organisation that provides IT systems to a user (customer). The organisation may be an internal IT department of the company you work for – the people who put the computers on your desks and fix them when they go wrong. Equally it may be a commercial organisation that provides IT services in exchange for money, in other words an Internet provider or IT outsourcer. In all cases these organisations are providing a service to their customers.

You'll find out much more about service management and these terms as you dive into this book. I describe the basic terminology in Chapter 2.

Equating Service Management with Customer Service

What annoys you when you go shopping, or go to a restaurant, or phone up your bank's call centre? Is it the service you get? Do bored shop assistants who are more interested in chatting with their friends really annoy you? Do you get frustrated when you arrive at the restaurant and are wilfully ignored for five minutes while standing by the door? Does the call centre assistant robotically ask the same questions as usual? These are examples of poor customer service that I'm sure you've experienced. If you're anything like me you'll think, 'Surely you can do better than that?' The concept of customer service has existed for such a long time now that it is considered quite basic, and there is no reason why customer service shouldn't be second nature.

But what, I hear you ask, has this got to do with service management. Well, you can think of service management as *customer service* for IT people. Customer service is a simple principle, one that says: find out what your customers want and give it to them – within reason. This principle should apply to computing and IT systems.

Seeing why IT service users complain

This book is about improving the management of IT services in order to improve the provision of IT services. A good starting point is to understand the users', or customers', point of view.

Pretty much everyone has a computer at home, often more than one. I remember, many years ago, laughing at a friend who had a computer network in his home. 'You must be a real geek', I said. Now I'm writing this book on one of the three computers (not including smartphones and e-book readers) that are in constant use in our house and are networked together. Who looks foolish now?

What's more, I live in a remote part of the UK, yet I'm still connected to the Internet by broadband; in fact I rely on it. When my broadband connection fails, I rant and rave at the provider, berating the organisation for not understanding my needs, and urging it to work faster to restore my service.

The point is that one of the difficulties associated with providing IT services is that customers have high expectations; because IT is so prevalent in modern times, users feel that provision is straightforward.

And whereas IT used to be the domain of the few geeks that took an interest in computers, now it's everywhere. Very few businesses don't rely on IT in some way, if only for sending emails or using the Internet. Most people have computers at home and know what they can do, therefore when they go to work or use other IT services, they have high expectations.

Understanding the IT provider's point of view

Providing IT services that please all users, all of the time, is a challenge because:

- ✔ **IT is complex:** IT systems aren't simple to set up and run, and users expect many different types of technology to work together.

- ✔ **IT is always changing:** IT systems change constantly with new upgrades, software applications and technologies appearing every week.

- ✔ **Users' needs change:** People use IT systems to help them do business, so as the business needs change, so do the requirements of the IT systems that support them.

IT providers therefore have to deal with constantly changing technology, constantly changing customer needs and high expectations.

Why can't customers and IT just talk to each other?

Customer service is about finding out what your customers want and giving it to them, so why don't the customers and providers just talk to each other?

I often I hear the following kind of exchange:

- ✔ IT says: 'The customers don't know what they want!'
- ✔ The customer says: 'IT people just talk jargon, they don't understand our business!'

In many organisations the IT department is thought of as just providing technology, not providing a service. So IT is just a bunch of technical experts providing IT systems. The IT department's view is that IT is specialised so only the experts know what you can have; therefore you get what you're given.

You may be thinking that this is an old-fashioned view of IT and times have moved on. Well, I assure you that through the training work I do, I meet many IT staff and users from many organisations who still think this way.

Improving IT services

The best way to improve IT service provision is to take a look at people and companies that do it well. A great idea, but difficult to know where to start. Well, wouldn't it be great if someone took all the experience and advice from many organisations and individuals who've been managing IT services for a while and put it in a book. Ta da! It's been done, and the books are ITIL.

The benefits of books such as the ITIL publications is that the advice in them is proven. The recommendations are not just theoretical: this is stuff that people have tried and actually works. It is a proven way of doing things.

ITIL's proven way of doing things has a lot to do with processes. Put simply, a *process* is a way of doing something. If you have agreed ways of doing things in your organisation, you're more likely to do things consistently and accurately, and achieve what you intend to achieve.

This book contains descriptions of all the main ITIL processes; most of them are in Part II.

Understanding ITIL: Best Practice Guidance

ITIL is an acronym, and when it was first established it stood for the Information Technology Infrastructure Library. But although people still use the acronym ITIL, you no longer find the definition in the ITIL books. I guess this is because the scope of ITIL has gone well beyond just the IT infrastructure.

Anyway, I'm less interested in what ITIL stands for and more interested in what it is:

- ✔ **Five books:** The core ITIL publications
- ✔ **Complementary guidance:** A set of publications that provide specific guidance to industry sectors or types

The books are a source of best practice for service management. *Best practice* provides some good ways of doing things. A bunch of people who have done this stuff have put their heads together and said 'Here are some of the things we have done and they work, why don't you have a go.' I don't mean to make it sound haphazard: ITIL has been carefully honed and developed over 20 years by industry experts. It is now a body of knowledge that represents guidance on how to manage your IT services.

The five core ITIL books are great but are quite thick and big – they're excellent reference books. *ITIL For Dummies* gives you an easy-to-digest description of the five core ITIL books and the processes that they contain.

The benefit of public frameworks such as ITIL is that the guidance has been verified across many industry types and organisation types, and so is easily transferable.

So what are the benefits of using best practice guidance? The benefits of best practice guidance are that it:

- ✔ **Can be adopted and adapted:** You can adopt the ITIL processes and practices and adapt them to suit your organisation.
- ✔ **Improves efficiency:** You can improve efficiencies in your organisation.
- ✔ **Satisfies customers:** You can increase your organisation's ability to provide services that meet the needs of your customers.
- ✔ **Is scalable:** One size fits all. It doesn't matter if you have three people in the IT department or 3000, ITIL is just as applicable.

The benefits of best practice include the fact that ITIL is for any service provider regardless of size, type of industry. Any organisation can improve what it does. So it doesn't matter whether your organisation is public sector or private sector, is manufacturing, service industry or financial– ITIL can still help.

Is ITIL for individuals or just the management teams? ITIL works best if the concepts and processes are adopted by the whole IT organisation. But this doesn't mean ITIL is aimed only at management. The management team must rely on their staff to perform the service management practices and make ITIL work.

From the point of view of an individual, even if your organisation doesn't intend to implement ITIL, it is still a great thing to understand. To have an ITIL qualification on your CV is a good thing.

Piecing Together the Jigsaw: The Content of ITIL

The ITIL guidance is all about managing IT services. I consider and describe four main elements in the chapters of this book:

- **The service lifecycle:** The life of an IT service from inception through a development project and introduction into day-to-day use
- **Processes:** Sets of ways of doing things
- **Functions:** Organisational departments – the source of the people who do the stuff needed to manage IT services
- **Roles:** Sets of responsibilities allocated to people or departments

I talk about processes, functions and roles in Chapter 2.

The ITIL guidance is structured around the service lifecycle, which I overview in Chapter 3. IT services don't just appear one day fully formed. If you want your IT services to meet the needs of your business then careful thought and planning must go into the development of those services, not least an understanding of how the service supports the business processes.

The service lifecycle consists of five stages, and ITIL dedicates a core publication to each. This book concentrates on these five core books:

- Service strategy (see Chapter 4)
- Service design (see Chapters 5 and 6)
- Service transition (see Chapter 7)
- Service operation (see Chapter 8)
- Continual service improvement (see Chapter 9)

At the heart of ITIL is a set of processes. It is the processes that make ITIL flexible. If I told you that in order to provide good IT services you must have 10 staff employed on your service desk and another 20 in second-line support, you would put this book down now. However, if I described a way of doing things that provides a number of coordinated activities that you can allocate to your existing staff, you might be more prepared to listen.

Debunking Some Common Misconceptions about ITIL

Over the years I've heard many reasons, in some cases excuses, as to why companies haven't adopted ITIL, or why they think ITIL won't work for them. I cover some common myths about ITIL in the following sections.

Treating ITIL as training only

I have trained many people in ITIL, and I'm pleased to see that many attend the foundation course as part of an awareness project (more on ITIL training in Appendix A). What concerns me is that the training course is sometimes viewed as just training to improve someone's skills, without realising that it should be paving the way for the implementation of the ITIL processes.

For ITIL to provide benefit to your organisation, the processes and practices should be adopted and implemented in your IT organisation. I describe how to implement the ITIL service management processes in Chapter 10.

Misinterpreting ITIL

Occasionally, people see what they want to see in ITIL. ITIL isn't a methodology and it's not prescriptive. It is guidance. Therefore, by its very nature it is open to interpretation and therefore also open to misinterpretation. I have heard stories of organisations that have implemented ITIL to the letter, doing *exactly* what it says in the books. They're missing the point.

You must understand ITIL and then adapt it to suit your organisation. There are some things you shouldn't change, such as the basic process flows; but how the activities that form the processes operate in your organisation is up to you to decide.

In Parts I and II of this book I provide guidance on how to interpret ITIL. Part III focuses on practical application.

Thinking ITIL is for the service desk and support staff only

ITIL is often perceived as being for customer- or user-facing people only. Or only for day-to-day operations people. I don't know where this idea comes from; however, it's not true. I have known delegates on my training courses who are developers or technical specialists and who state that they don't know why they've been sent, because ITIL is not relevant to them.

Everyone in IT has some involvement in providing the IT services to the business, and it is important that all staff are aiming to achieve the same ultimate goal.

Believing that processes introduce unnecessary bureaucracy

No, they don't. Without good processes, your organisation is probably wasting time, money and other resources. If your processes are considered to be bureaucratic then I respectfully suggest that there may be something wrong with them. Maybe they're not well written, or perhaps the reason and need for processes has not been properly communicated to the necessary people.

The ITIL guidance is just that– guidance. You should develop your processes in such a way that they work for your organisation.

Assuming that ITIL uses a lot of time, staff and money

Don't fall into the trap of thinking that ITIL requires your organisation to employ many more staff. This is untrue. The best value is to be obtained from using your existing staff in better ways. The processes that I describe include activities that can be performed by your existing staff. The processes will ensure that you staff are focussed on the important things – like providing IT services to your customers.

It is true that it will take time, money and commitment to implement the ITIL practices, and you should develop a sound business case before starting.

Appreciating the history of ITIL

ITIL first appeared in the late 1980s and was published by the UK Government department known as the Central Computer and Telecommunications Agency (CCTA). The CCTA was later absorbed into the Office of Government Commerce (OGC) which was, until 2011, the Government department that promotes best practice in industry. In 2011 there was a further UK Government reorganisation which meant that the ownership of best practice, including ITIL, moved to the Cabinet Office.

When it was first published, ITIL consisted of 10 core books and a further 30 complementary books. In 2000/2001 the ten core books were rewritten as two, followed over the next few years by a number of others. Later, the ITIL 2007 edition was published (known to many as ITIL Version 3). The major advancement of this (and the current) version of ITIL is that all the material has been rewritten and brought into five volumes structured around the service lifecycle. This emphasises the fact that no area of an IT organisation can divorce itself from the understanding that it plays some part in providing services to the organisation's customers.

In the ITIL 2011 edition, the books were updated to consolidate the improvements made in the 2007 refresh and improve consistency across the core books.

All this reference to versions is confusing – I'll just call it ITIL!

Taking the ITIL Qualifications

You can obtain a number of qualifications to prove that you know something about ITIL. The ITIL Foundation Certificate is the starting point for anyone wanting to become qualified in ITIL service management. You can find lots of details about the qualifications in Appendix A.

Parts I and II of this book include material that covers the syllabus of the foundation qualification. That's not to say that by reading this book you pass the exam. That depends on who you are, your background and your experience. No substitute exists for a well-run training course to bring the material alive. (I'm a trainer, therefore I'm bound by oath to tell you that!)

For those of you wanting to take the foundation exam only, you may find reading the five core ITIL books like using a sledgehammer to crack a nut. Happily, this book explains the main concepts and information to give you an introduction to ITIL without having to navigate the five core books. But after you've read this book and whetted your appetite, have a go. Read the proper ITIL books.

Chapter 2

Using the Building Blocks of ITIL

In This Chapter

▶ Understanding what 'services' and 'service management' mean

▶ Thinking about how you create value

▶ Looking at assets in terms of resources and capabilities

▶ Considering processes, functions and roles

*I*TIL-based service management is, among other things, a set of processes that you can adapt to any IT organisation regardless of size. But because ITIL is guidance, there are a few basic things to get your head around before I get into detail about the processes themselves. You can call these things the building blocks of ITIL – a bundle of terminology to kick-start your adventure into the wonderful world of ITIL. It's really tempting to throw yourself head-long at the chapters in this book that cover the service management processes. However, this chapter covers some key fundamentals that you'll find really helpful. So I urge you to read this chapter before you read the chapters in Part II.

This chapter covers some things you really should know before you get started: the basic ITIL definitions of 'service' and 'service management', and how you can create value for your customers.

Defining Services

This section begins with a description of services in general then focuses on IT services.

Whenever I talk to people for the first time about service management, I always start with the same question: 'What is service management?' And I always prompt people for the same answer: 'The management of your services'. I'm a great believer in stating the blindingly obvious and keeping things simple. We don't talk about service management for very long before one of us says, 'By the way, what's a service?' Another good question.

A *service* is something provided to a customer by a provider. It's usually something that the customer wants and, for whatever reason, cannot or will not do itself.

In ITIL speak, a service is a means of delivering value to customers by facilitating outcomes that customers want to achieve without the ownership of specific costs and risks.

I find it helpful to look at this definition in three parts. Here goes:

- ✔ **A means of delivering value to customers:** A service is something provided to a customer by a provider. The customer wants to use the service for a reason: it delivers value in some way. So the provider must understand and define that value. Consider the example of a bus. Why do you take a bus? Is it just because you want a jolly bus ride? Well, perhaps, but more likely you get the bus because you want to get from A to B. What is your destination? Is it the bus stop?

- ✔ **By facilitating outcomes customers want to achieve:** Customers use the service because they have a need that they want fulfilled, so the service provider must gain a good understanding of each customer's needs. In the bus example, is it adequate for the bus company to know that all customers want to get from one bus stop to another? How do they know where to put the bus stops? How do they know how often to schedule the buses? How big should the buses be? To answer these questions, the bus company needs to find out more about the intentions of the customers. Why do the customers want to take the bus? To go shopping, to get to an interview, to get to work, to go to the pub, to attend a training course or to get to Granny's house? When the bus company knows the answer to this question, it plans to run more buses in the rush hour to get people to work, and it puts bus stops by the out-of-town shopping centre. So the provider has to know what the customer is trying to achieve so that it can match its service to the customer's needs.

- ✔ **Without the ownership of specific costs and risks:** When you board the bus, before sitting down do you approach the driver and ask to see her driving licence, the MOT certificate and insurance certificate for the bus? Why not? You no doubt assume the paperwork is all part of the service. In fact, that may be the reason you chose to take the bus instead of the alternatives, because you don't want to bother with the costs and risks involved with owning a car. Or perhaps you can't face sitting in a traffic jam in your own car. The service provider must keep in mind that when people use services they often review the alternatives, and consideration of costs and risks sways the customer.

This is all well and good, but what's it got to do with IT services? Well, do you work for an IT department or organisation whose job it is to provide IT systems and software applications? Why do your users use your IT systems? In a business or commercial situation the customers use IT systems because they help them do their job. (Okay, people may play on the IT systems a little, but that's not the main use.) Like the bus company that knows where its customers want to go and understands their habits, do you know exactly why your users use your IT systems?

An *IT service* is a service provided by an IT service provider. An IT service is made up of a combination of information technology, people and processes. A customer-facing IT service directly supports the business processes of one of more customers, and its expected outcomes are defined in a *service level agreement* (SLA). Other IT services, called supporting services, aren't directly used by the business but are required by the service provider to deliver customer-facing IT services.

A user often perceives an IT service to be the software application that appears on the screen of the workstation or PC, but the application can't work alone without the PC and other pieces of equipment.

A common expression you hear is 'end-to-end IT service'. This expression derives from the fact that the user is at one end of the service, and the PC sends its messages through various components until they reach a computer server or mainframe at the other end. So, *end to end* describes all of the components required for the IT service to operate as required.

A final note about the definition of services; you may hear the following terms:

- ✔ **Customer-facing IT services.** This refers to IT services that the customer uses to support its business.
- ✔ **Supporting services.** Some customer-facing services are made up of a combination of other IT services which are not visible to the customers. These are also services, but referred to as supporting services.

Understanding IT Service Management

The previous section defines the word 'service' in IT terms. So what's *service management*? Well, the simple answer is the management of your services.

ITIL-speak has the same definition essentially, just a little wordier: service management is a set of specialised organisational capabilities for providing value to customers in the form of services.

Note this is a general definition of service management – the definition of IT service management (ITSM) is coming up. This first definition centres around the word *capabilities* (which I discuss in the later section aptly titled 'Capabilities') and includes such things as functions, processes and roles (which I cover in the section 'Exploring Processes, Functions and Roles').

When considering managing your IT services, another obvious question is 'How would you like me to manage your services on your behalf?' Here are some popular answers to that question:

- ✔ To my expectations
- ✔ So my staff and I can get on with our jobs
- ✔ Effectively and efficiently
- ✔ So that I don't have to
- ✔ To agreed targets

You can no doubt add your own thoughts to this list, but the key point is to remember the ITIL definition of a service – to deliver value to the customer – and ensure that you manage the service in such a way that you do just this.

Think of IT service management as customer service for IT people. I'm sure you've come across customer service philosophies – we're all customers and suppliers, the customer is always right, and so on. Put very simply, service management aims to find out what the customer wants, agree it with the customer and then give it to the customer. Note the importance of the word *agree* in that sentence. I want to give the customer whatever it wants, but within reason. I'll discuss with the customer what it really needs, and we'll come to an agreement about what it's prepared to pay for it (or what budget is available).

Is IT service management (ITSM) any different from service management in general? Well, not really, but the definition is more specific.

IT service management (ITSM) is the implementation and management of quality IT services that meet the needs of the business. IT service management is performed by IT service providers through an appropriate mix of people, process and information management.

Understanding Who Provides the IT Services

IT services are provided by an IT service provider. Great!

An *IT service provider* is a service provider that provides IT services to internal or external customers.

ITIL suggests three provider types:

- **Type I – internal service provider:** An internal IT organisation or department that serves one business unit.
- **Type II – shared services unit:** A single internal IT organisation or department that serves many business units.
- **Type III – external service provider:** A organisation that provides services to external customers. A commercial business.

Types I and II are internal providers, providing IT services to other parts of the same company. Type III providers are commercial organisations that provide services in exchange for money.

Knowing the IT Service Management Stakeholders

I use the words customers and users a lot in the pages of this book, but who are they and does it matter what you call them? Customers and users are some of the stakeholders that you need to consider when providing IT services. A *stakeholder* is someone who has an interest in, or is affected by, whatever you're doing. In this case, they have an interest in your IT services. Here are the explanations of some key stakeholders.

The user

The ITIL publications say 'a *user* is a person who uses the IT service on a day-to-day basis. Users are distinct from customers, because some customers don't use the IT service directly'.

You need to define users for many reasons. Users:

- Use the service
- Ring up your service desk
- Have varying degrees of understanding of computers and your services
- Often need training

The number of users that use a given service helps you get an understanding of the capacity requirements of a service. Often the SLA defines who the users of a service are, where they're located, the support they require and how many can use the service at any one time. I describe SLAs in Chapter 5.

The customer

People use the term *customer* in many different ways. Even the ITIL books use it in more than one way. However, when defining and managing services, one main definition exists.

A customer is someone who buys goods or services. The customer of an IT service provider is the person or group who defines and agrees the service level targets.

The customer is the one who pays. If your organisation is a commercial one, providing services in exchange for money, then this definition is reasonably clear and obvious. But what if you're an internal IT provider that delivers IT services to another part of the same organisation? Do you charge the business for the IT service? Sometimes the answer is yes, sometimes it's no. In these cases I like to think of the customer as the person in the corner office, in other words the department manager. Note that the second part of the definition states that a customer is the person who agrees to the service levels in the SLA. This is usually the person in the corner office.

Customers come in two flavours:

- **Internal customers.** The ITIL publications say 'they work for the same business as the IT service provider'.

- **External customers.** According to ITIL 'they work for a different business from the IT service provider and usually buy services from the IT provider'.

The supplier

A *supplier* is a third party (external to your organisation) from whom you obtain goods or services that are required to help deliver IT services. Examples of suppliers include commodity hardware and software vendors, network and telecom providers, and outsourcing organisations.

Creating Value

In the earlier section 'Defining Services' I give the ITIL definition of a service as 'a means of delivering value to customers'. But how do you define value? Ask two friends what value they expect when going to a restaurant, and I guarantee you get two different answers. One may say, 'somewhere to get a quick bite before going on elsewhere'; the other may say, 'somewhere to have a long, lingering, romantic dinner'. I'm sure you've heard the expression 'beauty is in the eye of the beholder'; well, I believe that *value* is also in the eye of the beholder.

The value a customer derives from a service is influenced by many things. If the success of your service depends on providing value to your customers then you'd better get a clear view of what your customers mean by value. You need to tie your customers down and get a clearer view of how *they* perceive value. Here's a formula:

Value = Utility + Warranty

The following sections explore utility and warranty.

Considering utility

In the ITIL publications, it says 'Utility is the functionality offered by a product or service to meet a particular need'. Utility is often summarised as '*what it does*'. What does a kitchen cooker do? Allows you to cook meals. What does a bus do? Gets you to your destination. What does an email service do? Allows you to send and receive emails. All these are examples of the basic functionality, or utility, of a product or service.

A service that provides the correct utility is said to be *fit for purpose*.

You must ask your customer to give you a good description of what it wants to do. In the earlier section 'Defining Services', I give an example of a bus service. In order to provide a good bus service, the bus company must understand why the public want to take a bus. The utility offered by a product or service is closely linked to the business outcomes that your customer wants to achieve. Examples of possible business outcomes are that the customer wants to:

- ✔ Provide a quotation to a client in less than one hour
- ✔ Pay its employees salary every Friday
- ✔ Manufacture enough toys for the Christmas rush

Of course the list is endless, but please note that none of these examples mentions IT. Once you get an understanding of what the customer wants to do then you can start to think about how you can provide an IT service to help the customer do it.

Weighing up warranty

ITIL defines *warranty* as 'the assurance that a product or service will meet agreed requirements'. Warranty is often summarised as '*how* it does it'.

When you go to the electrical store to buy a new washing machine, the sales-person is likely to ask you whether you'd like to take out the extended five-year warranty. What does this mean? The store is giving you some assurance that if the washing machine breaks down you'll be able to get it fixed as soon as possible. The warranty allows you to get the utility more often. In other words, if the utility of a washing machine is to wash your clothes, the warranty allows you to wash your clothes more often.

You can think of warranty as a guarantee, but mention the word *guarantee* to some IT people and they'll run screaming from the room. So if the g-word gets you hot and sweaty, consider warranty as the assurance that you can minimise the risks of *not* getting the utility from the service.

A service that provides the correct warranty is said to be *fit for use*.

Warranty has four main aspects:

- ✔ **Availability:** Is the service available – is it there and working when you want it? If it fails, can it be fixed quickly so you can get on with what you're supposed to be doing?

- ✔ **Capacity:** Is there enough of the service and does it work fast enough?

- ✔ **Continuity:** If the service breaks in a really bad way, can the customer get the service back in some way or can you provide an alternative?

- ✔ **Security:** Is the service secure and does it protect your information and your interests?

Think about the current account you have with your bank. The service, or *utility*, it provides is the means to store money and give you access to it whenever you want. What about the *warranty?* Availability refers to your money being available when you want it through the different access methods such as cash machines or online banking. *Capacity* refers to the amount that you can deposit or withdraw at any time and how quickly the bank adds the money to your account or gives you the money. *Security* refers to the bank ensuring that only you can get to your money, and that it keeps your details confidential. *Continuity* refers to the bank providing you with an alternative if the normal access method to your money is blocked in some way; for example, if all the cash machines fail, the bank allows you to withdraw money over the counter at a branch.

The definition of a service states that you want to deliver value to customers to *facilitate the outcomes that customers want to achieve.* So the utility and warranty focus on helping the customer achieve its business outcomes.

Having the Right Assets

The previous section considers how you look at the value a service provides from the point of view of the customer. Now look at it from the IT service provider's point of view and ask the question, 'How on earth am I (the IT service provider) going to achieve this?' The answer is relatively simple: make sure you have the right service. However, the service is only as good as its component parts, so now is the time to delve a little deeper and look in more detail at what an IT service is made of.

Every part of your services, whether tangible or intangible, is an *asset* – something of value. Your house is an asset. Your health is an asset. Your intelligence in an asset. All these things have value.

ITIL defines an asset as any resource or capability. The assets of a service provider include anything that may contribute to the delivery of a service. Assets can be management, organisation, process, knowledge, people, information, applications, infrastructure, and financial capital.

In the wonderful world of ITIL, assets are sorted into two types: resources and capabilities.

Resources

You know what a resource is, don't you? The stuff they dig out of the ground: water, gas, oil, minerals and metals. But often it doesn't come out of the ground in a useable form. Oil must be refined, and metals are extracted from the ore.

Resource is a generic term that includes IT infrastructure, people, money or anything else that may help to deliver an IT service.

ITIL suggests there are five rough groups of resources that you need to deliver IT services:

✔ Applications

✔ Infrastructure

✔ Financial capital

✔ Information

✔ People

These are the component parts that make up the service. Resources are the raw material, the inputs into your IT factory. But to be able to use them usefully, something more has to happen: capabilities.

Capabilities

Capabilities are the something more that have to be applied to resources (see the previous section) to make something happen. A capability is the ability or means to do something – the ability to take a resource and turn it into something useful.

In ITIL, capability is the ability of an organisation, person, process, application, component or IT service to carry out an activity. Capabilities are intangible assets of an organisation.

In service management terms, capabilities tend to represent the collective ability of your organisation to provide IT services. Capabilities are like the machinery of a factory that takes the raw material (the resources), does work on it and produces the finished product (the service), shiny and new and in a pretty box.

Capabilities are what make your organisation or service distinctive; what distinguish you from your competitors, or your services from other services. ITIL suggests there are five rough groups of capabilities that you need to deliver IT services:

✔ Knowledge

✔ People

✔ Processes

✔ Management

✔ Organisation

What makes your organisation special? Is it the staff you have that have particular knowledge and skills? Perhaps it's the way your organisation is managed and organised that allows you to provide excellent IT services that meet the needs of your customers.

Using your assets

The value that your services provide depends on using the right amount of your assets and organising them in the right way. If I asked you to set up a new company tomorrow, do you think you could just employ a bunch of people, buy some equipment, throw the people in a building and tell them to get on with it? I doubt it. You have to decide carefully how many people you need and what they will do, and then acquire the appropriate equipment and other assets to suit your overall purpose.

The same is true for your IT services. To be able to provide the value that the customer needs to achieve its business outcomes, you must select the right assets and configure (coordinate) them in the right way in order to create the IT services that meet the needs of your customers. Figure 2-1 shows an example of how an IT service is made up of its constituent assets.

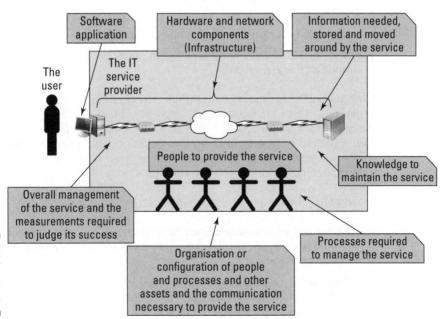

Figure 2-1:
An IT service and its assets.

Exploring Processes, Functions and Roles

Processes, functions and roles are what you may call the more organisational aspects of ITIL – who does what, and which part of the organisation people work for.

Understanding processes

Processes are one of the most important elements of ITIL-based IT service management. One of the most powerful things about ITIL is that one size fits all. No matter how big or small your IT organisation, it can still benefit from ITIL. ITIL isn't a methodology and it's not prescriptive. It provides a framework of processes that enable you to improve the IT services you provide to your customers.

A *process*:

- ✔ Is a structured set of activities designed to accomplish a specific objective
- ✔ Takes one or more defined inputs and turns them into defined outputs
- ✔ May include any of the roles, responsibilities, tools and management controls required to reliably deliver the outputs
- ✔ May define policies, standards, guidelines, activities, and work instructions if they're needed.

For now, just remember the first point: a process is a structured set of activities designed to accomplish a specific objective. Often, processes are described as a way of doing something. The point of using service management processes for your organisation is to describe how the organisation wants things to be done in order to manage your IT services. This, of course, involves telling people how to do their jobs.

So, what are the benefits of processes? Here are a few ideas:

- ✔ **Better use of resources:** Documented processes mean more predictable processes and fewer mistakes. This leads to less and more predictable resource usage.
- ✔ **Consistency and accuracy:** You provide a better service if things are done the same way every time regardless of who is performing them. Better accuracy should mean fewer mistakes.

✔ **Coordinating work across the organisation:** One of the most powerful aspects of processes is that they help you coordinate activities that take place in different parts of the organisation. This is often known as breaking down technical silos.

✔ **Recording and traceability:** Processes help you build up information about how well you perform your processes, and allow you to identify opportunities for improvement.

A process is a set of activities. There is usually a procedure to tell staff how to perform each activity. You give a piece of paper (procedure) to a staff member and ask the person to follow the instructions each time he or she performs this task.

If you're anything like me, when you buy a new bit of technology, say a new TV, you sit down and read the manual – oh, okay, you're not like me. Reading the manual tells you how you're intended to operate the TV. This is just like a procedure.

If your processes are going to provide benefits they must be carefully designed and implemented. This means working out what you want done and who's going to do it. When designing and documenting your processes, you have many things to consider. For more information about designing processes take a look at Chapter 10.

Understanding functions

What's a function? In ITIL terms, a *function* is a team or group of people and the tools they use to carry out one or more processes or activities – for example, the service desk. So a function is an organisational unit or, put simply, a bunch of people in a room doing something. Every organisation contains functions: departments and teams. The sales department, the accounts department, the application development team, the operations support group, are all examples of functions.

Functions are great because they provide structure. You can easily get an idea of what an organisation does when you describe what a bunch of people in a room do as a whole rather than describe the many individual jobs that exist. For example, you say you have a sales department rather than describing the jobs of the sales manager, the order takers, the call centre and so on. Functions also describe management and reporting structures and so give you a better understanding of where you fit in the organisation.

The functional units in your IT organisation are the source of the people who perform the activities of the service management processes.

Understanding roles

The previous sections explain process and functions. Roles link these two together.

A *role* is a set of responsibilities, activities and authorities granted to a person or team. A role is defined in a process.

One person or team may have multiple roles; for example, one person may carry out the roles of both configuration manager and change manager. And similarly a single role may be performed by many people; for example, many IT staff perform the role of second-line support, but some of them work in the application team and some work in the network team.

For some examples of crucial roles, skip to the later section 'Who Does What? Looking at Some Important Roles'.

Using processes, functions and roles in service management

The combination of processes, functions and roles allows you to make best use of service management in your organisation. Figure 2-2 provides a pictorial overview of how processes, functions and roles come together to organise service management.

Who Does What? Looking at Some Important Roles

Knowing who does what is essential to the success of ITIL. The ITIL books suggest lots of roles associated with each process, and I give a brief description of them in the relevant chapters. However, you benefit from knowing a few really important roles from the outset.

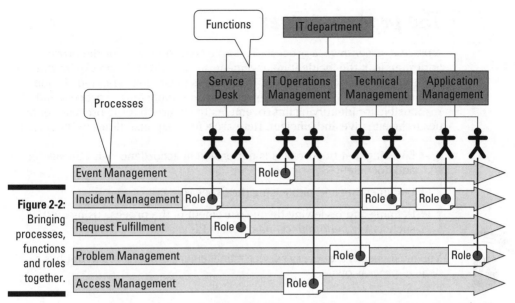

Figure 2-2:
Bringing
processes,
functions
and roles
together.

© *Crown copyright 2011. Reproduced under licence from the Cabinet Office.*

The service owner

The *service owner* owns a service. The service owner is usually someone in
the IT provider organisation, and the role provides a point of contact for a
given service. The service owner doesn't necessarily know everything about
the service, but he does know a man (or woman) who does.

Here are some responsibilities of the service owner role:

- ✔ Participates in internal service review meetings
- ✔ Represents the service across the organisation
- ✔ Represents the service in change advisory board meetings
- ✔ Is responsible for continual improvement of the service and manage-
ment of change in the service
- ✔ Understands the service and its components

The process owner

A *process owner* owns a process. This role is accountable for the process. For example, if the incident management process doesn't achieve its aim of restoring the service to the user, the process owner gets shouted at (hopefully not literally). The process owner is accountable for the process and is responsible for identifying improvements to ensure that the process continues to be effective and efficient. Here are a few responsibilities of the role:

- ✔ Ensuring that the process is performed in accordance with the agreed and documented process
- ✔ Documenting and publicising the process
- ✔ Defining and reviewing the measurement of the process using metrics such as *key performance indicators* (KPIs)

You must ensure that every service management process you adopt has a defined process owner.

The process manager

A process owner (see the previous section) is accountable for the process, but may not get involved in the day-to-day management of the process. This is a separate role often allocated to a different person: the *process manager*.

A process manager is responsible for operational management of a process. The process manager's responsibilities include planning and coordination of all activities required to carry out, monitor and report on the process.

One process may have several process managers, for example it may have regional change managers or IT service continuity managers for each data centre.

You must ensure that every service management process that you adopt has a defined process manager – though this may, of course, be the same person as the process owner.

The process practitioner

The *process practitioner* is the role that carries out one or many of the process activities. Basically, these people are the ones who do the work. However, it's important that they have a clear list of responsibilities related to the process that they get involved in.

Understanding Governance

Governance is concerned with control and the manner in which an organisation is managed. Particularly nowadays, governance includes the necessary controls, policies and guidance to ensure that an organisation is managed fairly and transparently so that no wrong-doing or fraud can occur.

The ITIL definition of governance is: ensuring that policies and strategy are actually implemented, and that required processes are correctly followed. Governance includes defining roles and responsibilities, measuring and reporting, and taking actions to resolve any issues identified.

So the controls we want to see in place are policies and processes along with clear definitions of the roles associated with the processes, and the procedures detailing how the processes should be performed. And, of course, a mechanism to ensure that the policies, processes and procedures are adhered to.

These controls can be driven by both internal and external influences. Internally, the board of directors may lay down guidance for how it wants the organisation to be run. Externally, many organisations find themselves required to conform to legislation and regulation by industry-specific bodies such as the Financial Services Authority (the UK finance industry body).

ITIL-based service management is a perfect bedfellow of governance. ITIL provides the guidance you need to implement suitable controls in the form of processes, along with the policies and procedures that go with them. An organisation with a mature set of service management processes is an organisation that finds it easier to comply with governance requirements.

Chapter 3

Outlining the Structure of ITIL

In This Chapter

▶ Fitting the service lifecycle to IT development

▶ Getting to know the set of ITIL processes

▶ Identifying who does what: the functions

*I*TIL is best practice guidance and describes capabilities for managing IT services. The four main elements of these capabilities are: processes, functions, roles and the service lifecycle. Chapter 2 gives definitions of process, function and roles; this chapter describes the service lifecycle. This chapter also provides an overview of the ITIL service management processes, which I describe in greater detail in the chapters of Part II.

Implementing ITIL in your organisation means using the ITIL service management processes. Processes provide a documented way of doing things. When adopting the ITIL processes you must consider who is going to do what. This brings me to functions. Functions are organisational units, like a team or department, and are the source of the people who perform the process activities. ITIL offers some advice about the functions you may have in your organisation. So, later in this chapter, I describe how you can roughly group people into teams or departments.

Getting to Know the Service Lifecycle

ITIL recommends that you structure your service management activities around the service lifecycle. But, what is it?

The *service lifecycle* is the lifecycle of a service – from cradle to grave. Have you ever wondered where IT services come from?

Perhaps you're an IT engineer and your boss asks you to investigate an error that causes an IT service to fail. Someone is using a software application and receives an error message. You investigate and discover that the software writer made a mistake. I wonder what you think. I'd be tempted to say, 'What dummy didn't spot the error when the program was tested?' You then investigate further and the thought crosses your mind: 'What dummy designed the software this way?' Then finally, after more investigation and thought, you say to yourself, 'What dummy thought this application was a good idea at all?' Well, you can now find out who those dummies are by working through the service lifecycle:

- ✔ **Service transition:** Where you find the dummy who does the testing.

- ✔ **Service design:** Where you find the dummy who does the design.

- ✔ **Service strategy:** Where you find the dummy who approves things at the beginning.

Some organisations don't give enough thought to the planning and designing of IT services. They cobble something together then, when the service is live and the users are using it, they tweak it to better align it with the needs of the business. Sounds familiar? Well, this is a costly way of doing things that doesn't impress your customers.

The success of an IT service depends on the success of every activity needed to conceive, design, build, test and implement the service, not just the ability to make it work after it's implemented. In order to provide an IT service, that service must be designed, built, tested and implemented with a clear understanding of the customer's needs and a will to fulfil them.

Figure 3-1 shows the ITIL service lifecycle. There are many ways that this lifecycle can be depicted, but the benefit of this diagram is that it shows the hub-and-spoke (like a wheel) nature of the service lifecycle: service strategy is the hub, and service design, service transition and service operation are the revolving lifecycle stages or 'spokes'. Like the rim of a wheel, *continual service improvement* (CSI) surrounds and supports all the lifecycle stages. Each stage influences the others and relies on them for inputs and feedback. While many service management activities are organised as projects, the service lifecycle does not consist of one single project but is an ongoing set of activities.

The five core ITIL publications are organised around the service lifecycle stages – one for each. Each of these five core books describes a number of processes. This does not mean that those processes have activities that are performed *only* in these lifecycle stages. The processes are described in the lifecycle stage with which they are most closely associated or in the stages where they should first be considered. The next sections introduce you to each of the five lifecycle stages, and the processes. The processes are described in more detail in Part II of this book.

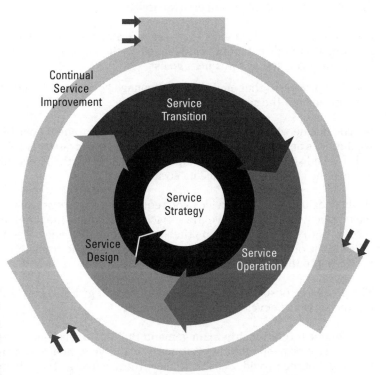

Figure 3-1:
The service
lifecycle.

© Crown copyright 2011. Reproduced under licence from the Cabinet Office.

Introducing service strategy

In the *service strategy* stage of the service lifecycle, you set the strategic direction of your IT services. Here you decide who your customers are and what services you'll provide for them. This stage encourages you to think in a strategic manner:

- ✔ How can we make best use of our services to benefit the organisation?
- ✔ How can we differentiate ourselves from competing alternatives?
- ✔ How can we create value for our customers?

Service strategy enables service management to become a strategic asset and to ensure that service provision always focuses on supporting business needs.

The service strategy stage covers two areas:

✔ How to use service management as a strategic asset, either to your organisation's competitive advantage in the marketplace, or to achieve your organisation's business goals

✔ The processes that enable you to manage your set of IT services throughout the service lifecycle

So, you decide which IT services you need in order to help your business do what it does and do it successfully. Then, when the strategy is set, you put policies and standards in place that make it easier for the IT organisation to achieve the strategy and hence its strategic goals.

Having decided what IT services you require, the service strategy stage includes activities to approve the services and acquire the funding and resources to develop them. You then realise your strategic objectives by utilising the other service lifecycle stages to design and transition these services into the live environment.

The processes described in the ITIL service strategy book are used throughout the service lifecycle. These processes are:

✔ **Business relationship management:** Building a relationship between the service provider and the customers, identifying their needs and ensuring that the provider is able to meet these needs as they change over time and in different circumstances.

✔ **Service portfolio management:** Managing a provider's set of services throughout the lifecycle and approving business cases for investment in IT services.

✔ **Financial management for IT services:** Managing budgeting, accounting and charging for IT services, and identifying the cost of providing the IT services.

✔ **Demand management:** Understanding the patterns of business activity and how these relate to the use of the IT services.

✔ **Strategy management for IT services:** Identifying, developing and managing a strategy for how a service provider will enable an organisation to achieve its business outcomes by providing and managing services that are matched to these outcomes.

To find out more about these processes and ITIL's service strategy stage, head to Chapter 4, except for strategy management for IT services – you'll find that in Chapter 11.

Considering service design

The main purpose of the *service design* stage of the lifecycle is the design of the new or changed services for introduction into the live environment.

The service design stage of the lifecycle is where you take an idea for a new service or a change to an existing service, and put meat on the bones. From the high-level business requirements that you establish in the service strategy stage (see the previous section), you make plans, designs and estimates of resources that help you understand what's involved in creating the new or changed service.

This is the stage that covers the gathering and analysis of the service requirements, and the design of the service. You must gather the detailed requirements of the service and then check that they are achievable; then you can design the service to meet the requirements.

The service design stage incorporates the following processes (some of these you also perform in the service transition and service operation stages):

- ✔ **Design coordination:** Ensuring that the goals and objectives of the service design stage are met, by providing a single point of coordination and control

- ✔ **Service level management:** Ensuring that a defined level of service is agreed and delivered

- ✔ **Service catalogue management:** Ensuring that a service catalogue exists and is a reliable source of information about live services

- ✔ **Supplier management:** Managing third party suppliers and the products and services they supply

- ✔ **Availability management:** Managing the availability of services to ensure they are offered to users as agreed

- ✔ **Capacity management:** Managing service capacity to ensure it is sufficient, and performance of the services to ensure they work fast enough

✔ **IT service continuity management:** Managing the recovery of the services when affected by a disaster or an event with a large impact on the business

✔ **Information security management:** Ensuring that the integrity of the information and data that is contained in and used by the IT service is maintained at the appropriate level to meet the business needs

For the low-down on ITIL's service design stage and its processes, check out Chapters 5 and 6.

Looking at service transition

Service transition helps organisations plan and manage changes to services and deploy releases (install software, hardware and related components and documentation) into the live environment successfully. Service transition is the bit between service design and service operation (which I explain in the sections before and after this one) – it focuses on how to ensure the business requirements identified in the service strategy and set out in service design are effectively realised in service operation, while controlling the risks of failure and disruption.

The overarching activities of the service transition stage are:

✔ Build

✔ Test

✔ Implementation

In other words, this is the phase in which you get physical.

Here are the processes that you need to control the implementation of new or changed services into the live environment:

✔ **Transition planning and support:** Providing coordination of all service transition activities

✔ **Change management:** Managing and controlling changes from request through to closure

✔ **Service asset and configuration management:** Maintaining a source of information about the services, their component parts, and the other assets required to deliver the services, and the relationships between them

✔ **Release and deployment management:** Managing the physical introduction of new or changed services and associated equipment into the live environment

✔ **Knowledge management:** Carrying out a lifecycle-wide process in which you improve the quality of management decision-making by ensuring that the right information and data are available throughout the service lifecycle

✔ **Change evaluation:** Ensuring that an independent view of any unexpected effects of a change has been evaluated, and that the customer's expectations are met

✔ **Service validation and testing:** Ensuring that components and services are tested and will provide the value in terms of utility and warranty that has been agreed with the business

Chapter 7 covers the service transition stage and processes in depth, except for change evaluation and service validation and testing which you will find in Chapter 13.

Moving on to service operation

In the *service operation* stage you coordinate and carry out the activities and processes required to deliver the services to business users and customers and manage them at agreed levels. Service operation also covers the ongoing management of the technology used to deliver and support services. So, the service operation stage is where you deliver and support your IT services – you make sure the service is working, and fix it quickly when it goes wrong.

The service operation stage is when you realise the strategic objectives. (See the earlier section 'Introducing service strategy'.) Wow!

The processes for this stage, which mainly focus on the delivery and support of the services in the live environment and ensure that services are provided as agreed, are as follows:

✔ **Event management:** Identifying electronic notifications that come from IT equipment and using them to ensure that the services are operating normally, and responding appropriately if services are behaving abnormally

✔ **Incident management:** Managing interruptions to or reductions in the quality of the services and ensuring that the service is restored within agreed timescales

✔ **Request fulfilment:** Managing requests that come from users; these may be simple questions about how to use an application, or requests for new equipment or software

✔ **Problem management:** Investigating and identifying the cause of incidents when considered necessary, and recommending permanent solutions

✔ **Access management:** Making sure that users have usernames and passwords for the services that they are allowed to use

Chapter 8 focuses on the service operation stage.

Maintaining success with continual service improvement

The primary purpose of CSI (which stands for continual service improvement, of course, in case any of you were thinking along the lines of Americans rooting about at crime scenes) is to continually align and realign IT services to changing business needs, by identifying and implementing improvements to IT services that support the business processes.

Service management delivers value to customers in the form of services that enable them to achieve their business goals and outcomes. So CSI has to ensure that the IT services align with changing business needs and continue to provide value.

The activities of CSI are primarily to:

✔ Identify, or help others identify, opportunities for improvement

✔ Prioritise improvements

✔ Set up and run (or help others set up and run) improvement projects

Note that CSI isn't one improvement project but a number of initiatives or projects, each aimed at improving an aspect of IT services.

CSI consists of many activities in which you analyse and report on services. In this stage you also identify opportunities for improvement and manage a service improvement plan to implement the improvement. ITIL refers to only one set of activities as a process: the *seven-step process*, an approach to measuring a service or service management process, analysing information and data about the service or process, and acting on the results.

To find out more about the CSI stage, take a look at Chapter 9.

Applying the service lifecycle to IT projects

The previous sections introduce you to the ITIL service lifecycle. I also mentioned that the service lifecycle can be depicted in a number of ways (one was in Figure 3-1). Another way is to relate the lifecycle to something you're familiar with: an IT development project. Figure 3-2 provides a rough overview of a typical IT development project and how it relates to the service lifecycle stages.

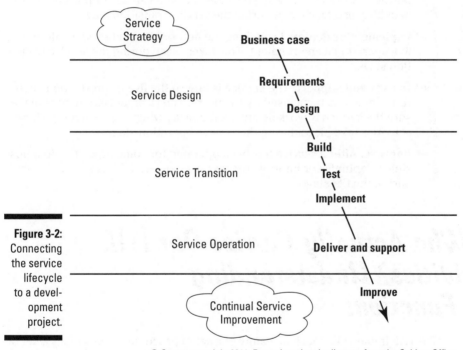

Figure 3-2: Connecting the service lifecycle to a development project.

Here's a brief description of each activity of a typical project and its relation to the service lifecycle:

✔ **Business case and project initiation:** You use a business case to justify the cost and effort involved in providing the new service or changing an existing service. The business case triggers the project initiation. These activities happen at the service strategy stage.

- ✔ **Requirements gathering and analysis:** You identify and analyse the detailed requirements of the service or change. These activities happen in the service design stage.

- ✔ **Design:** You produce a design of the service that meets the requirements. This is usually a paper-based design at this point. These activities take place in the service design stage.

- ✔ **Build:** The physical bit where you acquire the solution, such as building the hardware, the servers and networks, or programming the software application. These activities happen in the service transition stage.

- ✔ **Test:** Testing the service is essential to ensure it meets the needs of the business, works in the way you expected, and can be supported. These activities also take place during the service transition stage.

- ✔ **Implement or deploy:** Launching the new or changed service into the live operational environment. This takes place during the service transition stage.

- ✔ **Deliver and support:** The service is now in the live or production environment and is being used by the users. The IT organisation must make sure the service is working and fix it quickly when it goes wrong. These activities take place during the service operation stage.

- ✔ **Improve:** After a service has been operated for some time, it's often possible to optimise or improve the way it's delivered. These activities are part of the CSI stage.

So Who Actually Carries Out ITIL Activities? Understanding the Functions

The ITIL framework consists mainly of a set of processes. A *process* is a set of activities coordinated to achieve an objective. But who in your organisation carries out the activities?

Some people, when introduced to ITIL for the first time, immediately assume they have to employ more staff to do ITIL. For example, when they see mention of a problem management process they think to themselves, 'I must set up a problem management team.' This isn't always the right approach. Although many organisations do have a problem management team, this is (I hope) because they've decided that it's the most appropriate thing to do for their organisation. ITIL has over 20 processes, and you can't set up a team for every one. One of the strengths of ITIL is that it describes processes that organisations can adapt to suit their needs without employing a fleet of new staff.

People already perform many of the ITIL activities in your organisation. Maybe what they lack is a bit of coordination. You need to be sure that the activities your staff perform focus on the goals of your organisation. The ITIL processes give you the coordination you need.

But I still haven't answered the question 'Who actually does all this stuff?' Here's why: ITIL can't come along and tell you that you need 15 network engineers, 30 staff on your service desk and 95 support technicians. If it did, I suspect you would put this book down right now. You and your organisation have to decide who does what. The good news is, ITIL does provide guidance.

In Chapter 2, I define a *function* as an organisational unit. This could be a team, department, division – whatever you call them. In other words, a bunch of people in a room doing stuff. To help you decide which of your staff should do what, ITIL suggests four main functions (four main bunches of people in different rooms):

- ✔ Service desk
- ✔ IT operations management (which splits into two sub-functions: IT operations control and facilities management)
- ✔ Technical management
- ✔ Application management

The functions are the source of the people who take on the roles that perform the activities that are part of the processes (read it again slowly; you'll get it!). ITIL describes the functions as providing the resources for the various stages of the service lifecycle. It also describes the functions as the owners of certain skills and knowledge.

The service desk and the IT operations management functions provide resources for the service operation stage. The technical management and application management functions provide resources for *every* stage of the lifecycle.

So, the technical management and application management functions have an understanding of the skills and knowledge required to design and manage the technology and applications. They know what type of skills are required. They can then compare the skills required to the skills available within the organisation, by carrying out a skill analysis. This enables the technical management and application management functions to understand any gaps and ensure that your organisation has access to the skills needed to provide the services to your organisation or customers.

Suppose I want to set up a project to design and transition a new email service. I ring up the technical manager and ask whether he has two email server engineers to help with the hardware requirements and design, and three support staff to help with the build, test and deployment. In addition I ring up the application manager and ask whether he has some staff I can second to my project to help with the software requirements, design and testing. In both cases, the managers may say, 'Sorry, I haven't got them at the moment. However, I've got some friendly contractors – I'll get them for you.' Whatever the solution, I now have the staff I need for each stage of the service lifecycle of my project.

Figure 3-3 summarises the functions. It also illustrates the potential for overlaps to exist between the functions. For example, both IT operations management and technical management can get involved with resolving incidents and problems. This is also true of IT operations management and application management.

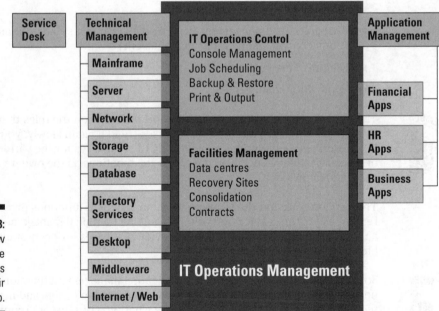

Figure 3-3: Overview of the functions and their overlap.

© Crown copyright 2011. Reproduced under licence from the Cabinet Office.

In the next sections I describe each function in a bit more detail. To see some examples of the functions in action, have a look at Chapter 10.

Dealing with the Users: The Service Desk

I'm sure, like me, you have wonderful stories of hanging on the phone trying to get through to a call centre, being told every 30 seconds that your call is important to the organisation, forgetting why you rang by the time you get through to a human being, and haranguing the innocent call centre operator about how awful the automatic phone system is and why can't you just get through to a nice person straightaway. Or is that just me? At least it gives you something to talk about down the pub.

Are all help experiences like this? When something goes wrong with your PC, who do you call? The IT service desk. And your users don't, I hope, have the same problems as I do with call centres when trying to get help for their IT issues.

Over the years, IT help has been called many things (some of them printable): help desk, support desk, IT service centre. ITIL suggests that the current best practice name is service desk. To be honest, I don't think it matters what you call it as long as the users know what it is, how to contact it and what to expect.

The main aim of a *service desk* is to provide a single point of contact between the service provider and the user.

Providing a single point of contact (sometimes referred to as a SPOC) means giving the users someone to contact when they need help. The definition of an *IT service* is a means of delivering value to customers to enable them to do what they need to do. The IT provider must therefore want the users to get that value as much as possible. So if, for some reason, the users can't use the services to get value, you must give them an easy means of getting their issues resolved and getting up and running again. The issue may be anything from a simple query such as 'Will the IT services be running at the weekend, because I need to do some overtime to catch up?' to a major failure with one of the IT services. Whatever the issue, the user needs a simple, consistent method of getting a resolution.

So how do you help the user? Basically, you give users a single phone number for IT and tell them 'whatever you need from IT, just ring this number'. Sounds simple. But then, of course, the staff on the receiving end need to be prepared and ready to take that call. By telling all users to ring one number, you're putting all your eggs in one basket. The service desk is the shop window of the IT department or organisation. To some users, the service desk *is* the IT department or organisation. So whatever response the users get from the service desk staff influences their opinion of the entire IT department or organisation.

The following sections take you through the role of the service desk function and the strategic decisions you must make about your service desk, like: how many service desks do I need, what sort of staff should be at the service desk, and what skills will they have?

Knowing what the service desk does

In short, the service desk fixes a technical fault, fulfils a service request, answers queries, and helps users to return to work. The list of things that the service desk does is very long, but the following gives you some idea:

- Log incidents and service requests and allocate categories and priorities.
- Provide first-line investigation and diagnosis.
- Resolve incidents and service requests, where possible.
- Escalate incidents and service requests to other parties to resolve within agreed timescales.
- Keep users informed of progress.
- Close all resolved incidents, service requests and other calls.
- Conduct satisfaction surveys.

As I explain in the earlier section 'So Who Actually Carries Out ITIL Activities? Understanding the Functions', the service desk is a function – a bunch of people in a room. This book is mostly about processes. So how does the service desk coordinate its activities? The service desk function has most involvement with the following processes:

- Incident management
- Request fulfilment
- Access management

The service desk owns the incident or service request. This means that the service desk staff are collectively responsible for the incident or service request from the point that it is reported to the service desk until it is closed. This includes the periods of time when the call is escalated to other IT teams for resolution. The timescales for responding to incidents and requests are agreed and recorded in a *service level agreement* (SLA; see Chapter 5).

If you want to know more about the three processes that the service desk gets involved with, have a look at Chapter 8.

Choosing a service desk structure

The physical structure of the service desk must match the needs of the business. You have to make a decision here. If you have users at more than one site, do they need their own service desk at each site, or will they be happy to phone a centralised service desk?

ITIL makes a few suggestions for the structure of your service desk. You can choose between four structures:

- ✔ **Local service desk:** A desk is physically located near the users. This most likely means that if you have more than one user site, you have several service desks, one at each site.

- ✔ **Centralised service desk:** A single service desk at a single fixed location serves users at multiple sites.

- ✔ **Virtual service desk:** The physical location is invisible to the users. The service desk appears to be a centralised service desk, but the users don't actually know where the service desk is. In truth, there are many service desks, possibly scattered geographically, and the users' calls are distributed to different service desks in some way. The calls may be routed by:

  - The type of help needed
  - The language of the user
  - The site the user is ringing from
  - The length of the queue at each service desk
  - The time of day

  A virtual service desk relies on good use of tools and technology to make sure the calls get to the right place, and that the calls are properly logged and shared with the appropriate staff.

- ✔ **Follow-the-sun service desk:** This is a type of virtual service desk where the calls are routed by the time of day. So if my IT organisation has sites in several countries, I can use these locations to provide a 24/7 service desk. As an example, using UK time: between 08:00 and 18:00 the service desk calls will be dealt with in the UK; between 18:00 and 00:00 calls are dealt with in the USA; between 00:00 and 08:00 they're dealt with in India. Staff are cheaper to employ when they are awake or when the sun is up. So it makes sense to route the calls to staff in these countries.

Table 3-1 outlines the pros and cons of each type of service desk, to help you determine the best fit for your organisation or client.

Table 3-1	Pros and Cons of Service Desk Types	
Type of Service Desk	*Pros*	*Cons*
Local service desk	Service desk staff are more likely to have better knowledge of the staff and the business activities that happen at that site. Users may be able to physically visit the service desk and ask for help.	Users may think they can jump the queue by walking into the service desk office and standing by a service analyst's desk This is not always the best use of resources: for example, if you have six service desks each supporting a site of a different size, you may have to provide staff to be at each desk the whole time, but they may not be busy for all that time dealing with calls. Experience and details of resolutions are not shared. Resolved issues may not be communicated to the other service desks unless good processes and systems are put in place. Several service desks may resolve the same incident independently and therefore duplicate effort.
Centralised service desk	You can gain the benefit of economies of scale. Issues and details of resolutions are more likely to be shared, therefore providing better services.	The service desk may lack the local knowledge that you sometimes get from a local service desk.

Type of Service Desk	Pros	Cons
Virtual service desk	Can make use of home-workers and technology such as self-help websites where users can log their own issues.	The technology can be complex and difficult to get right.
Follow-the-sun service desk	Makes good use of local resources and therefore is sometimes a relatively low-cost solution.	This approach relies on technology again. Good escalation and handover procedures are required.

Getting the right service desk staff

A single point of contact also means a single point of perception. As I mention in the introduction to this section, the response the users get from the service desk staff influences their opinion of the entire IT department or organisation. If users are greeted by a monosyllabic Neanderthal grunt, they'll have little confidence that their issues will be resolved. On the other hand, if users are greeted by an efficient, confident voice that sounds willing and able, users will feel much more optimistic about getting their issues fixed.

So how do you ensure that the latter response is the common one for your service desk? Training. Well, recruitment and training. Service desk staff must have an appropriate collection of skills and knowledge. Make sure service desk staff have:

- **Interpersonal skills** such as good communication and empathy

- **Business awareness** such as knowledge of what the business does and of the organisational structure

- **Technical awareness** – at a minimum, basic IT literacy, knowledge of how to use the service desk software application, and some basic knowledge of the IT services supported

- **Understanding of procedures and documentation** such as service level agreements, escalation procedures, known errors and knowledge bases

How techie does a service desk need to be?

You design service desks to provide the service you've agreed with the business customers (or the management if you're in the IT department of an organisation). So not all service desk staff are technical experts, and getting a deeply technical issue resolved in a short time isn't necessarily an indicator of a good service desk. If the agreement is that the service desk quickly deals with all calls and resolves issues, then this should be the case. But in other cases, the agreement may be that the service desk has the skills required only to log calls and resolve simple issues.

You agree the level of support the service desk provides with senior management, and take into account the needs of the business and the cost of providing the desk. Then, after you agree the type of service desk and set it up, you tell the users and set their expectations.

Managing the Day-to-day Stuff: IT Operations Management

IT operations management consists of the staff that do the day-to-day tasks that keep the IT infrastructure and the IT services going. This, of course, has to be done to meet the service levels that are agreed with the business.

The IT operations management function has a dual role, being:

- ✔ Responsible for executing the activities and performance standards defined during service design and tested during service transition (see the earlier section 'Getting to Know the Service Lifecycle'); that means maintaining the stability of the IT infrastructure and the consistency of the IT services

- ✔ Part of the process of adding value to the business by being able continually to adapt to business requirements and demand

This is a bit of a balancing act. On the one hand nothing must go wrong and the infrastructure must be as stable as possible. On the other hand the infrastructure and staff must be able to adapt to the changing needs of the business. A bit of a tricky one.

Considering teams and skills

In order to achieve a balance between stability and adaptability, the IT operations management team needs the following:

- ✔ An understanding of how technology is used to provide IT services
- ✔ An understanding of the relative importance of the services and their impact on the business
- ✔ Clearly differentiated metrics to report to the business on the achievement of service objectives
- ✔ IT operations staff who understand exactly how the performance of the technology affects the delivery of the IT services
- ✔ Procedures and manuals that outline the role of IT operations

Looking at typical activities

In order to distinguish between IT operations management and the other functions (especially technical management and application management; see the earlier section 'So Who Actually Carries Out ITIL Activities? Understanding the Functions') it's useful to consider the sort of activities that IT operations management will get involved with. Activities comprise:

- ✔ Delivering and measuring the value of the services
- ✔ Ensuring that a device or system is actually working
- ✔ Focusing on shorter-term, repetitive day-to-day activities
- ✔ Turning plans developed in other service lifecycle stages into actions

The IT operations management function splits into two sub-functions: facilities management and IT operations control:

- ✔ **IT operations control** is what many experienced IT people think of as the old-fashioned view of a mainframe operator: someone staring at a screen, waiting for something to happen. IT operations control consists of the following activities:
  - Backup and restore of data on behalf of technical and applications teams
  - Console management – observation and monitoring of components and services (this uses the event management process; see Chapter 8)

- Involvement in resolving incidents and problems, part of second-line or higher-level support

- Job scheduling – management of routine jobs and scripts

- Print and output – collation and distribution of centralised printing or electronic output

Sometimes an operations bridge or *network operations centre* (NOC) is set up as a focus for operations control activities. Even if your organisation doesn't have one, I'm sure you've seen the sort of thing on television. It's a bit like the bridge of a futuristic space ship: banks of screens with staff sitting in front of them waiting for something to happen. Inevitably, the person in charge sits in the centre of the operations bridge in a big leather chair.

✔ **Facilities management** refers to the management of the physical IT environment and is often outsourced to specialist companies. It can include the following:

- Coordination of large-scale projects such as the movement of a data centre

- Management of the physical IT environment, including data centres, computer rooms and recovery sites

- Management of power and cooling equipment

Managing the Technology

The *technical management* function has a dual role as:

✔ Custodian of technical knowledge and expertise related to managing the IT infrastructure

✔ Provider of the resources to support the service lifecycle (see the earlier section 'Getting to Know the Service Lifecycle')

Considering teams and skills

So the technical management function is the bunch of people with the appropriate skills and knowledge who perform activities at any stage in the service lifecycle. Sometimes staff are allocated permanent roles; other times they get involved in project work as and when required. It depends on the size and type of your organisation.

The exact skills and teams you have in your organisation depend on the services you provide and the technology that supports them. However, you likely have some, or a combination of, teams dealing with:

- Databases
- Directory services
- Mainframes and servers
- Network support
- Storage
- The Internet

Not only does technical management provide resources for the service life-cycle, but it's the service lifecycle that prompts consideration of the necessary knowledge and skills during the design of the services.

A project to provide a new service is at the design stage. Jane, the technical architect, decides that a technology platform that the organisation has not used before will provide the best service. So, during the design activity for the new service, Jane and the John (the manager of the technical management function) identify the skill and resource requirements for providing the new service. John takes these requirements and ensures that the new skills and any additional new resources are in place in time to deliver and support the new service.

Looking at typical activities

Note that the second role of the technical management function is to plan and provide the technical resources to support the service lifecycle. This ensures that the knowledge and resources required to design, test, manage and improve IT services is identified, developed and refined. This implies ensuring that your organisation has, or has access to, the right type and level of human resources. In other words, you need the right people. You may need to train staff to be able to design, transition and support your services. This is, of course, not as easy as it sounds, and maintaining the balance between the skill level, utilisation and cost of human resources is quite a feat.

The technical management function is involved with many activities. I list just a few below to give you a flavour:

✔ Defining standards and architectures during the strategy and design stages

✔ Designing and delivering training programmes for technical staff, service desk and users

✔ Getting involved in projects during service design, service transition, CSI and operational projects, such as operating system upgrades, server consolidation projects or physical moves

✔ Identifying and documenting skill needs, including developing skills inventories and conducting training needs analyses

✔ Identifying the knowledge and expertise required to manage and operate the IT infrastructure and deliver IT services

✔ Recruiting or contracting in resources

✔ Resolving incidents and problems as part of second-line or higher-level support

Managing the Applications

The *application management* function is similar to the technical management function I describe in the earlier section 'Managing the Technology', but in its own technical domain. In this case the technical domain is that of your software applications. So, nearly everything I say about technical management applies here – just substitute the word *application* for *technical*.

One thing I must point out is that ITIL distinguishes between application management and application development:

✔ **Application development** tends to involve the programming of applications and often the analysis of application requirements and the design of the application. These activities are quite well established in many organisations.

✔ **Application management** provides the overall control of applications, along with a strategy for how applications are acquired and developed in the organisation. Whereas software programs are often acquired from a multitude of sources, it's important that your organisation has an overall strategy and policy for how it wants to manage software applications through the service lifecycle.

Application management has a dual role as:

- ✔ Custodian of knowledge and expertise related to managing applications
- ✔ Provider of the resources to support the service lifecycle

Considering teams and skills

The application management function is the bunch of people with the appropriate skills and knowledge who manage software applications through each stage of the service lifecycle. Staff may be permanent roles, or they may work on projects.

How your application management teams are organised depends on the applications you provide. Sometimes teams are divided by application: a team for the manufacturing planning application and another for the payroll application. On the other hand the teams may be organised by when they get involved in the service lifecycle.

Looking at typical activities

However the teams are organised, application management involves such things as:

- ✔ Assisting in the design and deployment of applications
- ✔ Assisting in the on-going support of those applications
- ✔ Defining overall strategy, policies and application architectures
- ✔ Getting involved in the testing and validation of applications
- ✔ Identifying functional and manageability requirements for application software
- ✔ Providing guidance to IT operations about how best to manage applications

In common with the technical management function, in application management the defining of the requirements for skills and resources needed to support applications starts in service strategy, is expanded in service design, and developed through the remainder of the service lifecycle (see the earlier section 'Getting to Know the Service Lifecycle').

In the earlier section 'Managing the Technology' I explain that the second role of technical management is to plan and provide the technical resources to support the service lifecycle – and the information I supply there also applies to application management. The application management function carries out many activities in line with those I list in 'Managing the Technology'. The function is also responsible for research and development of solutions that can expand the service portfolio.

Part II

Getting to Grips with the Service Lifecycle and the Processes

The 5th Wave   By Rich Tennant

"I have 3 of the best selling ITIL core books. 'Service Strategy and the Philospher's Stone,' 'Service Design and the Prisoner of Azkaban,' and 'Service Transition and the Goblet of Fire.'"

Part II

Getting to Grips
with the Service
Lifecycle and the
Processes

In this part . . .

*E*quipped with the basic ITIL toolkit by Part I, now
you can dive into the ITIL processes proper. A fair
number of these processes exist, and this part takes you
through each. Calmly. Each chapter covers a different
set of processes in the service lifecycle, taking in service
strategy, service design, service transition, service operation and continual service improvement.

Chapter 4

Thinking It Through: Service Strategy

In This Chapter

▶ Having a strategy for your services

▶ Understanding what the customer wants

▶ Managing your entire collection of services

▶ Bringing together financial management

▶ Knowing the demand for your services, and how to supply

*W*hen you start a new project at home – decorating the bathroom, clearing out the garage, tidying the garden – do you just jump in head first? I suspect you sometimes do. Perhaps you regret doing so and ask yourself why you didn't sit down first and plan your project. Most things work better if you plan them first. And a good plan starts with a good strategy.

Many IT organisations grow their IT services organically. They just respond to business needs as and when they occur and implement other good ideas suggested by IT staff. Over time, organisations discover that they have a set of services. I think this is somewhat haphazard. You gain a lot by sitting down and doing a bit of planning – Rome wasn't built in a day. Building a good set of services takes time and effort.

This chapter provides an overview of the ITIL service strategy stage in the service lifecycle, as described in the ITIL service strategy book. When you have a strategy for your IT services, you use it as a guide to direct your IT organisation to build up a set of IT services that support the business and make best use of your IT assets.

The ITIL service strategy book describes five processes. Four of them I explain in this chapter: service portfolio management, financial management for IT services, demand management and business relationship management. The final process, strategy management for IT services, I explain in Chapter 11.

Understanding Strategy

What is a strategy? Think of a *strategy* as a high-level plan to achieve something.

Put simply, a strategy is a plan that outlines how an organisation will meet a defined set of objectives.

The definition implies that first you must know what your defined objectives are. So, in any piece of work, deciding what you want to achieve so you can then set a plan in place to achieve it is common sense. By laying down your strategy you make it easier to tell others about your plans and get support for them.

Not only does defining strategy make you consider *what* you want to do, but it also prompts you to consider *why* you should do things. Sometimes an IT department blindly implements what management tells it to do, without much thought. Stopping and asking why you're doing something can lead to better, more innovative solutions.

Some people run screaming from the room at the mere mention of the word *strategy*. But don't be afraid. In this chapter I just prompt you to think about having a plan for deciding which IT services you should offer to your customers or organisation. This inevitably means talking about money, because developing services costs money. It also involves thinking about whether a strong demand exists for the service.

An organisation without a strategy has no idea of how it will achieve its goals. It's groping around in the dark. Things may happen accidently and turn out right – but can you take the risk?

The activities you use to create a strategy for your IT service are described by the ITIL process called strategy management for IT services. I describe this process in Chapter 11.

Understanding the Purpose of the Service Strategy Stage

The service strategy stage sets the strategy for your IT services. This stage helps you decide who your customers are and what IT services you want to offer them. This allows you to define the complete set of IT services that you want to provide. This complete set of services is known as a *service portfolio*.

The strategy you create provides a sense of direction for all your service management activities. Your strategy will influence all the activities you perform in other service lifecycle stages. (In Chapter 3, I describe the service lifecycle; Figure 3-1 shows the service lifecycle, with service strategy at the centre.)

The purpose of the ITIL service strategy stage is to allow you and your organisation to make decisions such as:

- ✔ What services should we offer and to whom?
- ✔ How do we differentiate ourselves from competing alternatives?
- ✔ How can we create value for our customers?
- ✔ How can we make a case for strategic investments?
- ✔ How should we define service quality?

Thinking about strategy gets you thinking about how to use service management as a strategic asset, that is how to use service management to the benefit of the organisation, either to the organisation's competitive advantage in the marketplace or to achieve the organisation's business goals. IT services and systems are ever more relied upon by businesses to help them do what they do.

For example, some companies must respond quickly to their customers in order to win business, and therefore a fast and reliable email service may be the difference between winning and losing an order. In another organisation, a sales quotation IT system may contribute to quickly offering customers a good deal and thus winning business. These are both examples of achieving a strategic advantage.

When the strategy is set, in the service strategy stage you put policies and standards in place that make it easier for the organisation to achieve the strategy and hence the strategic goals. I like to think of this as putting signposts in place that direct you towards your goal or destination. The policies and standards help prevent you and your colleagues reinventing the wheel each time you do something to your services. It's a little like saying, 'We've done it before and here are the things that we discovered that should make things easier for you.'

Take a simple example of going on a journey. Say you have to travel a hundred miles to a major city. I'm your boss, and your strategic objective is to reach the city. An example of a policy may be: 'Take the train. We find that you arrive fresh and ready to do business as opposed to enduring a stressful drive.' Or the policy may be: 'Travel the evening before, because train travel is cheaper in the evenings than during the morning peak hours.'

Understanding Some Basic Principles

In order to identify and manage a strategy there are couple of aspects of your services and your organisation that you must understand and identify.

The value proposition

The *value proposition* helps you understanding how your customer gets value from each IT service. The value proposition refers to the little equation:

Value = utility + warranty

Briefly, *utility* refers to what the service does; a service that does this is *fit for purpose*. *Warranty* refers to an assurance that the customer receives the appropriate levels of availability, capacity, security and continuity for the service; a service that provides warranty is *fit for use*. (For a more detailed explanation of these terms, have a look at Chapter 2.) Your organisation must understand how the customer derives value from each and every service the organisation provides. This is part of the high-level business requirements of the service.

The level of utility and warranty the customer requires affects the assets you use to provide the service. Two types of assets exist: *resources* and *capabilities*. (I describe these assets in more detail in Chapter 2.) For example, if a customer demands higher availability, say 22 hours a day with no failures, you have to use up a lot of knowledge to design a more resilient service, and you have to spend money to acquire additional hardware and software and possibly support staff. So the value the customer gets from the service is linked to the assets needed to deliver the service.

Understanding what the customer wants

Value is linked to the business outcomes that customers want to achieve. Customers don't necessarily *want* to use your IT services. But they recognise advantages exist to using IT in general. Using a PC is often faster, more accurate and less labour-intensive, but users expect the software applications to be easy to use and focused on their needs. Additionally, they expect the IT services to be there when they need them and to work at the right speed. In other words, they expect the IT service to be a help not a hindrance.

A vehicle roadside recovery organisation is discussing how IT can support its business needs. The business states that an important business outcome is the ability to despatch the nearest available driver and vehicle to a stranded customer at any time of day or night. The IT service provider discusses the basic levels of utility and warranty to fulfil this need and provide the value that the customer requires.

Service providers

You can't set a strategy for your IT services unless you know what sort of IT provider you are. ITIL suggests three provider types:

- ✔ **Type I – internal service provider:** A provider embedded within the business unit it serves. For example, the research and development department of a pharmaceutical organisation has such specialised IT needs that it employs an IT department to provide IT services exclusively to that business unit.

- ✔ **Type II – shared services unit:** A single function that provides services to the whole organisation. This is a common form of internal provision. An example is a central IT department that fulfils the needs of all business units in the organisation. In this case, IT is often bundled with other departments such as HR and finance, and they work as a combined, shared-services unit.

- ✔ **Type III – external service provider:** An organisation that provides services to external customers. A commercial business.

Overview of the Service Strategy Processes

As I explain in Chapter 3, a *process* is a set of activities coordinated to achieve a specific outcome. What follow are descriptions of many activities that are required to set and manage the strategy for your IT services. You don't perform each process in isolation; you coordinate the processes to achieve an overall aim. Take a look at Figure 4-1 for a quick overview of the processes of service strategy.

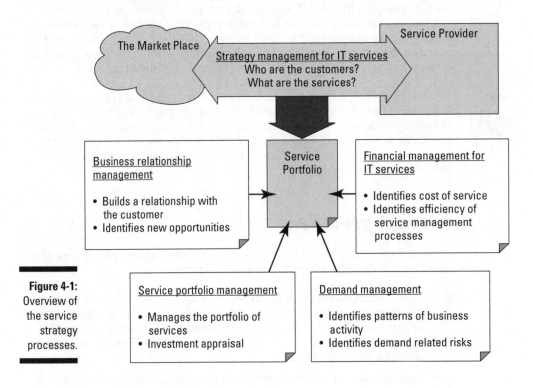

Figure 4-1: Overview of the service strategy processes.

The Market Place

Service Provider

Strategy management for IT services
Who are the customers?
What are the services?

Service Portfolio

Business relationship management

• Builds a relationship with the customer
• Identifies new opportunities

Financial management for IT services

• Identifies cost of service
• Identifies efficiency of service management processes

Service portfolio management

• Manages the portfolio of services
• Investment appraisal

Demand management

• Identifies patterns of business activity
• Identifies demand related risks

The processes are:

✔ Strategy management for IT services (see Chapter 11)

✔ Service portfolio management (see the later section 'Knowing Your Services: Service Portfolio Management')

✔ Financial management for IT services (see the later section 'Managing Your Finances: Financial Management for IT Services')

✔ Demand management (see the later section 'Identifying the Demand: Demand Management' and Chapter 11)

✔ Business relationship management (see the later section 'Getting Friendly with Your Customers: Business Relationship Management')

Knowing Your Services: Service Portfolio Management

Does everyone in your IT organisation know what IT services you've got? Do they know what new developments are in the pipeline? Does your organisation spend money in the right places? Do senior management have the right information at their fingertips to make good investment decisions? Put simply, *service portfolio management* is the process (set of activities) that manages your portfolio (the complete set) of services.

Defining some service portfolio management terms

No doubt you're keen to know what service portfolio management entails. . . . The following sections give you the low-down, starting with an explanation of the service portfolio.

What's a service portfolio?

According to the ITIL books, 'The *service portfolio* is the complete set of services that are managed by a service provider'. A service portfolio isn't just a list of services; it's usually a set of software tools and databases you use to manage your IT services throughout the service lifecycle. The service portfolio is used to manage the entire lifecycle of all services, and includes three categories of service:

✔ **Service pipeline:** This includes the services you're thinking about, and those that are proposed or in development. So these are the services that are in the early stages of the service lifecycle, in the service strategy stage or possibly the service design stage. (See Chapters 5 and 6 for details on the design stage.) Services that are still in the service strategy stage are those that are proposed and have a business case created for them. Therefore a value proposition has been created and a cost–benefit analysis has been developed, but the decision about whether to approve and charter the service for introduction into the live environment has not been made. (For more on business cases and cost–benefit analyses, head over to the later section 'Business case'.)

✔ **Service catalogue:** This includes the services that are currently live plus those you're preparing to go live: the services that are live or available for deployment. So the service catalogue contains services that have been *chartered* (approved and with money made available to develop them). Some of these services are live; others may still be in the service design or service transition (see Chapter 7) stages of the lifecycle. The service catalogue is often managed as a separate entity – see Chapter 5 for details of the service catalogue management process.

When your organisation starts to develop services, do you keep quiet and not tell anyone? Hopefully not. With any luck, you communicate your plans to the rest of the IT department and to the business or customer in order to prepare it for the new service. Think of the service catalogue as a selling aid in the same way that you go into a car showroom and the salespeople show you the catalogue (or brochure) of all the cars that are available for you to buy. Some of the cars may be sitting on the forecourt, and you can drive them away today, and some may have to be ordered for you, and you may have to wait. In fact, for new models, the car manufacturer may start advertising the new vehicle and take orders well in advance of the date when the car will be available. The IT service catalogue works in a similar way: some services are available now, some are available for deployment, and others can be ordered for delivery some time in the future.

The decision to move services from the service pipeline to the service catalogue is often made on a case-by-case basis – it's a good idea to have a policy for how you make the decision in your organisation.

✔ **Retired services:** This includes the services that you used to offer but have now withdrawn. It can be useful to keep information about these services in case they're needed again in the future. As part of the service portfolio, the section for retired services allows you to manage the withdrawal of services in a controlled manner and also provides information about any assets (resources or capabilities) that have been released and can be redeployed elsewhere.

You may have come across the word *portfolio* in different contexts. Maybe you invest in shares in the stock market. If so, your portfolio consists of all of the companies you invest in. I suspect you also maintain information about the companies you're planning to invest in, in order to decide on the right time to invest. You may also keep information about the companies you used to invest in, in case you want to reinvest. In other words, you keep information about your complete set of investments.

Figure 4-2 shows a picture of the service portfolio. It illustrates how developments to a service can be managed through the lifecycle by recording their status in the service portfolio. For example, when the new version of the sales service is moved into the live environment, it will be given the status of 'operational'.

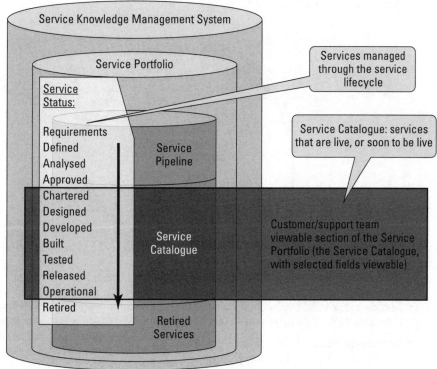

Figure 4-2:
The service portfolio and its content.

© Crown copyright 2011. Reproduced under licence from the Cabinet Office.

What's service portfolio management?

The ITIL service strategy book describes service portfolio management as a dynamic method for governing investments in service management across the enterprise, and managing them for value. Sounds a bit grand!

In simple terms, service portfolio management enables your IT organisation to manage all your IT services as a complete set. This means you can understand where your assets are being used and which services consume most assets, both resources and capabilities.

A bunch of portfolios

The ITIL service strategy book describes several portfolios. A portfolio is simply information about a collection of things. There's no need to get confused. Each portfolio is defined in a database or structured document, and is just an organised source of information. This figure shows all the portfolios.

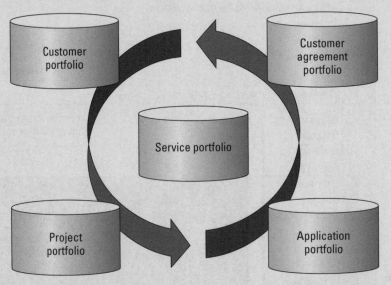

- ✔ **Service portfolio:** See the section 'Defining some service portfolio management terms'

- ✔ **Customer portfolio:** See the section 'Getting Friendly with Your Customers: Business Relationship Management'

- ✔ **Customer agreement portfolio:** See the section 'Getting Friendly with Your Customers: Business Relationship Management'

- ✔ **Application portfolio:** A database or structured document used to manage applications throughout their lifecycle, and which contains the key attributes of all applications

- ✔ **Project portfolio:** A database or structured document used to manage projects throughout their lifecycle, and which is used to coordinate projects

Service portfolio management enables you to answer questions and make decisions about the entire set of services. What questions would you want to ask? Well, the service portfolio (see the previous section) should contain adequate information for you to be able to answer the following questions:

✔ Why should customers buy these services?

✔ Why should customers buy these services from us?

✔ What are the pricing or chargeback models?

✔ What are our strengths and weaknesses, priorities and risks?

✔ How should our resources and capabilities be allocated?

Having answered the questions, you can now use the service portfolio to:

✔ Make investment decisions

✔ Prioritise investments

✔ Manage resources

✔ Approve the movement of services from one lifecycle stage to the next

The boundaries between the three parts of the service portfolio can represent milestones, or gateways, where the project stops and senior management make a decision about whether to continue, based on estimates of the time and cost involved.

Figure 4-3 is a suggestion of one of the outputs of a service portfolio – in this case, an overview of the services recorded in the service portfolio. I include the figure to give you an idea of some of the information that's in the service portfolio. Please bear in mind this is just a rough sample; the service portfolio should contain a lot more information to help you manage your services.

Note how the payroll service is in the service portfolio twice. Each is a different version. So you can manage upgrades and new releases by using the service portfolio.

As a lot of service portfolio management is about making investment decisions, there are a couple of important aspects to take into account:

✔ **Financial aspects:** You must look at the financial case. This involves reviewing the business case and looking at the *return on investment* (ROI). In other words, is it a sound investment financially speaking? In making this decision you use the financial management for IT services process. (See the later section 'Managing Your Finances: Financial Management for IT Services'.)

✔ **Demand for the service:** You must consider what the business need for the service is and understand how the business will use it. This can constitute a risk. If you don't have a clear understanding of the frequency, duration and volume of use of the IT service, you can end up buying lots of expensive equipment or acquiring specialised resources only to discover that it's not used. In investigating this issue you use the demand management process. (See the later section 'Identifying the demand: Demand Management'.)

Service	Version	Description	Portfolio part	Status	Business outcomes	Utility & Warranty	Resources used
Customer Relationship Management (CRM)	V1	New service	Service Pipeline	Defined	To be agreed	To be agreed	To be agreed
Payroll	V5	New version. In design phase	Service Catalogue	Built	Pay staff on time	Click for more information	Click for more information
Email	Standard	Part of standard desktop	Service Catalogue	Operational	Internal and external business communication	Click for more information	Click for more information
Payroll	V4.7.3	Current live version	Service Catalogue	Operational	Pay staff on time	Click for more information	Click for more information
Production planning system	V9.1.3	Current live version	Service Catalogue	Operational	Optimise use of factory resources	Click for more information	Click for more information

Figure 4-3:
Example of a service portfolio status report.

Based on ITIL® material. Reproduced under licence from The Cabinet Office.

Do you do service portfolio management?

You may be reading this section thinking 'I don't think anyone in my organisation does this.' Well think again. Service portfolio management manages investments in IT – how does this happen in your organisation? Think about the round of budget activities that inevitably take place each year. I'm sure you're familiar with the rush of activity prior to each new budget period, when managers have to decide what money is required for the next year. Funding through budgets is always limited, so senior management have to decide how the money is best spent. IT staff make suggestions for new IT

services or improvements to existing services throughout the year. The response from senior management is often 'That's a good idea, but we can't afford it now. We'll have a closer look at budget time when more money becomes available.' Senior management assess each of these suggestions along with new services that are needed to meet the needs of the customers, and decide which will be invested in this year and which will have to wait until another time. ITIL views all this activity as part of service portfolio management.

Looking at the activities of service portfolio management

The following activities are normally performed in the service strategy stage of the service lifecycle. You can perform them on your complete set of services or just one service. These activities take the service to the stage where it has been approved and the resources identified and made available. Once the service has been chartered, it moves through the other stages of the service lifecycle.

In the service portfolio management process, the decisions to move the service through these subsequent phases – to approve the design (see Chapters 5 and 6) and promote the service to service transition (see Chapter 7) – must be made by senior management. Whenever management make such a decision, you update the service portfolio to change the status of the service and to allocate the necessary resources in the service portfolio.

The following sections look at each activity of the service portfolio management process in turn.

Initiate process

Because service portfolio management is the main means of managing new services and changes to existing services, and prioritising these investments, you must have a formal method of triggering these activities. Service portfolio management can be initiated in many ways such as:

- ✔ **Strategy management for IT services:** This is the process that defines the strategy for your IT services. The strategy will provide guidance on which services you introduce, modify or retire. Deciding to act on your strategy will trigger the service portfolio management process. (See Chapter 11 for more about strategy management for IT services.)

- ✔ **Business relationship management:** This process maintains a relationship with your customers and so will receive requests from them for new services or changes to services. (See the later section 'Getting Friendly with Your Customers: Business Relationship Management'.)

- ✔ **Continual service improvement (CSI):** CSI will identify initiatives for improving your services and processes; the investment will require authorisation. (See Chapter 9 for more about CSI.)

- ✔ **Other service management processes:** Each service management process identifies options that need investment. Often these are initiated through change management. However, if significant investment is required, this should be handled through service portfolio management.

Define

As the name suggests, the *define* activities of service portfolio management define the IT service. You should maintain a standard set of information for each service, so that each time you add a new service to the service portfolio you collect the same set of information.

One key task is to establish a business case. Every service in the service portfolio must have a *business case*: the high-level business requirements of the service and a cost– benefit analysis that helps to establish the ROI of the service. (For more details, check out the section 'Business case', later in the chapter). The high-level business requirements include a description of the value proposition. (See the section 'The value proposition', earlier in this chapter.) The business case describes how the business will get value from the service in terms of utility and warranty.

For more information about defining IT services, have a look at Chapter 11.

Analyse

The *analyse* activities of service portfolio management analyse the service to establish its alignment with your strategy for service management. (The earlier section 'Understanding the Purpose of the Service Strategy Lifecycle Phase' covers establishing a strategy for your IT services.) You compare each IT service with your strategy to establish how well the service contributes to the achievement of the strategy. This provides a way of establishing the relative priority of each service, and enables you to carry out an investment appraisal of each service.

Approve

Based on the analysis of each service (see the previous section), you can decide whether to invest in the IT service now, or delay or reject the investment. If the answer is 'invest now', the service is *approved* and the service and resources are authorised.

The service portfolio management 'approve' activities will include a regular review of all services in the service portfolio, including those in the service catalogue. (There's more on the catalogue in the earlier section 'What's a service portfolio?'.) For existing services, the outcome of the review falls into one of the following six categories:

- ✔ **Retain:** Keep the service as it is.

- ✔ **Replace:** Replace the service.

- ✔ **Rationalise:** Make better use of the assets required to provide the service.

- ✔ **Re-factor:** In cases where some of the functionality of the service can be better achieved by removing it to a different service.

- ✔ **Renew:** A service that may require some technical updating.

- ✔ **Retire:** Retire the service.

Approving change proposals

Having decided the general approach, when investing in new services or major changes to existing services, a change proposal should be submitted by Service Portfolio Management to Change Management for authorisation.

A *change proposal* is a document that includes a high level description of a potential service introduction or significant change, along with a corresponding business case and an expected implementation schedule.

The change proposal allows change management to assess the impact of the proposed change on other services and on the availability of resources. It also provides change management with advanced warning of the change (if it is authorised) and warns them to expect a number of requests for change (RFCs) to be raised to manage the introduction of the service and its constituent components.

Change management will assess the proposed design and resource requirements in order to discover if the new or changed service is feasible. This is only high-level work at this stage – the full design of the service will commence once the service has been chartered. The result of the assessment is either the authorisation or rejection of the change proposal.

Charter

Having made the decision to approve the service and commit the resources and capabilities necessary to develop it (see the previous sections), you must now communicate the decision and get the ball rolling. A *charter* is a document that contains details of the new or changed service and is used to communicate the steps, and the costs and benefits, to the organisation, and to plan to implement the approval. In many cases the 'approve' and 'charter' steps are similar to your project approval and project initiation activities.

Managing Your Finances: Financial Management for IT Services

IT isn't free! Someone has to pay for it, or at least account for it. Do you budget in your personal life? You may think me sad, but I've been known to sit down and write a list of what I spend and what I earn. After I've done the calculations, I decide how much money I have left to spend at the pub.

The IT department never seems to have enough money, so you have to make sure you spend what you have wisely.

The purpose of the financial management for IT services process is to secure the appropriate level of funding to design, develop and deliver services that meet the strategy of the organisation.

Financial management for IT services acts as a gatekeeper to ensure that an IT provider does not commit to a service it cannot afford. To do this, financial management for IT services identifies the balance between cost and quality of service, and maintains the balance of supply and demand between the service provider and the customer.

Financial management for IT services provides the business and IT with the quantification, in financial terms, of the value of the IT service. To do this, it must quantify, in financial terms, the value of the assets that make up your services.

An organisation needs to know the cost of its services so that it can secure the funding for them. If your organisation is a commercial organisation, it recovers the cost of the services by charging for them, and hopefully makes a profit. If you're an internal provider delivering IT services to other people in the same organisation, you must forecast what it will cost to provide the IT services and you must ensure that the budget is available.

Financial management for IT services provides data and information to enable the forecasting of the operational costs associated with providing and operating the IT services – it aggregates financial information. This means that financial management for IT services is like a sponge. It collects and soaks up, from across the organisation, information about the costs of providing and managing the IT services. It then slices and dices the information into an understandable format so that it can be used by all of the IT department to make decisions about how to provide better management of the IT services.

Creating a cost model

A *cost model* is a framework which allows the service provider to determine the costs of providing services and ensure they're allocated correctly.

Cost models can be used to allocate costs in many ways: by department, by customer, by location or by service. For example, what does it cost to provide IT services to the sales department (cost model by internal customer), or what does it cost to provide the email service (cost model by IT service)? It depends on your organisation and its policy how you do this. The cost of a service is the sum of its parts, those parts being the assets that make up the service – hardware, software, people, and so on. To understand what it costs the IT provider to deliver the services, you need to know the amount of assets used in each case. Not all assets are dedicated to a single service; some are shared. I'm sure in your organisation some hardware is shared between services, for example the network is usually used by many services. Similarly, IT staff (you and your colleagues) no doubt work on several IT services – so how will you allocate their time? Your time and effort should be accounted for and allocated to one or many services. I'm sure you've experienced the joy of filling in time sheets!

To make things easy, classify your costs as:

- **Direct costs:** those that are used exclusively for a service or customer. For example, the server hardware that is used only for the email service will have its cost allocated to the email service.

- **Indirect costs:** costs that cannot be allocated to a single service are shared costs. For example, the service desk costs are shared among the services or customers that use the service desk.

Classifying costs in this way makes it easier to understand where each asset is used and how it should be accounted for. These costs are inputs to your cost model. Another classification is used to separate out the day-to-day costs from the large purchases or investments:

- **Capital costs:** these are usually large purchases such as servers and network equipment. They are assets that your organisation keeps for a long time and which will provide value for a number of years. For this reason, finance departments usually allocate, or spread, the costs over a number of years. You'll hear this special allocation referred to as depreciation. *Depreciation* is the measure of the reduction in value of an asset over its life.

- **Operational costs:** the operational expenditure resulting from running the services on a day-to-day basis, for example staff costs, maintenance costs and overheads such as electricity. Once spent, this money is gone – it has no future value.

By far my favourite cost model is the one that calculates the cost of providing each IT service – cost by service. When you know the total cost of providing the IT service, you can decide how best to charge for the service or how best to account for it.

For example, what's the cost of providing the email system to all your users? Table 4-1 gives an example. First you decide which components form part of the email service. You identify the assets that are dedicated to the service (direct costs). For those components or assets that are shared (indirect costs), you decide how to share the cost. Then you add up the cost of the assets to get a total cost for the email service.

Table 4-1	Calculating the Cost of Providing an Email Service	
Asset	*Amount Used for Email (%)*	*Cost Per Year (£)*
Server hardware (direct)	100	40,000
Server software (direct)	100	10,000
Network usage (indirect)	25	5,000
Engineers – for technical support (indirect)	20	18,000
Service desk staff – to deal with incidents and requests (indirect)	15	12,000
Total cost of providing the email service		85,000

© Crown copyright 2011. Reproduced under licence from the Cabinet Office.

Table 4-1 is simply an example of *part* of a cost model; it's not the complete model. In real life it is more complicated.

All this calculating could become very complicated. However, think about what happens if you get the calculations wrong. If your organisation is a commercial supplier of IT services, and someone miscalculates the cost of the services, your organisation may not recover its costs and could lose money. Not a good thing.

Creating a business case

ITIL describes a *business case* as a business support and planning tool. A business case is usually a document that describes the reasons and costs involved in a course of action. Organisations use a business case to justify the expenditure on a project. The main section of a business case is the *cost–benefit analysis:* an analysis of the costs and benefits of the project.

As an example, the sales department has asked the IT department to develop a new *customer relationship management* (CRM) service. This involves a new software application along with the related hardware and support. Have a look at Table 4-2, which shows what this cost–benefit analysis might look like.

Table 4-2	Example Cost–benefit Analysis
Benefits	Improve ability to identify customer needs
	£100,000 per year increased sales from identifying new customer opportunities
Costs	£50,000 cost of developing new software application
	£30,000 cost of hardware upgrades
	£20,000 per year additional support costs
Risks	Software not completed on time
	Lack of expertise of related technology
	Availability of business staff to identify requirements

© Crown copyright 2011. Reproduced under licence from the Cabinet Office.

Here's a suggested outline for a business case for a new or changed IT service:

- **Introduction:** Set the scene and link the project to the business objectives.
- **Methods and assumptions:** Provide the scope of the project.
- **Business impacts:** Describe the benefits to be gained and the costs that will be incurred: a cost–benefit analysis.
- **Risks and contingencies:** What may go wrong, and how you can get around it.
- **Recommendations:** Give specific actions.

In the service portfolio management process (which I discuss in the earlier section 'Knowing Your Services: Service Portfolio Management'), one of the main activities is to decide which services to invest in. One of the main inputs to this decision is the financial cost of the service. For each new service or significant change to a service, you must calculate the costs involved and the financial benefits. You produce a business case so that the service portfolio management process can compare the financial aspects of various proposed investments and help senior management make a decision.

Looking at the activities of financial management for IT services

The main activities of the financial management for IT services process are:

- **Budgeting:** Getting hold of the money. You predict how much money you'll need next year to provide the IT services, and then you try to secure the money. Your cost models provide a useful structure for predicting costs.

  The budgeting activity can turn into a bit of a game, with each department in the organisation competing for its share of the corporate pot. So you must have a clear understanding of what it costs to provide your services, and how costs may change in the coming period. This means you must find out what the business plans are. Does it intend to expand the business, contract the business, add more staff? Consider anything that may affect the use and cost of the IT services.

- **Accounting:** Calculating the costs – working out where the money has gone. You put structure in place and code the stuff you buy (and get rid of) so that you have an accurate record of what you've spent. The structures are often suggested by your organisation's main finance department, but you may have to change some to suit the types of IT expenditure. Much of this structure is provided by your cost models.

- **Charging:** Deciding whether and/or how to charge. If your organisation is a commercial one then you charge for the IT services with the intention of at least breaking even, and hopefully making a profit. If you're providing IT services to internal customers (people in the same organisation), you don't have to charge. In some cases the financial department does some funny stuff to account for the IT budget. In other organisations the internal IT department does charge. This helps staff and customers understand the cost of IT and sometimes influences how the business uses the IT services.

If you do charge you must have a clear understanding of what it costs to provide the service – see the earlier section 'Creating a cost model'.

Identifying the Demand: Demand Management

Where does the demand for your IT services come from? How do you know when and how often your IT services will be used? The answer is: from the business. Your IT services are only used when the business needs them. Users only use your email system when they want to send a message. The sales department only uses the sales ordering system when one of your organisation's customers contacts the sales department to place an order. Therefore, the IT services must work when the business needs them, not the other way around. Your users don't use the IT services simply because they exist. They use them because they fulfil a need. So if you want to know how much of a service is needed, you have to look at the business activities that the service supports.

The IT department of a manufacturing organisation is running low on network bandwidth at the busiest times of day. In order to share the available network capacity the sales department is asked to reduce the number of sales orders it receives from customers between 10:00 and 12:00 a.m. What do you think the sales department's response is!

If you were managing a supermarket, how would you decide how many staff to put on the checkouts each day? How do you know how many staff are required? Hopefully, you identify the busiest times for the supermarket, when most customers visit, and then match the number of staff at the tills to the ebb and flow of the customers throughout the day. Of course, what is the consequence of getting this wrong? A queue builds up. Not a problem; you may say, when a queue forms I'll put more staff on. Well, if you don't have spare staff in the building already, you won't be able to cope. The queues will get longer, and some customers may not return. On the other hand, if you ask a lot of staff to come in just in case, there may be nothing for them to do.

The moral of the story is that you have to plan ahead and do your best to predict the busy times.

The purpose of the *demand management* process is to understand, anticipate and influence customer demand for services, and to work with capacity management to ensure the service provider has capacity to meet this demand.

Demand management gets involved in every stage of the service lifecycle to ensure that services are designed, tested and delivered to help achieve the business outcomes at the appropriate levels of activity.

Demand management provides an important input into service portfolio management by helping to decide the risks associated with investigating new or changed IT services. You can't manufacture IT capacity in advance and store it for later use, and excess capacity generates cost without creating value. Therefore demand management:

- ✔ Establishes whether demand exists for a service
- ✔ Contributes to the business case for a service (see the earlier section on the business case)
- ✔ Ensure that the cost of production is factored in to the cost of the service

Defining some demand management terms

Here are a couple of bits of terminology used in the ITIL books.

Pattern of business activity

In the words of the ITIL books 'A pattern of business activity (PBA) is a work-load profile of one or more business activities. PBAs are used to help the IT service provider understand and plan for different levels of business activity'.

Business processes are the primary source of demand for services, so identifying the usage of the business processes establishes patterns for the usage of the services – PBAs. You need to identify, analyse and document patterns of usage of business processes, and in doing so you identify the demands that business processes put on the IT services.

Record the following information about the PBA:

- ✔ **Frequency:** How often this pattern occurs in the business
- ✔ **Volume:** The amounts of activity; for example, how many sales orders are processed in one day
- ✔ **Location:** Where in the organisation the business activity takes place – which department, building or country
- ✔ **Duration:** How long the PBA lasts

A theatre ticket agency wants to be sure it has enough telephone operators to handle the demand for ticket requests for concerts and shows. It monitors its customer activity to discover the peaks and troughs of demand. The agency discovers that 70 per cent of customers request tickets on the first day of release, and that demand slowly decreases over time. However, the agency notes that within two weeks of the event, demand increases again. This fluctuation in demand is the PBA.

You can read more about PBAs and see some examples in Chapter 11.

User profile

The ITIL books say 'A *user profile* is a pattern of user demand for IT services. Each user profile includes one or more PBAs' (see the previous section).

A user profile is a combination of many PBAs. User profiles are based on roles and responsibilities, and are typically used to group PBAs into common activity groups. So a user profile represents a typical work profile of a user.

For example, a member of the sales team has three main business activities:

- ✔ Contacting customers – for which he or she uses the customer relationship management IT service
- ✔ Taking orders – for which he or she uses the sales ordering IT service
- ✔ Creating invoices – for which he or she uses the financial management IT service

Each activity is associated with a PBA, which tells you how often and when the activities are performed. By combining the three PBAs you get a good idea of all the business activity performed by the salesperson and hence the demand for all three IT services. The IT department can now use this to calculate the extra load each new salesperson will put on the IT services.

Looking at the activities of demand management

Understanding PBAs helps you to plan and manage the services throughout the lifecycle:

- ✓ **Service strategy:** Identify the services and outcomes and the associated PBAs. Using the service portfolio management process you can approve investments for additional capacity, new services and changes to services.

- ✓ **Service design:** In the service design phase (see Chapters 5 and 6) you can optimise the design of the service to suit the demand patterns. Availability management and capacity management will identify the assets needed to meet the PBAs.

- ✓ **Service transition:** Demand management is a valuable input to testing and validating services to ensure that they can meet the demands of the PBAs.

- ✓ **Service operation:** Technical staff will monitor the service to ensure that service levels are met. If necessary, they'll make better use of resources by adjusting the allocation of resources and consolidating demand.

- ✓ **CSI:** Demand management can identify trends in the PBAs over time that may give rise to improvements and changes.

The demand management process encompasses many activities. Here is a brief description:

- ✓ **Identifying sources of demand forecasting:** The information that allows you to identify PBAs can come from many sources including business plans, marketing plans, production plans and sales forecasts.

- ✓ **Identifying PBAs and user profiles:** Unsurprisingly, the activities that identify PBAs and user profiles (see the previous section).

✔ **Activity-based demand management:** The activities involved in identifying the capacity requirements of a service from the analysis of the business activities that are enabled by the service. So, you analyse how and when the business does what the business does, and then you use this to predict how much IT capacity you need: how much server power, network bandwidth and disk storage, and how many software licences and possibly staff to support the service.

Activity-based demand management involves:

- Identifying PBAs

- Grouping them into user profiles

- Documenting and coding PBAs so all of IT can use them to manage various aspects of the service

✔ **Developing differentiated offerings:** By identifying and understanding PBAs, you may detect that your customers require different levels of service at different times of the month or year. By working with the service portfolio management process, you can identify different service packages matched to the needs of the customers.

✔ **Management of operational demand:** Generally speaking, the IT organisation has to ensure that services meet the service level targets agreed with the business. However, sometimes you may use demand management at a tactical level to influence the users to use the service when *you* want them to use it.

Take the example of telephone service providers. You often get a deal in which evening and weekend phone calls are free. They're giving them away! Well, the majority of phone usage is in business hours, so the phone companies have to have enough kit and staff in place to fulfil business usage. In the evenings and weekends, when most businesses have gone home, the phone companies are left with spare capacity that costs money. It's better for them to appear to give it away for free than not have it used at all. By charging you less, or nothing at all, the phone companies hope to balance out the demand so that all in all they make better use of their resources. So, you can do the same. If you have limited capacity at certain times, you can agree with your customers that you'll charge less if they use it at off-peak times. However, be warned: customers must agree. Customers mustn't perceive the off-peak agreement as the IT service failing to provide a proper service.

If you want to know more about demand management, turn to Chapter 11.

Getting Friendly with Your Customers: Business Relationship Management

Business relationship management pretty much does what it says on the tin: it aims to build a relationship with the customer. Why would you want to do that? Surely customers are best kept at arm's length aren't they? Well, I argue that you need to know what your customers want. Service management is all about identifying what customers need, agreeing it with them and then delivering the service. So it all starts with the customers.

Business relationship management has a duty of care to customers. It makes sure that the needs of customers are taken into account in all service management activities, to ensure that customers will be happy with the outcome.

The purpose of the business relationship management process is two-fold:

- ✔ To establish and maintain a business relationship between the service provider and the customers, based on understanding the customers and their business needs

- ✔ To identify customer needs (utility and warranty) and ensure that the service provider is able to meet these needs as business needs change over time and in different circumstances

So the business relationship management process provides a focal point for customers in order to identify opportunities to provide value to customers in the form of services. These opportunities may be identified by the customer, such as the launch of a new business product that needs the support of a new IT service. Opportunities can also be identified by the IT provider; for example, the use of emerging technology such as cloud computing services, that may allow the customer to perform business processes more effectively and efficiently.

The service provider must understand how the customers' needs change over time, and the business relationship management process will provide this information. Business relationship management needs to be pragmatic: it must ensure that customers' expectations do not exceed what customers are prepared to pay for, and that the service provider can actually meet the customers' expectations before agreeing to deliver the service.

In this section it's important to be clear of the distinction between the customer and the user. If you're not sure how this distinction is viewed by ITIL then have a look in Chapter 2 for more details.

A user is a person who uses the IT service on a day-to-day basis. A customer is someone who pays for the service or agrees the level of service.

Explaining the terminology

There are one or two bits of terminology that it is useful to get out of the way first.

What's the difference between business relationship management and service level management?

You may notice some similarity between business relationship management activities and *service level management* (SLM) activities. (You'll find SLM described in Chapter 5 – so go and have a quick look if you like.) But it's more straightforward than you may imagine. *Business relationship management* is the overarching process. It maintains a relationship with the customer from cradle to grave and deals with many types of contact. On the other hand, SLM manages service levels. SLM gets involved once a service has been chartered, develops the service level agreements in conjunction with the customer and the business relationship manager, and ensures that the service is provided in accordance with agreed service targets.

Customer portfolio

A *customer portfolio* is a database or structured document used to record all customers of the IT service provider. The customer portfolio is the business relationship manager's view of the customers who receive services from the IT service provider. So the customer portfolio is a resource that provides details of all the customers to whom you provide services – a useful source of information.

The customer portfolio is defined and maintained as part of the business relationship management process.

Customer agreement portfolio

A *customer agreement portfolio* is a database or structured document used to manage service contracts or agreements between an IT service provider and its customers. Each IT service delivered to a customer should have a contract or other agreement that is listed in the customer agreement portfolio.

Getting confused about roles

This section is about the business relationship management process. ITIL also describes the role of a business relationship manager. It's easy to get confused here. Don't forget that a role is not necessarily performed by one person. A role is not the same as a job title. The activities of the business relationship management process may be performed by more than one role and more than one person. The activities of the business relationship management process are many and various. They often involve interfaces with other service management processes, for example service portfolio management and SLM.

In my experience, the business relationship management role is often performed by some-

one with the job title of account manager. This person initiates contact with the customer. This person is often engaged in initial bidding processes that engage a new customer, or discusses a new opportunity with a customer. Once the bid progresses and a service is developed, other processes start to get involved.

Again, another common job title is that of service delivery manager. This person tends to get engaged when the detailed service levels are defined and agreed. This is part of the SLM process, and at this point the service delivery manager is performing the role of service level manager.

For every customer to whom you provide a service there is an agreement. Hopefully there should be a written agreement: an SLA for internal customers and possibly a contract for external customers. It's likely that the SLM process will have some involvement in maintaining the customer agreement portfolio.

The benefit of a customer agreement portfolio is that everything is in one place. This means that a service provider can review and compare its commitments to all its customers.

The activities of business relationship management

There are two overarching activities of business relationship management which encompass all the activities of business relationship management:

- ✔ To represent the service provider to its customers through coordinated marketing, selling and delivery activities

- ✔ To work with service portfolio management and design coordination to ensure that the service provider's response to customers' requirements is appropriate; this process facilitates customer advocacy throughout the lifecycle

Funny word *advocacy,* isn't it? In this context it means that the business relationship management process will ensure that the interests of the customer are represented in all service management activities.

Business relationship management is not a single end-to-end process but a number of sets of activities performed in response to a particular trigger. The type of activities these are depends on the trigger and the situation. For example, if the customer contacts the business relationship manager requiring a change to be made to a service, the business relationship manager will facilitate the completion of a *request for change* (RFC) and submit it to the change management process.

Initiating business relationship management

There are many triggers for the business relationship management process. However there are some important occasions in which business relationship management needs to get involved.

It's important the customer has a point of contact for all requests, be they requests for new services or changes, or other requests. The use of the business relationship management process should provide customers with the confidence that they have a contact with the service provider and that their requests will be followed up.

- ✔ **Opportunities:** Customers may have new needs that can be fulfilled by a service, or the IT provider may be able to offer customers an opportunity that they can take advantage of. The business relationship manager will make sure that the customers' needs are explained well and that the IT provider gains a good understanding of the value (in terms of utility and warranty) that the customer wants to achieve.

- ✔ **RFCs:** RFCs are one of the main methods used by service management to get things done. The RFC form (as designed by the change management process) should be easy to use. However, there will be occasions when the business relationship manager will act as a facilitator to ensure that a customer's requirement is expressed in the clearest way and subsequently understood by the service provider.

- ✔ **Complaints and compliments:** Both complaints and compliments provide an opportunity for a service provider. Complaints provide a possible opportunity for improvement. Compliments may provide conformation that the service provider is providing the service as required and is achieving customer satisfaction. In both cases, there should be an agreed method of handling this type of contact with the customer.

Business relationship management through the service lifecycle

The activities of business relationship management vary depending on which part of the lifecycle the service has reached. It's part of the purpose of business relationship management to represent the customer's interests throughout the service lifecycle. The following are just a few of the possible activities of the business relationship management process, organised by the stage of the service lifecycle:

- ✓ **Service strategy:** Primarily identifying opportunities, but this can also involve specifying strategic requirements and funding, defining outcomes and business cases, or validating PBAs

- ✓ **Service design:** Validating requirements; ensuring the customer is appropriately involved in design activities

- ✓ **Service transition:** Coordinating customer involvement in service transition, in other words testing, release schedules, training

- ✓ **Service operation:** Communicating scheduled outages, providing updates on major incidents, and providing an escalation point

- ✓ **CSI:** Reporting service performance, conducting customer satisfaction surveys, and initiating service improvement plans

Using Technology for Service Strategy

ITIL emphasises the use of technology in helping you provide the IT services to your customers. The following sections look at two areas: the use of technology to support the service strategy activities, and the use of automation throughout the service lifecycle.

Technology to support the service strategy activities

You can use many software packages to support the service strategy activities:

- ✓ **Service portfolio management:** With a quick exploration using your favourite Internet search engine you can discover many service portfolio management tools. These store information about your services, making it easier for you to make decisions about them.

✔ **Financial management:** You can use a simple spreadsheet package to manage your finances. In larger organisations this can prove impractical. Many software packages are designed for managing finances.

✔ **Demand management:** You need to understand and model the PBA. (See the earlier section 'Defining some demand management terms'.) For simple calculations, you can use a spreadsheet. Or a quick Internet search reveals many tools designed for complex modelling.

Automation

Automation refers to the use of tools and technology to automate the activities of service management. You can use automation in many ways, from planning staff resources like shift patterns, to using network management tools that can automatically reconfigure infrastructure equipment to cope with peak business demands. Here are some other examples:

✔ It's possible to automate service management process flows, such as by routing incidents to second-line support.

✔ Users can select 'standard' services from an electronic service catalogue; this self-help takes the load off the service desk, leading to better use of resources.

✔ You can set up the system to automatically raise an RFC when a monitoring tool discovers an unauthorised component in your infrastructure.

Your organisation should have a strategy for how you use automation to support IT services. There may be some activities that must be performed by a person and should not be performed by a computer program. These should be decided and documented.

Chapter 5

Are We All Agreed? Service Design Part 1: The Relationship Management Processes

In This Chapter
▶ Knowing how the service design stage of the lifecycle works
▶ Seeing how to manage service levels
▶ Cataloguing information about live services
▶ Managing third-party suppliers

Some years ago on a Saturday night, my wife and I invited friends to dinner. It was the first time I had cooked for them. When my friend arrived, he introduced his wife and said, 'I did remember to tell you she's a vegetarian, didn't I?' The answer was no. Panic! After a quick bit of rethinking, my meat dish separated itself into both a vegetarian and non-vegetarian version. The evening went well and we're all still very good friends to this day. The moral of the story? Make sure you establish the requirements *before* you start.

In Chapter 3 I introduce you to the service lifecycle, of which service design is one part. The service design stage includes eight processes – a lot to cover in one chapter, so I've split the content between this chapter and Chapter 6. This chapter covers service level management (SLM), service catalogue management and supplier management – I like to call these the relationship management processes (this is my description, not an official ITIL term). This chapter also covers the design coordination process. Chapter 6 covers the other four processes: availability management, capacity management, IT service continuity management and information security management. The chapters are designed for you to read separately, but to get the whole picture you may want to read both in order.

Before you dive in, here's the essence of the service design processes: find out what the customer wants, design a service to meet those requirements, talk to the customer about the design, and get agreement.

Understanding the Purpose of the Service Design Lifecycle Stage

How do you know whether you're doing decent job? How do you know whether your organisation is providing the IT services required by the business? You won't know unless you've agreed up front what the customer wants from you and how it will measure your success. You will think about these things in the service design stage.

The main purpose of the ITIL *service design* stage of the lifecycle is the design of new or changed services for introduction into the live environment.

The service design stage of the lifecycle is where you take an idea for a new service or a change to an existing service, and put meat on the bones. From the high-level business requirements that you establish in the service strategy stage (which I explain in Chapter 4), you now create plans, designs and estimates of resources that help you understand what creating the service or change involves – if you choose to go ahead. So this is the stage that covers the gathering and analysis of the service requirements, and the design of the service. You must gather the detailed requirements of the service, check that they're achievable, and then design the service to meet the requirements.

Understanding Some Basic Principles

Before you launch into service design, you need a grounding in some basic principles of this stage of the service lifecycle.

Keeping in mind the four Ps of service design

You must consider four areas when designing service management:

- ✔ **People:** Ensure you have the right people in place with the right skills and training.
- ✔ **Processes:** The service management processes! Make sure they're properly designed and suit your needs.

✔ **Products/technology:** The IT services themselves along with any tools or underpinning technology. Again, ensure they're appropriate.

✔ **Partners/suppliers:** Ensure you have the right third-party suppliers in place that are able to help you deliver and support the service.

Knowing the five aspects of service design

I could have titled this section 'The *scope* of the service design stage'. What sort of things do you design in this stage? Clearly, you design the service, but when doing so you must also identify the impacts on other areas that may be affected by the design. ITIL refers to these areas as the five aspects of service design. Here they are:

✔ **Service solutions:** Designing the new or changed services. You gather and agree all the functional requirements and estimate the resources and capabilities you need to develop and operate the service.

✔ **Service management systems and tools:** Any service management tools you use, for example a service desk call-logging tool. You must establish a set of requirements and acquire or develop the tools to meet these requirements. ITIL gives special mention here to the service portfolio (which I cover in Chapter 4), from which you extract the high-level business requirements for new services.

✔ **Technology architecture and management systems:** The architecture, tools and systems that must be in place to support the design of the infrastructure, data and environments.

✔ **Processes:** Designing the service management processes. Designing and implementing these processes can be time-consuming and complex. I include more advice on implementation in Chapter 10.

✔ **Measurement systems, methods and metrics:** Not the actual monitoring tools themselves, though you use them to gather much of your measurement data – the emphasis here is on designing a structure to collate the right measurements and metrics that provide the necessary visibility and ability to control the service and the service management processes.

Creating a service design package

A *service design package* (SDP) is a package of documents that define all aspects of the design and requirements. This package is one of the main outputs of the service design stage of the service lifecycle. You produce a SDP for each new service, major change or service removal. The SDP details all aspects of the service through the subsequent stages of the service lifecycle.

The following is a brief overview of what a typical SDP includes:

✔ Business and service requirements

✔ *Service level requirements* (SLRs) or *service level agreements* (SLAs) (more on these in the following section)

✔ The design of the preferred solution

✔ Organisational readiness assessment

✔ Service lifecycle plan for the introduction of the service

✔ Service acceptance criteria, including criteria for sign-off of the service by the business

Managing Service Levels: Service Level Management

You don't know whether you've hit the target if you don't know where the target is. Everyone needs standards, otherwise you're fighting in the dark.

What do you think the service level management process does? Yep – it manages the service levels. I like to summarise the service level management process in the following way. Service level management:

✔ Defines, agrees and documents service levels

✔ Monitors, reports and reviews service levels

✔ Improves service levels

The purpose of the *service level management* process is to ensure that all current and planned IT services are delivered to agreed, achievable targets.

Your service level management process must maintain a close relationship with your business relationship management process. Many of the triggers of the service level management activities can come from business relationship management. You will find the business relationship management process described in Chapter 4.

Defining some service level management terms

Oh, how ITIL loves jargon. Never fear; in this section I explain the terms you come across in the service level management process.

Service level agreements

According to the ITIL books, 'An SLA is an agreement between an IT service provider and a customer. The SLA describes the IT service, documents service level targets, and specifies the responsibilities of the IT service provider and the customer'.

The SLA is the main agreement. Without it the customer doesn't know what it's getting and the provider doesn't know what to provide. The SLA should be in clear, unambiguous business language and cover aspects such as availability, capacity, security and IT service continuity. Gone are the days when the IT department deliberately included vague targets so that it could tweak the reports to make things look good, or when you could inherit SLAs and continue with them without any understanding of whether they were achievable or measurable.

To negotiate, agree and set up SLAs with the customer is a time-consuming and sometimes challenging task. So why bother? Table 5-1 helps you see the merits of these agreements.

Table 5-1	The Benefits of SLAs
With SLAs . . .	*Without SLAs . . .*
You set the expectations of both parties	You don't know whether you're any good at providing the service
You can measure the service	You may either over- or under-achieve
You have clear targets to achieve	You can never be right

© Crown copyright 2011. Reproduced under licence from the Cabinet Office.

You must make sure that all those who help provide the services understand the part they play in delivering them. That means putting underpinning agreements in place. These are *operational level agreements* (OLAs) and *underpinning contracts* (UCs) (see the next two sections).

Operational level agreements

The ITIL books say 'An OLA is an agreement between an IT service provider and another part of the same organisation', for example between teams within the IT department. An OLA supports the IT service provider's delivery of IT services (in accordance with the SLA) to customers. And now you're among friends, so you can talk techie!

Sample SLA

Here's a sample of an SLA. It's by no means perfect or a template for all situations, but you will get a rough idea of what to include.

Introduction and signatures

This is the SLA for the production planning system. It's an agreement between the production business unit and the IT department.

Service description

Provides ability to plan the manufacturing schedule, identify raw material needs and place purchase orders.

Service level targets

Service hours

24/7

Planned maintenance can take place between 2 and 5 a.m. on weekdays, up to a total of 5 hours per week.

Availability and reliability

The service will be available over all service hours (except for agreed planned maintenance). In the case of unplanned outages due to incidents, the service must be restored within two hours. No more than three unplanned outages are allowed in any one seven-day period.

Response to incidents

P1: Interruption to critical service; service to be restored in 2 hours

P2: Degradation of critical service; service to be restored in 8 hours

P3: Incident impacting low-criticality service with low urgency; service to be restored in 48 hours

P4: Planned work

Capacity and performance

Maximum number of concurrent users = 100

System response time to be no greater than 2 seconds when all users are using service.

Security

Refer to security policy.

IT service continuity

In the event of a disaster, service to be restored within 2 hours to recovery site.

Support

The service desk will be the first point of contact for users for all IT issues. Standard service desk hours are 8 a.m. to 6 p.m. Out-of-hours support for this service will be provided via the same contact number.

Reporting and review

Service reports of service levels versus service targets to be issued on the first Monday of each month. Monthly service reviews to be held on the second Monday of each month.

EXAMPLE

The IT department of a manufacturing organisation has a total of 20 SLAs in place for the various services it provides to its internal customers. The network team leader has commented to the service level manager that his department finds it difficult to understand what level of service it has to provide to which customers at what time. The service level manager suggests they sit down and draft an OLA. They review all the SLAs and identify how each service target relates to the network service. They note where a common level of service is needed across many customers and where special levels of service are required for particular customers. They now create one simplified set of service targets and document them in the OLA. Now the network team has a single set of targets to meet that allows it to meet the targets in the SLA.

Underpinning contracts

According to the ITIL books 'A underpinning contract (UC) is a contract between an IT service provider and a third party supplier. The third party supplier provides goods or services that support delivery of an IT service to a customer. The UC defines targets and the responsibilities required to meet agreed service level targets in an SLA' (see the earlier section 'Service level agreements').

No difference exists between a *contract* and an *underpinning contract*. The term just reminds you that the contract must underpin the targets in your SLA.

You negotiate and manage the contracts you have with your suppliers by using the supplier management process (see 'Getting Friendly with Third-party Suppliers: Supplier Management' later in this chapter). The service level manager ensures that the supplier manager is clear about the requirements of the part of the service to be provided by the supplier, and between the service level manager and supplier manager ensure that the contract underpins the SLA with the customer.

Service level requirements

Service level requirements (SLRs) are the documented requirements of the customer prior to the SLA being agreed. Here is the starting point for negotiation. For a major development project, the SLR is the starting point for the design of the service. As the project goes through the service transition stage (see Chapter 7), testing provides confidence that the requested requirement can be fulfilled. At this stage, you create a draft SLA. As the service is deployed, the significance of the SLR fades and the SLA becomes the operative document. The SLA is signed as agreed by both parties.

SLA frameworks

Ask yourself how many business units and how many IT services you have. For example, say you have 10 business units and 50 IT services. If every customer uses every service then potentially you may have 500 SLAs. Hands up anyone who'd like to manage 500 SLAs! Now, I can already hear you shouting at me, 'But not all my customers use the same services.' So hopefully you can simplify the number of SLAs you have. Here come some suggestions:

- **Service-based SLA:** An SLA for *one* service that describes the targets for *many* customers.

- **Customer-based SLA:** An SLA for *one* customer that describes the targets for *many* services.

In addition to these two, you can also have multi-level agreements:

- **Corporate level:** An agreement covering the generic issues appropriate to all customers, for example: service levels for common services such as the email service; how to contact the service desk; how to request changes.

- **Customer level:** An agreement covering issues relevant to a particular customer or business unit, regardless of the service being used.

- **Service level:** An agreement covering issues relevant to a specific service for a specific customer.

I've now given you a choice of five agreement types to choose from. Which is best? As ever, the answer is 'it depends'. You probably find that a combination of types works for you, but you have to sit down and plan the best combination.

Customer satisfaction

Customer satisfaction may seem an odd thing to cover in a section on jargon. But do you know what the term means? Of course, *customer satisfaction* means keeping the customer satisfied. However, often the IT department thinks it's doing a good job, and the opposite is true. For example, you look at the service level reports prior to the monthly service review meeting with a customer. You read the results and think, 'Wow, we've achieved all the service targets. I bet the customer will be really happy.' But when you enter the meeting room, the customer tells you what an appalling month it has had!

The provider and the customer can have a different perception of the same achievements for many reasons:

- The SLA doesn't meet the customer's needs.

- The customer hasn't communicated the agreed service levels to the users, and the users have complained.

- The SLA targets can't be measured accurately.

- The SLA targets don't reflect the relative criticality of the services or the critical business periods.

- The customer or provider has misinterpreted the requirements.

- The SLA isn't underpinned by appropriate OLAs or contracts.

The moral of the story is that you must measure customer satisfaction as well as achievement of the service targets. Often the service desk sends out surveys to users. Service level management should collate and review this feedback to form a better overall view of the quality of the service. Customer satisfaction is a prime concern of the business relationship management process. Service level management and business relationship management must work closely together. Business relationship management is covered in Chapter 4.

Service improvement plan

In the words of the ITIL books 'A *service improvement plan* (SIP) is a formal plan to implement improvements to a process or IT service'.

That's as good and clear as definitions go – for a change. Don't get over-excited: a SIP is very simple. It's just a plan, or a small project, to investigate the factors that lead to a poor quality of service and to suggest actions to improve the service or service management processes.

Looking at the activities of service level management

The following sections explore the main activities of the service level management process.

Determining, documenting and agreeing requirements for new services (creating SLRs) and producing SLAs

This activity involves a discussion with the customer of the service to discover its SLRs. (I explain SLRs in the earlier section 'Defining some service level management terms'.)

Here's how the activity works:

1. **The service level manager gains an understanding of the business activities performed by the customer.** Then the manager can communicate the importance of the service to others in the service provider organisation. The requirements are documented.

2. **The service level manager returns to the IT provider to establish whether the requirements are achievable.** This triggers other service management processes, especially availability management, capacity management, IT service continuity management and information security management. (Chapter 6 has the low-down on these.) These processes ensure that the specific aspects of the service requirements are fully assessed and the impacts of meeting the requirements are understood.

3. **The service level manager negotiates with the customer regarding the level of service that is achievable and affordable.** This can take several goes. Inevitably, the customer modifies its requirements during the negotiations, and you have to return to the technical staff to double-check.

I can't emphasise enough the importance of getting the steps right. Once agreed, these are the service levels you must stick to, and on which your success as a service provider will be measured. Also, by using so few words, I may have made this activity sound easy. It isn't! You may be left tearing your hair out or mumbling in a corner after the tenth round of negotiations and fifteenth draft of the SLA. You must persevere. Once you start providing the services in accordance with the SLA, there will be laughter and happiness all around.

Reviewing and revising SLAs, service scope and underpinning agreements

This set of activities relates to the previous set, and is often part of the same process. Whenever you receive a new set of requirements, you must check that they are achievable, and what it will cost to achieve them. This involves negotiating and agreeing the necessary underpinning agreements. These agreements are usually the OLAs and UCs. (More on these in the earlier section 'Defining some service level management terms'.) You use the supplier management process (which I cover in the later section 'Getting Friendly with Third-party Suppliers: Supplier Management') to negotiate and set up the UCs. The service level manager ensures that the contracts underpin the SLA that has been agreed with the customer.

The service level manager negotiates and sets up the OLAs. They represent a commitment from other parts of the service provider organisation to fulfil their parts of the bargain. So for example, if the server team believes it can fix all priority-2 incidents in less than two hours, it should be willing to sign an OLA confirming this fact.

Monitoring service performance against the SLA and producing service reports

Unfortunately, once you have agreed and signed your SLAs, you can't throw them in a drawer, shut it and forget about them. You must measure and report on your service achievements. How often do you monitor your service levels? As often as you committed to do in your SLA. The service operation people are monitoring your services and components all the time. You must ensure that they collect and collate the appropriate information that you need to go into your service reports.

You have to produce and circulate reports regularly in line with what you agreed in the SLA. When reporting to customers, keep things simple: don't flood customers with unnecessary information and data. Also, don't get too techie – unless customers ask for the complex stuff.

Exception reports are a good idea. As the name suggests, you report on exceptions only – so SLA breaches or service outages. This prevents you from printing page after page of data that simply tells the customer things are okay. Another popular report goes under many names: RAG chart (*red, amber, green*) or traffic light chart. ITIL calls this a SLAM chart – *service level agreement monitoring* chart. Have a look at the example in Figure 5-1.

Service	Target	Week 1	Week 2	Week 3	Week 4
X	Availability	G	G	G	G
	System response time	G	A	G	G
	Service Desk response time	G	G	R	G
	Incident response time	G	G	G	G
Y	Y1	G	G	G	G
	Y2	G	G	G	G
	Y3	A	R	G	G

Figure 5-1: Example of a SLAM chart.

G	A	R
Light Gray – Service Target Met	Gray – Service Target Threatened	Dark Gray – Service Target Breached

Conducting service reviews and instigating improvements within an overall service improvement plan

Service reviews are regular reviews between the service provider and the customer. Aim to hold these meetings at least quarterly, though I know many organisations that hold them monthly. These aren't reviews of the SLA – not an opportunity to renegotiate the SLA – but an opportunity to review service achievements for the last period. Of course, service achievement can be both good and bad.

Send out your reports a few days before the meeting so that the customer has time to review them. You don't want to waste time in the meeting reading reports together. How dull. Instead, spend the time discussing any outages or breaches in the last period and reviewing any points either party needs to be aware of in the forthcoming period.

Service reviews are great for identifying opportunities for improvement. The customer may be looking at the SLAM chart (see the previous section) and say, 'Looks like you've had a lot of amber lights recently – wouldn't you like to do something about it?' The amber lights indicate a number of outages in the last period that the IT department should investigate. The appropriate response is for the service level manager to set up a SIP. To do this, he probably calls on the help of his very good friend the *continual service improvement* (CSI) manager, and they work together to set up the plan to investigate the outages and recommend improvements.

Collating, measuring and improving customer satisfaction

You must get a qualitative feel for the service you're providing to the customer. Customer satisfaction surveys are a good way of doing this.

Be careful. What do you do when walking down the street and someone grabs you and asks you to complete a survey? Similarly, you may be sitting at home watching your favourite TV programme, and the phone rings and the caller asks you to complete a survey – it won't take long! What's your reaction? Most people have a natural aversion to surveys, so you take that into account when surveying your users and customers. Keep surveys simple and don't ask users to complete them too often.

The service desk often helps with surveys. It can send out email surveys after an incident, or ask users their opinions of the service while on the phone, and then pass this to service level management to be included in reports and service reviews.

Developing contacts and relationships, recording and managing complaints and compliments

Hopefully, if all the activities I describe in the preceding section are performed well then the natural consequence is a good relationship with your customers. However, natural happenstance isn't enough: you have to make building a positive relationship an objective of the process. The necessary negotiations and service reviews go much better if you build a relationship based on openness and trust.

This activity also includes dealing with complaints and compliments. The service level management process acts as the escalation point for service issues from either party. The customer should contact the service level manager with any complaints or issues. Similarly, if the service provider can anticipate possible service breaches or issues, these should be escalated to the service level manager, who can discuss them with the customer. The business relationship management process is concerned with the customer's overall satisfaction with all the service received, so make sure you understand who does what and that the lines of communication don't get crossed (business relationship management is covered in Chapter 4).

Keeping Information about the Live Services: Service Catalogue Management

What does *service catalogue management* entail? Managing the service catalogue. What's a *service catalogue*? Basically, a catalogue of your services.

The purpose of the service catalogue management process is to provide and maintain a single source of consistent information on all operational services and those being prepared to be run operationally, and to ensure that it's widely available to those who are authorised to access it.

Defining the service catalogue

In ITIL-speak, the service catalogue is a database or structured document with information about all live IT services, including those available for deployment. The service catalogue is the only part of the *service portfolio* (the complete set of services managed by a service provider) published to customers, and you use it to support the sale and delivery of IT services (there's more about the service portfolio in Chapter 4). The service catalogue includes information about deliverables, prices, contact points, ordering and request processes.

At its most basic, a service catalogue is a simply list of your live IT services plus those being prepared to go live. It includes a summary of the main attributes of each service and an overview of the agreed service levels. But the service catalogue can be much, much more than a list of services. Often, complex software applications are used to allow staff to drill down and view details of each service.

Figure 5-2 gives you an idea of what a service catalogue may look like.

Service	Service Description	Business Units	Service Hrs.	SLA	Support	Support Hrs.
Customer Relationship Management (CRM)	Customer contact information system. Used for all customer contact processes.	Sales	7am–8pm Mon-Fri. Saturday on request	Refer to Sales SLA	Service Desk	Normal Service Desk hours
Payroll	Employee payment system.	Accounts	9am–6pm Mon-Fri. Critical period – every fourth Friday.	Refer to Accounts SLA	Service Desk	Normal Service Desk hours
Production Planning System	Provides ability to plan the manufacturing schedule, identify raw material needs and place purchase orders.	Production	24 × 7	Refer to Production Planning service SLA	Service Desk. Operations Bridge for out of hours support.	24 × 7
Desktop services	Standard desktop workstation including office applications and email.	All business units	Dependent upon other services used.	Refer to Corporate SLA	Service Desk	Normal Service Desk hours

Figure 5-2: Example of a simple service catalogue.

Based on ITIL® material. Reproduced under licence from The Cabinet Office.

Uses of the service catalogue

Here are some suggestions of how you can use the service catalogue:

✔ As an essential tool for the service level manager and supplier manager to understand and manage the customer-facing services and underpinning services in their care

✔ To show the relative criticality of each service – using the results of a business impact analysis

✔ To provide relevant information to business relationship managers so they can recommend or sell services to customers (a bit like a shopping catalogue)

✔ As a quick reference guide for service desk staff

✔ As a product catalogue for users, identifying standard service, products and requests available from the service desk via the request fulfilment process

✔ As a tool to enable business relationship managers to match customer demand patterns to under-utilised services

---

The information in your service catalogue can be presented in many ways; these are often called *views*. A service catalogue view restricts the information you show to specific groups of people. ITIL provides the following examples:

✔ **Two-view service catalogue:**

  • **Business service catalogue:** The business service catalogue is the customer view of the service catalogue. This is the only bit you show to the customers. It contains the details of all the IT services delivered to the customers, along with the relationships to business units and business processes that rely on the IT services.

  • **Technical service catalogue:** The technical service catalogue is the technical view of the service catalogue. This is the bit you keep to show your technical staff. It contains the details of all the IT services delivered to the customers, along with the relationships to the supporting services, shared services and other components and assets.

✔ **Three-view service catalogue:**

  • **Wholesale customer view:** Shows the details of services available to wholesale customers, along with the relationships to the customers the services support.

  • **Retail customer view:** Shows the details of services available to retail customers, along with the relationships to the customers the services support.

  • **Supporting services view:** This view is similar to the technical service catalogue described above and provides details of the supporting services required to deliver the services displayed in the wholesale and retail customer views.

Looking at the activities of service catalogue management

The service catalogue management process is straightforward and consists of those activities needed to ensure that the service catalogue is accurate and reflects the current details, status, interfaces and dependencies of all services that are being run, or being prepared to run, in the live environment.

In order to achieve this you:

- ✔ Agree and document a service definition.
- ✔ Produce and maintain the service catalogue and its content, ensuring consistency with the service portfolio.
- ✔ Interface with all parts of the business and the IT function who help supply information to the service catalogue or rely on information from the service catalogue.

Getting Friendly with Third-party Suppliers: Supplier Management

You can't do everything yourself. Sometimes it makes sense to get someone else to do it. However, whenever you get some else to do something for you, you hope they'll do it to an acceptable standard.

This is where you turn the tables. Service management is all about providing a good service to your customers. However, sometimes you're the customer, so what do you expect from your suppliers? If you believe in the philosophy of customer service, you expect to receive a similar quality of service from your suppliers as you give to your customers. But, as with all things to do with service management, you need a clear understanding of, and agreement about, what you expect from your suppliers.

Suppose you're planning to build an extension on your house. You choose not to do it yourself but to pay a building organisation to do it. Do you tell it what to do? Well, you give it the plans and tell it what the final extension should be like, and you set a standard for the quality of the workmanship. You also agree a price. Do you now stand over the craftsman every minute of the day, telling everyone how to do their job? I think not. But you check every now and again and look for indicators that everything is going to plan.

Why outsource?

Why do organisations use suppliers to provide part or all of their IT services?

- **Cost:** Using suppliers may be cheaper for many reasons such as the economies of scale that a supplier can get from offering the service to many customers.

- **Flexibility:** If your need for the service is likely to change over time, it's sometimes easier to get a supplier to do it for you. This means you don't have the hassle of employing new staff in the busy times, or laying off staff in the less busy times – the supplier can deal with this for you.

- **Risk:** Sometimes there are risks associated with doing something yourself, especially if it's something new to your organisation. Getting someone else to do it may be a good way of putting your toe in the water without investing a lot of money.

- **Skills:** You may not have, or want to have, specialist skills in your organisation. You often hear companies talking about their *core competencies* – things they think they're good at that are essential to their business; for everything else, they get a supplier.

The purposes of the *supplier management* process are to obtain value for money from suppliers, and to provide a seamless quality of IT service to the business by ensuring that all contracts and agreements with suppliers support the needs of the business, and that all suppliers meet their contractual commitments.

As ITIL definitions go, this one is fairly straightforward:

- **Value for money:** Commercial companies are in business to make money. If you ask a supplier to provide a service for you, then I'm sure you expect to pay for it, but how much are you prepared to pay? The important thing is to get value for money.

- **Seamless quality of IT service:** Your customers aren't interested in seeing the joins between the bits that you do and the bits you get someone else to do. One of the most frustrating things you may hear an assistant say when you phone a call centre is, 'I'm sorry, we can't deliver your goods. Our supplier has let us down.' My reaction to this is, 'I don't care; that's your problem. Get it sorted.' Or is it just me? You must ensure that the bits that your suppliers provide are integrated into the end-to-end service and are able to contribute to the level of service you have agreed with your customer.

Defining some supplier management terms

Jargon be gone! Here's some demystification to help you get to grips with the supplier management process:

- **Supplier:** According to the ITIL publications, a supplier is 'A third party (external to your organisation) responsible for supplying goods or services required to deliver IT services. Examples of suppliers include commodity hardware and software vendors, network and telecom providers, and outsourcing organisations'.

- **Supplier and contract management information system (SCMIS):** A set of tools, data and information about your suppliers and the contracts you have with them. This useful repository of information and data allows you to manage your suppliers and the relationship you have with them. Your supplier management policy drives the actual detail of what you keep in the SCMIS, which is usually:

  - All supplier details

  - Details of contracts

  - Details of the services and products provided by each supplier

  - A categorisation of each supplier and its products, such as 'commodity', 'service' or 'partner'

You also come across the word *contract* or *underpinning contract* (UC) in the supplier management process; I cover this in the earlier section on service level management.

The relationship between service level management and supplier management

There must be a close relationship between the service level management process (see the earlier section 'Managing Service Levels: Service Level Management') and the supplier management process. The service level manager agrees the service levels with the customer and so has a clear understanding of the requirements. When a decision is made to outsource part of the provision of the service, the service level manager liaises with the supplier manager to pass on a clear understanding of what is needed from the supplier. In fact, the service level manager should not confirm anything with the customer until he knows what the supplier can do and what it will cost. So you can see that several rounds of discussions may occur between the various parties.

Looking at the activities of supplier management

Read through the following sections to gain an understanding of the supplier management process.

Supplier strategy and policy

Having a policy for when you use a supplier and when you do a task yourself is sensible. Your policy can be as simple as: all application development is done by a supplier; all wide-area networks are done by a supplier; everything else we do ourselves.

Here are some other areas of strategy and policy that you should address:

- ✔ Should we have a preferred supplier list?
- ✔ Who is responsible for managing suppliers?
- ✔ How do we ensure that all contracts are legally sound?

Definition of new supplier and contract requirements

The service design stage includes designing the service and producing a requirements specification. (You can read more about this in Chapter 12.) This must be authorised before you search for a supplier to provide the service for you. Supplier management often works with service level management to gain a clear understanding of what is needed from a supplier.

Evaluating new suppliers and contracts

Welcome to the whole world of *procurement*. You may use other words in your organisation, but I'm referring to the process of identifying potential suppliers, getting their interest, and then evaluating and selecting the appropriate suppliers. This is often called the *invitation to tender* (ITT) process. Your organisation may already have its own (sometimes long and complex) method of procurement for all purchasing, not just IT. In fact, some industry sectors impose regulations on how to procure.

You must have a consistent way of fairly assessing all potential new suppliers and services to ensure you select the ones that can best provide the service you need and best match your organisation.

This stage also includes the contract negotiations with the prospective suppliers. This, of course, must be done with care and honesty to ensure that both parties enter into a successful and mutually beneficial relationship.

Establishing new suppliers and contracts

When engaging new suppliers, ensure you assess and record any risks. Carry out checks on the supplier's past performance and its financial status. Once the contracts are signed, you add the supplier to your SCMIS.

Depending on the type of supplier, you may perform other activities in the service transition stage (see Chapter 7) to ensure that the supplier's service is integrated into your IT service; for example, network suppliers connecting their equipment to yours; an infrastructure outsourcer transferring your data to its systems. In some cases, the supplier may need regular access to your building, in which case you must familiarise them with your ways of working.

Supplier, contract and performance management

Regularly measure and report on the performance of your suppliers to provide factual evidence that they're providing the service as agreed, and to enable you to spot any issues in time to do something about them. Hold regular performance reviews (meetings) with your suppliers, similar to those you hold with your customers, to review:

✔ Service performance against targets

✔ Any incidents or problems

✔ Any changes or issues expected in the forthcoming period

✔ Any improvement plans

Contract renewal or termination

All good things come to an end, and so might your contracts. Contracts are rarely open-ended, but may need renewing. The SCMIS tells you the end dates or renewal dates for all your contracts, and you can use the information to help you plan what to do when the contract runs out. The obvious choices are renew or terminate. However, you can also take the opportunity to renegotiate the contract to take into account any business changes.

Supplier categorisation, and maintenance of the SCMIS

Not all suppliers are equal. Some absorb more management time and effort than others. The clever bit is knowing which you handle in what way.

For example, if a supplier provides commodity products such as paper or printer cartridges, you probably don't have an intimate relationship with a single supplier and phone each other every day. More likely, you maintain a list of preferred suppliers and choose whoever has the best discount on the day you want to place the order. On the other hand, if you have outsourced a critical part of your infrastructure upon which most of your services rely, then you likely have a much closer relationship with the supplier.

Here are some typical categories for your suppliers:

- ✔ **Strategic:** The sort of thing negotiated and managed by senior managers in your organisation, like major network provision that's integrated with your services. Needs frequent communication.

- ✔ **Tactical:** Usually managed by middle managers in the organisation. Includes support contracts for hardware and software, and needs regular communication and performance reviews.

- ✔ **Operational:** Products and services like Internet access and non-critical website hosting. This needs regular contact, but less often than for tactical suppliers.

- ✔ **Commodity:** Generally low-value stuff like paper or printer cartridges. Contact is as and when required.

Design Coordination

There's quite a lot going on in the service design stage – it makes common sense to coordinate it.

If you have a programme or project office in your organisation, you may be familiar with the role it has in the high-level planning and coordination of projects. The design coordination process performs similar activities for your design projects. Service design activities are often carried out as projects, or are part of other projects.

The purpose of the *design coordination* process is to ensure that the goals and objectives of the service design stage are met, by providing and maintaining a single point of coordination and control for all activities and processes within this stage of the service lifecycle.

Here's a brief look at the activities of the design coordination process. The activities of the design coordination process are divided into two groups: those applied to all design activities, and those applied to a specific design:

- ✔ **Overall activities:**

    - Defining and maintaining policies, standards and guidelines, and ensuring they are used

    - Planning the resources needed for service design activities

- Managing design risks and issues
- Improving service design

✔ **Activities performed for each design:**

- Planning, coordinating and monitoring individual designs; these are three separate activities, all aimed at ensuring the smooth management of a project to create the design of a new or changed service
- Ensuring the production of the SDP from documents and inputs provided by the application and technical teams involved in the design activities

Identifying Service Design Roles

Each service management process should have a process owner and a process manager. I explain these two roles in Chapter 2. For the relationship management processes, the relevant process manager roles are:

✔ Service level manager

✔ Service catalogue manager

✔ Supplier manager

✔ Design coordination manager

Each role is responsible for the activities described in the appropriate section of this chapter.

In addition to the process-related roles, you may want to consider some general service design roles. These are associated with design activities such as the gathering and analysis of requirements and the subsequent production of designs. These roles are:

✔ IT planner

✔ IT designer/architect

Chapter 6

Designing Services to Be Fit for Use: Service Design Part 2: The Warranty Processes

●●●

In This Chapter

▶ Making sure you can provide what the customer wants

▶ Checking you have enough capacity

▶ Preparing for all eventualities

▶ Keeping IT secure

●●●

*W*ould you agree to doing something for someone without checking you have the ways and means of achieving it? If someone asks you for a lift, do you check whether your partner is using the car that day? If someone asks to borrow some money, do you check you have enough spare after you've paid your bills? In other words, do you check you have the right assets, and that the assets are properly configured and ready to go?

This chapter and Chapter 5 cover the service design stage of the ITIL service lifecycle. (I introduce the service lifecycle in Chapter 3.) This is the stage that covers the gathering and analysis of the service requirements, and the design of the service to meet the requirements. Chapter 5 covers the design coordination process and the relationship management processes: service level management, service catalogue management and supplier management. In this chapter, I cover what I call the warranty processes: availability, management, capacity management, IT service continuity management, and information security management.

Think of the ITIL warranty processes as being similar to the warranty you get when you buy a new washing machine. The warranty means you should be able to get the machine fixed quickly if it breaks, ensuring that you can wash your clothes as often as you like. Warranty closely relates to the service levels that are described in your *service level agreements* (SLAs) (more on these in Chapter 5). In this chapter, I cover the four areas of warranty: availability, capacity, continuity and security. They don't wash your clothes for you, but they do allow your customers to get value from the IT service as often as agreed.

Making Sure the Service Is Available: Availability Management

What do the users do when the service breaks – that is, it becomes unavailable? They complain. Why? Because they can't achieve their business goals – they can't get the value that they expect from the service. Think how you feel when you're at home and your broadband connection or satellite connection fails. I bet you use a few choice expressions to describe your providers!

So what do I mean by *availability?* The availability of what? The IT service. In accordance with what? The SLAs (see Chapter 5) or agreed business needs. Asking the business about availability is the equivalent of asking, 'When do you want it?' So the aim is to keep the users happy by ensuring that the service is actually there and working when they want it.

'Availability' is just a clever way of saying that the service is working and you can use it. Your phone works – so you can make and receive phone calls.

The purpose of the *availability management* process is to ensure that the level of availability delivered in all IT services meets the agreed availability needs and/or service level targets in a cost-effective and timely manner. Availability management is concerned with meeting both the current and future availability needs of the business.

To give you a better idea of what availability management does, here are some other objectives:

- ✔ Ensure that service availability meets agreed targets, by managing services and resource-related availability performance.
- ✔ Ensure that services are designed to meet agreed availability requirements.
- ✔ Assist with the diagnosis and resolution of availability-related incidents and problems.
- ✔ Produce and maintain an up-to-date availability plan.

Providing good availability of your service isn't something that should happen by accident. Some IT departments provide an IT service that they think is about right and then tweak it when the business complains. But ideally, you start thinking about availability when designing the service – in the service design stage of the service lifecycle.

Seeing the process in action

Through the use of the service level management process, the IT department liaises with the business and identifies its needs. For example, if a project has been approved and set up for the development of a new IT service, then, at some point early in the project, the service level manager gathers the *service level requirements* (SLRs). These include the customer's requirements for the availability of the service. I don't know how your organisation measures availability, but often it's expressed as a percentage – for example, the email service will be available 99 per cent of the time.

Using the availability management process, you perform the activities to review these requirements and check to see whether they are achievable. If the requirements are not achievable, then you make suggestions on how the availability of the service can be improved to meet them, and report back to the service level manager, who can discuss the requirements further with the business. This discussion includes considering who will pay for the necessary improvements.

Once the requirements are agreed, availability management ensures that the service is designed to meet these availability requirements. This is part of the service design stage. During the service transition stage, availability management can get involved in testing to ensure that the design works in the way expected. In the service operation stage, availability management monitors the availability of the service to ensure that the requirements have been met.

Beryl, the sales manager, has a requirement for the sales IT service. She has stated that 'The service must be available from 8 a.m. until 6 p.m.; if it breaks, you will fix it within 30 minutes; it will not break more than twice in any one week. And by the way, Friday morning is our busiest time, so please keep the service going all morning.' Your technical staff look at these requirements from an availability point of view. They may calculate the required availability of the service: 98 per cent (the maths isn't that difficult!). A review of the infrastructure that supports the new service shows that availability is currently 95 per cent – so not enough. Your technical staff (technical architects) now redesign the service by building in greater resilience and more reliable components, and calculate that 98 per cent availability can be achieved. However, the increased cost will be £10,000. The service level manager (business relationship manager) discusses this with Beryl, who agrees that this is a worthwhile return on investment and agrees to make the money available.

Defining some availability management terms

Availability, reliability, maintainability, serviceability and resilience – these are terms you find in the availability management process. That's a lot of jargon (much of it designed by someone with an *-ability* passion); but don't worry, in the next sections I explain each term. To begin:

- ✔ **Availability:** According to ITIL, this is 'the ability of a service or component to perform its agreed function when required'. Availability refers to both the end-to-end service and the components. You normally refer to the availability of the overall service in your SLA. Availability management must consider two levels: service availability and component availability. Component availability depends upon reliability and maintainability.

- ✔ **Reliability:** The ITIL books define reliability as 'a measure of how long a service or component can perform its agreed function without interruption'. In other words, for how long will it work before breaking? Technical staff have a couple of ways of measuring this:

  - • **Mean time between failures (MTBF):** On average, how long does the component work before failing?

  - • **Mean time between service incidents (MTBSI):** On average, how frequently does the component fail?

- ✔ **Maintainability:** ITIL defines maintainability as 'a measure of how quickly and effectively a service or component can be restored to normal working after a failure'. So, when a component breaks, can you fix it quickly? For example, if a user's PC breaks, how long will it take you to fix it and help the user get back to work? This is usually measured using *mean time to restore service* (MTRS): on average, how long does it take to fix this type of component?

- ✔ **Serviceability:** In ITIL's words this is 'the ability of a third-party supplier to meet the terms of its contract'. So, for components or services that you outsource, you need to be sure that the supplier sticks to its part of the bargain. Serviceability is a bit of a strange term because it just refers to the contractual arrangements you have with a supplier, and you can't measure this. However, you should be able to measure the agreed levels of availability, reliability and/or maintainability for a supporting service or component.

- ✔ **Resilience:** ITIL's definition of resilience is 'the ability of a component or IT service to resist failure or to recover quickly following a failure'. For example, you may have two network routers sitting side by side, both doing the same job at the same time. If one fails, the other carries on as if nothing has happened. In this case, the user still receives the service and is blissfully unaware that anything has failed. A second example would be having a spare laptop ready to replace a user's desktop system – an example of restoring the service very quickly.

Improving availability

Generally speaking, you improve the availability of a service in two ways: increase uptime and decrease downtime (no, these don't mean the same):

- **Increasing uptime:** Keeping the IT service there for as long as possible requires you to design for availability: use reliable components or build resilience into the design of the service so that if a single component fails, the whole service doesn't fail. One form of resilience is to build in *redundancy:* have two components doing the same job, so if one fails the other takes over. If you apply this principle to the entire end-to-end service, you can eliminate any *single points of failure,* where the failure of a single component can affect many services (for example, a network switch failure can affect many services and many users). Building in a lot of resilience costs a lot of money, so you need to justify the business requirement and have someone who's prepared to pay.

- **Decreasing downtime:** The ability of your staff to restore the service in a timely fashion when it fails. This includes taking a look at your incident management and problem management processes (see Chapter 8) to ensure they take into account the needs of your critical services. You review your processes and procedures, especially how people contribute.

The speed of recovery relies on the following:

- **Detecting the failure quickly:** Don't wait for the user to tell you an incident has occurred; use monitoring tools.

- **Diagnosing the fault quickly:** Have the right staff available at the right time who can point at a component and say, 'That's the one that's failed.' You can sometimes use monitoring tools.

- **Fixing the fault quickly:** Have spare parts available and staff that have practised various scenarios and know what to do to fix the fault and restore the service.

Looking at the activities of availability management

ITIL groups the activities of the availability management process into those that are proactive and those that are reactive.

Proactive activities

The *proactive activities* of availability management take place during the service design stage of the service lifecycle. This is where you ensure that you have clear requirements for the availability of the service, and the design activities focus on creating a service that meets these requirements. The activities are as follows:

Is your car available?

Would you think I was mad if I asked whether your car was available? You might wonder what I meant by this. Perhaps I'm asking whether your car is available for use. To be available for use, is it parked outside? Is there fuel in it? Is it roadworthy? In fact everything necessary for you or I to use the car as expected. In general terms, I imagine your car normally works the way you expect, as and when you want it to.

Let me ask you a question. What do you think the manufacturer considered when designing your car? More specifically, what did it consider when designing the components of your car? Surely it must select components that contribute to the successful operation of your car as a whole. I think there are two main factors. First, I expect it chose components that have good reliability, that is ones that work for a reasonable amount of time without failing. Second, I hope it chose components that are maintainable, that is ones that are easy to repair or replace when they break. Imagine you go into your local garage and ask the mechanic to replace your brake pads; I expect you would be surprised if the reply was 'Sorry, but in your car I have to take the engine out to replace the brake pads.' That's not very maintainable.

This, of course, is an analogy. Your IT services are no different. For your whole service to be available, you have to ensure that each component of the service (for example servers, network equipment, PCs, software) has the appropriate level of reliability and maintainability.

✔ **Risk assessment and management.** You review the assets and components that make up the service, and identify any potential risks to the availability of the service – what could cause a failure. Then you suggest cost-justifiable improvements to reduce the risks. (You can find out a bit more about risk management in Chapter 9.)

✔ **Planning and designing new or changed services.** You get the requirements for new or changed services and ensure they translate into requirements of availability. Designing the service involves the factors I describe in the previous section 'Improving availability'. This activity also involves the design and selection of the components and how they contribute to the overall service availability.

✔ **Implementing cost-justifiable countermeasures.** The previous two activities yield many suggestions for improving the availability of your IT services. Each suggestion is likely to cost money, and you can't justify every one. So you review the various options and choose the most appropriate.

✔ **Reviewing all new and changed services and testing all availability and resilience mechanisms.** You continually review your services and regularly test the fail-over mechanisms you have in place. Only through such activities can you be sure everything will work the way you expect it to, when you want it to.

✔ **Continual review and improvement.** Nothing remains stable for long: customer needs change and technology progresses. Availability management must be aware of changes coming from the business as well as from other parts of the IT provider organisation, and react accordingly. Regular reviews are an ideal way to ensure that changes don't go unnoticed and opportunities for improvement and optimisation are captured and acted on.

Reactive activities

The *reactive activities* of availability management take place during the service operation stage of the service lifecycle. These activities aim to ensure that the targets for availability of the service are met and that any issues are spotted before outages occur:

✔ **Monitoring, measuring, analysing, reporting and reviewing service and component availability.** You do this to ensure that availability targets are met. You provide much of this data to the service level management process (see Chapter 5) to contribute to the regular reports that are delivered to the customers, usually on a day-to-day basis, by your service operation staff.

✔ **Investigating all service and component unavailability and instigating remedial action.** Here availability management gets involved with the incident management and problem management processes (see Chapter 8). You can think of this activity as providing expert help when there are availability-related incidents and problems. In addition, availability management ensures that previous problems influence the design of future services.

Have We Got Enough? Capacity Management

After availability (which I cover in the earlier section 'Looking at the activities of availability management'), what annoys users most is IT services that run slowly. Oh, how they complain. But sometimes speed is a matter of perception: how do you know whether the IT service is running as fast as intended?

Asking the business about *capacity* is like asking, 'How much do you want and how fast should it work?' *Capacity management* is concerned with both the capacity and performance of the IT service. So the aim is to keep the users happy by ensuring that there is enough of the service to meet the needs of all the users, and that the service works fast enough.

The capacity of the service depends on the component parts. So this may include having enough network bandwidth, enough server processing power, enough data storage, powerful enough PCs. Also consider software. Poorly written software code can lead to an application that uses more resources than necessary. Then you have people. Having enough people may be a management issue not an IT service management issue, but you may be able to use some similar concepts or methods of capacity management to help.

The purpose of the capacity management process is to ensure that the capacity of IT services and the IT infrastructure meets the agreed capacity- and performance-related requirements in a cost-effective and timely manner. Capacity management is concerned with meeting both the current and future availability needs of the business.

Eh? You've got to know how much is needed then provide what you've agreed.

Other objectives of capacity management include:

- ✔ Ensure that service performance achievements meet their agreed targets, by managing the performance and capacity of both services and resources.
- ✔ Assist with the diagnosis and resolution of performance- and capacity-related incidents and problems.
- ✔ Ensure that services are designed to meet agreed performance and capacity requirements.
- ✔ Produce and maintain a capacity plan – in line with the budget lifecycle.

Much of capacity management is a balancing act – in fact, two balancing acts:

- ✔ **Cost against resources:** Balancing the need to ensure that the appropriate capacity is present with making the most efficient use of capacity-related resources.
- ✔ **Supply versus demand:** Ensuring that the available supply of IT processing power is matched to the demands made on it by the business.

In common with the availability management process (see the earlier section 'Making Sure the Service is Available: Availability Management'), the requirements for capacity are gathered via the service level management process (see Chapter 5). Will the customer understand what is meant by the capacity of the IT service? I suspect not. But you should be able to ask the customer how many staff use the IT service and when are the busiest times of day. You then follow the same process that I outline in the earlier section 'Seeing the process in action'.

Capacity management and demand management

A close relationship exists between capacity management and demand management. Demand management is a process described in the service strategy stage and is concerned with identifying the patterns of business activity or patterns of use of the IT services. The information gathered is a valuable input to the capacity management process because it represents the requirements that have to be met by the resources that contribute to the capacity of the IT service. If you want to know more about demand management, take a look at Chapter 4.

Beryl, the sales manager, has requirements for capacity and performance. In response to my questions, Beryl says, 'I have 100 users in the department. The busiest time of day is between 10 and 12 a.m., and all 100 users may need to use the system. At lunchtime we get very few calls, but in the afternoon things pick up again, though not quite as much as in the morning. By the way, when all 100 users are using the service, the system should respond in less than two seconds when users hit the return key.' Your technical staff look at these requirements from a capacity point of view. They calculate the technical resource required to provide this service, in other words how much network bandwidth, processor power and disc storage. They discover that they can meet the requirements on most days; however, on Wednesday afternoons the response time may be greater than two seconds if all 100 users use the service. This is because of processing that takes place in the finance department. The service level manager discusses this with Beryl, who agrees that this is acceptable because it's unusual for the sales department to be that busy on a Wednesday afternoon.

A similarity between availability and capacity is that the capacity and performance of the service depends on the quality of the contributing components and assets. So, for a train company to run its service, it must have enough trains and they must run fast enough. There must also be enough staff, and they must be in the right place at the right time. This is exactly true of IT services as well.

Defining some capacity management terms

Here are a couple of bits of terminology:

✔ **Performance:** Performance refers to how quickly the computer system processes your data and responds to requests from users. Performance is often measured by system response time or transaction response time. This is usually the time it takes from when the users press the return key to when something appears on screen.

Think about when you are using the Internet at home. Perhaps you are on your favourite Internet shopping site. How long will you wait for the web page to refresh – 30 seconds, 15 seconds, 5 seconds or just 1 second – before you give up and go to a competitor's site? Response time is important to users; it can slow down their productivity or just simply frustrate them.

✔ **Capacity plan:** You use this plan to manage the resources required to deliver IT services. The plan contains scenarios for different predictions of business demand, and costed options to deliver the agreed service level targets. You usually create the plan once a year in line with your budget cycle. The plan has many purposes. One is a method of asking the organisation for more money. Capacity costs money, therefore it makes sense to plan carefully any increase (or decrease) in capacity. The capacity plan documents the need for additional capacity for the coming year, and can be used to justify the expenditure.

Understanding capacity management sub-processes

Capacity management carries out many activities, but the purpose of the activities can vary depending upon which sub-process you consider:

✔ **Business capacity management (BCM):** Translates business needs and plans into requirements for the service and IT infrastructure to ensure that the future business requirements for the IT services are planned and implemented. To do this, the BCM sub-process receives requirements from the business (via service level management or the service strategy) and reviews them to see whether anything will create a change in demand for the IT services (the process looks for things that may trip up IT).

Typically, market campaigns and promotions cause issues. I have heard of many cases where business units have 'forgotten' to mention a TV campaign that led to a large increase in usage of the IT service, and the IT department was unable to plan for it. Even when events are planned for, it's sometimes difficult to forecast them correctly. For example, in 2011 the UK Government launched a website that allows the public to see crime figures for their region. So many people tried to use the site that it crashed and was taken down.

✔ **Service capacity management (SCM):** Focuses on the end-to-end IT service and is concerned with whether the agreed service capacity levels are provided to the customers. This involves the management, control and prediction of the end-to-end performance and capacity of the live services. So the key is to monitor and measure against the targets in the SLAs.

✔ **Component capacity management (CCM):** Focuses on the underlying technology of the service that provides the capacity. You need to understand how each component contributes to the service. Similarly, each component may become a bottleneck. So this sub-process includes the management, control and prediction of the performance utilisation and capacity of individual IT technology components.

Looking at the activities of capacity management

Here are the main activities of the capacity management process:

✔ **Reviewing current capacity and performance.** When you receive a set of service requirements, you review them to see whether you can achieve them from a capacity and performance point of view. This involves reviewing the current design of your services.

✔ **Improving current service and component capacity.** You can use many capacity management techniques to identify how to make improvements to your services; check out the ITIL service design book, which has plenty of suggestions.

✔ **Assessing, agreeing and documenting new requirements and capacity.** Requirements for changes or new services will most likely be received through the service level management process (see Chapter 5). You translate the requirements into detailed capacity requirements. Capacity and resources cost money, so you carefully assess each requirement, and any improvements must be cost-justifiable.

✔ **Planning new capacity.** After you review capacity requirements and decide how you are to meet the requirements, you must plan to make the resources available. The capacity plan contains your recommendations for achieving this, along with the costs. The plan should be regularly reviewed and kept up to date.

Being Prepared for Anything: IT Service Continuity Management

Imagine your main computer centre is located near a main road. One day a tanker carrying a toxic substance crashes on the main road and the police create an exclusion zone and evacuate the area. How long can you operate your IT service for? Your services are still available and they still work; technically, there has been no failure. The organisation's business is evacuated along with the IT staff. How long is it before you need access, which you are denied by the police, to the services? Is this an occasion when you invoke your disaster recovery – or IT service continuity – plan?

IT service continuity management (ITSCM) is more or less another name for disaster recovery.

The purpose of the ITSCM process is to support the overall business continuity management process by ensuring that, by managing the risks that may seriously affect the IT services, the IT service provider can always provide the minimum agreed business-continuity-related service levels.

Business continuity management refers to the activities that your business performs to decide what to do in the event of a disaster or other large event that prevents the business from operating. So, the business comes first. It decides what business processes are essential to the viability of the organisation. The prime concern of an organisation when faced with some unexpected event is to remain in business. It should plan for this. This is business continuity management. When the business realises that one or many of these activities involve an IT service, the IT provider must get involved in planning how to recover the essential IT services. Once you've got the requirements from the customer, you then identify the appropriate way of recovering the service. This, of course, costs money.

The service level manager asks Beryl, the sales manager, what should happen if there is some sort of disaster. Her response is, 'Because the sales department represents the main means of generating income for the business, the sales IT service must be recovered within 24 hours.' Once your technical staff review these requirements, they discover that there is already a recovery site that supports one of the manufacturing department's IT services which uses similar technology. They decide that, for a small amount of investment, the recovery site can be extended to support the sales IT service as well. The service level manager returns to Beryl with the good news, and Beryl says she agrees with this solution.

Defining some IT service continuity management terms

The following sections explain some of the terminology you come across in the ITIL service continuity management process.

Business impact analysis

In the event of a disaster, it's important for the IT department to have a plan in place that tells it which IT services should be recovered and in what order. Who tells IT what to do first? Simple answer: the business. The severity of the disaster is determined by the size of the impact on the business.

An important part of IT service continuity is to perform a *business impact analysis* (BIA). This is, of course, an analysis of the impact of a disaster on the business.

Think of a supermarket that has to close unexpectedly for a day; what would be the business impacts? I'm sure you've just said 'loss of revenue'. So straight away the supermarket is losing money because it isn't selling anything. Second, there's a loss of reputation: customers won't be impressed and will shop elsewhere. Third, additional operational expense is incurred: store staff hanging around doing nothing; IT staff running around trying to fix things.

Disasters can have an impact on businesses in many ways, and not all impacts occur at the same time. If a bank's main trading IT service were to fail, the impact would occur immediately and the bank would lose money. However, if the human resources system failed, the bank might be able to manage without it for several days.

A bank has just completed a BIA which involved members of the IT provider organisation. One of the outcomes is a set of requirements for IT stating that in the event of a disaster the IT services should be recovered in the following order:

- ✔ Number 1: The trading service. To be recovered in ten minutes.

- ✔ Number 2: The email service. To be recovered in four hours.

- ✔ Number 3: The human resources service. To be recovered in two days.

Risk analysis

The BIA (see the previous section) helps you determine which services you have to recover. Now you can look more closely at these services to identify the risks to them. You may consider threats such as flood, fire and pestilence (disasters have been caused by rodents eating through cables). You can then consider how vulnerable your systems are to the threats. For example, the river that your IT data centre is near is not the only source of a threat of flooding. The threat could just as easily be that the pipe which feeds the coffee machine in the corridor situated over the top of the computer room bursts and floods your equipment.

After you identify and value risks, you must decide whether to take action. This may be risk reduction – in other words, move the coffee machine! Or the appropriate action may be to set up a recovery plan. You can find out a little more about risk by looking at Chapter 9.

IT service continuity strategy

Your IT service continuity strategy is your decision about how you intend to recover your IT services in the event of a disaster. There are a couple of extremes:

- ✔ **A complete duplicate of your computer room, or data centre:** You have duplicate servers, data storage and network connections in another location some distance away from your main computer room. You ensure that the data is duplicated on both systems, so when you have a disaster you simply switch to your second system. Great, but very expensive.

- ✔ **An empty room available that you can use as your backup data centre:** This must be far enough away from your main system so that both cannot be affected by the same disaster. So when you have a disaster, you have to acquire some hardware and software from your favourite computer store and take it to this empty room and rebuild your systems from scratch. In reality, I hope this is less ad hoc. You have a proper plan in place. However, it does describe the other extreme at which recovering your IT services is likely to take several days.

Other strategies exist in between these two extremes, and the clever bit is to decide which is most appropriate to your organisation. You make the decision based on the result of your BIA and risk analysis (see the preceding sections).

Looking at the activities of IT service continuity management

These activities aren't a process for invoking disaster recovery but a process for recognising the need to plan for significant events and for setting up the appropriate facilities:

- ✔ **Initiation:** Getting started. This requires recognition of the importance of business continuity management and ITSCM from senior management. Hopefully this is followed by getting approval, funding and support to establish business continuity management and ITSCM. To get started, someone must decide whether you need a project team, a department or just an individual to be responsible for ITSCM. Then you must create a plan to introduce ITSCM.

✔ **Requirements and strategy:** This activity is split in two:

- **Requirements:** This is the point at which you must perform a BIA and a risk analysis (see the earlier sections on these). The results of these two activities tell you which IT services you must recover in the event of a disaster, in which order you must recover them, and how long you have to recover each IT service.

- **Strategy:** You take the output of the business impact analysis and risk analysis and decide the type of recovery site. You can decide to have no recovery system or a fully equipped duplicate system.

✔ **Implementation:** This doesn't mean implementing or invoking your continuity plan. Now you've decided what recovery mechanism you need, you set it up, which usually involves:

- Developing the ITSCM plans and procedures

- Organisational planning – deciding who'll do what

- Building or acquiring the recovery site and systems

- Initial testing of the recovery systems

✔ **Ongoing management:** Once you have your continuity plan in place, for how long will it remain up to date? Not long! As soon as someone makes a change to one of your IT services, your continuity plan is out of date. That's life! Here are some ideas of things you can do to ensure the continuity plan remains up to date:

- Education, awareness and training of all those affected or involved

- Regular review and audit of your ITSCM processes

- Regular testing of your recovery systems

- Linking in to the change management processes (see Chapter 7) so that you can trap anything that may alter your recovery plans

Ensuring Security: Information Security Management

Where are your valuables stored? Don't worry, I'm not going to come round and steal them! I hope they're secure. I expect that your money is in the bank and your valuable possessions are stored somewhere safe. What do you do when young children come to your house? Do you put your favourite vase or ornaments out of reach so they don't get damaged? I'm sure children don't deliberately break things, but accidents happen. Mind you, do you set expectations? I still remember from my childhood, a friend's parent telling me, 'This is how you behave when you are in our house: be careful not to touch anything.' So what has this got to do with information security management? The point is, we all have valuable possessions, and we do whatever we have to do to protect them. What's more, one of the best ways to protect things from accidental damage is to set expectations and encourage people to act in a specific way when they're in your domain.

Instead of the word possession, ITIL uses the word *asset*. An asset is something of value. Not all your assets have the same value. So here's what you do:

1. **Decide which are your most valuable assets.** Start with the ones you can't manage without.

2. **Decide what the risks are to the assets.** For example, could the assets be stolen by a burglar or damaged in a fire?

3. **Decide the best way of protecting your assets.**

According to ITIL, IT assets can be resources (things like infrastructure, applications, information and people) and capabilities (things like processes and knowledge). You can find out more about IT assets in Chapter 3.

One of your most valuable IT assets is likely to be the information and data that is stored on and used by your systems. This is one of the most important things to protect. The data is at the heart of your organisation. It may be data about the products you sell, what they cost, and the customers you sell them to. Each organisation's data will be different. In IT terms, this data is stored on hard discs and data volumes scattered around your IT systems. The data must be protected against deliberate or accidental damage. In order to do this you also have to protect your IT infrastructure and applications. This is the same as locking your house when you go out in order to protect your valuables that are hidden inside. Your house is the equivalent of the infrastructure, and your valuables are the equivalent of your IT data.

The purpose of the information security management process is to align IT security with business security and ensure that the confidentiality, integrity and availability of the organisation's assets, information, data and IT services always matches the agreed needs of the business.

So, the information security management process:

- ✔ Provides strategic direction for security activities

- ✔ Ensures that a management system is in place to manage all aspects of IT security

✔ Manages information security risks

✔ Protects the interests of those relying on information, and the systems and communications that deliver the information, from harm resulting from failures of availability, confidentiality and integrity

Relating this information to the other warranty aspects, the users cannot get value if the service is not there (unavailable), or it goes slow (lack of capacity), or if the data and information they use is missing, corrupt or unavailable due to a security incident.

So what is the point of view of Beryl – the sales manager on security? 'We are bound by the Data Protection Act to protect our clients' information. Also our discount calculations are company confidential and must be secure. All sales data must be protected and must be restorable in the event of a cyber-attack.' The technical staff review these requirements. Happily, you discover that Beryl's view conforms with the standard level of security you have in place, so the service level manager once again delivers the good news to Beryl.

Defining some information security management terms

The following sections Dummify some ITIL technical terms.

Confidentiality, integrity and availability

One way of considering the most appropriate way of protecting your IT assets is to think about confidentiality, integrity and availability:

✔ **Confidentiality:** Making sure that only the right people know where your assets are, and that the information is seen by only those who have a right to know. IT has clever ways of doing this, including setting access (when you're given a username and password), and encryption of highly confidential data (electronically coding it so that the recipient's system has to know the code in order to read it).

✔ **Integrity:** Making sure your assets don't get damaged. IT data and information can easily get corrupted if not protected correctly, so you need to be sure that your information is complete, accurate and protected against unauthorised modification. This is what your anti-virus system does.

✔ **Availability:** Making sure the assets are there when needed. Ensuring that information is available and usable when required, and systems can resist attacks and recover from or prevent failures.

Security risks

Once you've established the customer's security requirements, you must identify any risks that may prevent you from achieving what the customer wants. This includes a review of the assets and components used to provide the IT service. The review identifies anything that's a risk to security. Here are some examples of risks:

- ✔ Systems that don't have password control
- ✔ Personal USB devices brought in from home and connected to a PC
- ✔ Users who write their passwords on sticky notes and leave them on the side of the PC

In one organisation, part of a network failed at the same time every day, at about 7:30 every morning. After much investigation it was discovered that a staff member was unplugging a network router (positioned on a windowsill!) in order to plug in and charge a mobile phone. A risk certainly – possibly a security risk.

Getting things under control

Once you have established the sort of risks you are facing (see the preceding section) you need to put controls in place to deal with them.

What is a *control*? When you add a lock to your house, you're adding a control. Similarly, when you take out insurance, this is also a control. So you must add similar control to protect your IT services. Here are some examples of security controls:

- ✔ Installing firewalls to detect and prevent intruders
- ✔ Taking regular data backups so you can restore corrupt data
- ✔ Mechanisms that, when your systems are attacked, shut them down to prevent further harm
- ✔ User access controls (usernames and passwords) to prevent the wrong people getting access to your systems

Information security policy

Once you understand the need for security in your organisation, don't keep it a secret – tell everyone how important it is. The best way to do this is to create an *information security policy:* a document that makes it clear to the entire business how seriously the organisation takes security. Circulate the policy to everyone, not just within the IT provider organisation, but to the users and customers.

Here are some ideas for what to put in your information security policy:

- ✔ **Access control:** Who is allowed to use your IT services and how they get access

- ✔ **Anti-virus policy:** What the anti-virus system protects and how often it is updated

- ✔ **Email and Internet policies:** What websites users can and can't visit; what they can and can't download

- ✔ **Use and misuse of IT assets:** What users can and can't do to their desktop system

Information security management system

The *information security management system* (ISMS) is a framework of activities. Have a look at Figure 6-1.

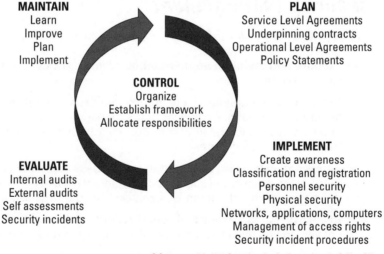

MAINTAIN
Learn
Improve
Plan
Implement

PLAN
Service Level Agreements
Underpinning contracts
Operational Level Agreements
Policy Statements

CONTROL
Organize
Establish framework
Allocate responsibilities

IMPLEMENT
Create awareness
Classification and registration
Personnel security
Physical security
Networks, applications, computers
Management of access rights
Security incident procedures

EVALUATE
Internal audits
External audits
Self assessments
Security incidents

Figure 6-1: The information security management system.

© Crown copyright 2011. Reproduced under licence from the Cabinet Office.

This framework of activities wasn't invented by ITIL but is based on stuff taken from a standard called ISO/IEC 27001. Best not to reinvent the wheel then. The ISMS provides a simple approach to planning and implementing the controls and measures needed for information security management:

- ✔ **Control:** The controls needed to maintain information security to support the business needs; includes the organisational structures, roles and responsibilities needed to manage information security

✔ **Plan:** Identification of the requirements of information security and the planning of how they will be achieved

✔ **Implement:** Implementation of the controls and mechanisms for achieving the planned level of security

✔ **Evaluate:** The review and measurement of the success of the controls and mechanisms

✔ **Maintain:** The continual improvement of information security

If you think the approach of the ISMS looks familiar, you're right. It's based on a well-known quality management approach known as the Deming Cycle. The cycle is the plan, do, check, act method for gradual improvement in any organisation. You can find out more about the Deming Cycle in Chapter 9.

Looking at the activities of information security management

The activities of the information security management process are as follows:

✔ **Produce and maintain an information security policy.** Does what it says on the tin.

✔ **Communicate, implement and enforce adherence to all security policies.** You must make it clear how seriously security is taken by your organisation. Some organisations link not adhering to the security policy to disciplinary procedures.

✔ **Assess and categorise information assets, risks and vulnerabilities.** This involves allocating some relative value to each security risk, so that you know which risks are most significant to your organisation.

✔ **Regularly assess, review and report security risks and threats.** Things change, so you need to do this regularly and keep things up to date.

✔ **Impose and review risk security controls, and review and implement risk mitigation:** Here you implement the controls and mechanisms that you've identified to support your information security policy.

✔ **Monitor and manage security incidents and breaches.** Breaches must not go unnoticed. Your policy will not be taken seriously if you don't police it.

✔ **Report, review and reduce security breaches and major incidents:** You must learn from the things that happen in your organisation.

Identifying Service Design Roles

Each service management process should have a process owner and a process manager. I explain these two roles in Chapter 2. Some of the service design roles are listed in Chapter 5. For the warranty processes, the relevant process manager roles are:

- Availability manager
- Capacity manager
- IT service continuity manager
- Information security manager

Each role is responsible for the activities described in the appropriate section of this chapter.

Using technology for service design

In each of the five core ITIL publications (one for each lifecycle stage), a chapter is dedicated to the use of technology in helping you provide the IT services to your customers. IT services, of course, largely consist of technology. But technology is also used by the staff who manage and deliver the services.

Tools can be used in the service design stage for hardware design, software design, environmental design, process design and data design. Such tools can help by:

- Speeding up the design process
- Helping you and your colleagues stick to standards and conventions
- Aiding prototyping, modelling and simulation
- Validating designs

Chapter 7

Getting Physical: Service Transition

In This Chapter

▶ Maintaining control of changes

▶ Knowing what assets you've got and where

▶ Deploying new or changed stuff

▶ Improving decision-making

▶ Planning for and supporting transitions

*H*ave you ever created great plans only to discover that when you put them into action it all goes horribly wrong? What looks great on paper doesn't necessarily work the way you planned. When it comes to IT projects, can you afford to get it wrong? To add insult to injury, you'll probably look a bit of an idiot if all goes pear shaped. So how do you prevent this happening? By having good service transition processes, of course.

Service transition is the stage in which you build, test and implement the new service or changed service. In other words, this is where you get physical. In all, there are seven service transition processes. This chapter introduces five of them: change management; service asset and configuration management; release and deployment management; knowledge management; transition planning and support. You can find the remaining two processes (service validation and testing, and change evaluation) in Chapter 13.

Understanding the Purpose of the Service Transition Lifecycle Phase

Service transition is the stage between service design (see Chapters 5 and 6) and service operation (see Chapter 8). This may seem to be an odd or rather obvious thing to point out; however, it's worth stopping and pondering for a moment what this means.

One of the main inputs into a service transition is a *service design package* (SDP). The SDP is produced during the service design stage and contains all the information required in order to decide whether to go ahead with the transition of the new or changed service. It's important to note that this is simply documentation; the design phase doesn't start to build anything. The main output of a service transition is a new or changed service that is handed over to service operation and can be used as required and intended. So service transition does the bit in between: everything needed to build, test and implement the new or changed service.

The purpose of the service transition stage of the service lifecycle is to ensure that new, modified or retired services meet the expectations of the business as documented in the service strategy and service design stages of the lifecycle.

Service transition can include any of the following:

- ✔ The introduction of new services
- ✔ Changes to existing services
- ✔ Decommissioning and discontinuation of services
- ✔ The transfer of services from one provider to another, including:
  - • Outsourcing services to a supplier
  - • Bringing services back in-house from a supplier
  - • Transferring services from one supplier to another

Looking at an Overview of the Service Transition Processes

You can divide the seven service transition processes up as follows:

- ✔ **Processes that support all service lifecycle stages:**
  - • Change management
  - • Service asset and configuration management
  - • Knowledge management
- ✔ **Processes that mainly focus on service transition:**
  - • Release and deployment management
  - • Transition planning and support
  - • Service validation and testing
  - • Change evaluation

A *process* is a set of activities that are coordinated to achieve a specific objective. So, what follows are descriptions of many activities that are required to build, test and implement a new or changed service. You don't perform each process in isolation; coordinate them to achieve an overall aim. Most of the activities for a specific transition are coordinated as a project. After you read about the processes here, look at Chapter 13 for more practical advice and examples of service transition projects.

Controlling Change: Change Management

Change management ensures that IT changes are recorded, assessed and authorised, and then implemented into the live environment in a controlled manner. The changes may be to any component of any IT service or infrastructure. Changes may affect hardware, software, documents – in fact anything that is under control. ITIL refers to IT changes, so changes to the business aren't normally within the scope of IT change management.

People often see change management as a bureaucratic waste of time. This is usually because they don't understand the benefits of change management. The natural consequence of a badly assessed and badly implemented change is an incident that creates downtime and adversely affects the business. What a stupid thing to do! To fail to assess and control changes correctly is to wilfully risk downtime to your services. I'm sure we have all experienced those occasions when a colleague quickly makes a change to a setting to a server just before going on holiday and forgets to mention it to anybody. The change affects something which creates an error. The consequence is an unforeseen and unidentified failure that wastes a large amount of time and effort to resolve. Many IT environments are huge, and no one person can hope to understand the effect a change may have on the IT enterprise. The change management process aims to ensure that all proposed changes are considered appropriately before any build, test and implementation work commences.

The purpose of the change management process is to control the lifecycle of all changes, enabling beneficial changes to be made with minimum disruption to IT services.

Anyone should be able to request that the IT department makes a change to one of the services. This includes business as well as IT staff. Changes are requested in response to many things, including regulatory or legal changes, changes in the business, software enhancements and technical improvements, and resolution of errors.

Change management doesn't have to be bureaucratic. Plenty of advice in the ITIL books (some of it included here) allows you to create a flexible and adaptable change management process. After you decide how change management will work in your organisation, make sure you document your policy and process – and then tell everyone about it!

Defining some change management terms

To understand the change management process, you need to understand some terminology:

- ✔ **Change:** ITIL states that a change is 'the addition, modification or removal of anything that may have an effect on IT services. The scope should include changes to all architectures, processes, tools, metrics and documentation, as well as changes to IT services and other components'. Any IT change, however big or small, can potentially have an effect on an IT service and hence an impact on the business in some way. ITIL defines three types of change: normal, standard and emergency. All changes follow the normal change management process, but standard and emergency changes are exceptions:

  - • **Standard change:** In ITIL's words, this is 'a pre-authorised change (also called a business-as-usual change) that is low risk, relatively common and follows a procedure or work instruction – for example, a password reset or provision of standard equipment to a new employee'. Most standard changes follow a pre-defined procedure or work instruction; this may be a change model or request model, that describes the established path that should be followed. (Request models are described in Chapter 8)

    Standard changes don't have to be initiated by a request for change (see the later bullet). Standard changes are often initiated by the service desk as service requests and dealt with using the request fulfilment process (see Chapter 8). This lifts some of the load off change management and improves the flexibility of your change management process. But bear in mind that not all standard changes are dealt with as service requests, and not all service requests are standard changes.

    Emergency change: According to ITIL this is 'a change that must be introduced as soon as possible – for example, to resolve a major incident or implement a security patch'. Emergency changes follow a pre-defined procedure – they adopt a change model.

    Emergency changes must not be used simply to speed up the change management process. Emergency changes are required to correct a situation where there's a great impact on the business, and should be kept to a minimum.

✔ **Request for change (RFC):** The ITIL publications state that this is 'a formal proposal for a change to be made, including details of the proposed change. Can be recorded on paper or electronically'.

✔ **Change proposal:** In ITIL's words this is 'a document that includes a high level description of a potential service introduction or significant change, along with a corresponding business case and an expected implementation schedule'.

Change proposals are used for major changes and for new service introductions proposed via the service portfolio management process (see Chapter 4).

✔ **Change model:** ITIL states that a change model is 'a repeatable way of dealing with a particular category of change. For each category of change, a change model defines specific agreed steps that will be followed. Change models may be very complex with many steps that require authorisation (for example, a major software release) or may be very simple with no requirement for authorisation (for example, a password reset)'. A change model is similar to a pre-defined template procedure for handling a particular type of change.

For example, the implementation of a service pack to a server is a relatively common change. I'm sure in your organisation you know who handles such a change, and I suspect that the same people get involved every time. The common-sense approach is to document this as a procedure, or change model, to ensure that all changes of this type are always dealt with in the same way.

✔ **Change advisory board (CAB):** In ITIL terminology, this is 'a group of people who support the assessment, prioritisation, authorisation and scheduling of changes. The group is usually made up of representatives from all areas within the IT service provider organisation, the business, and third parties such as suppliers'. The CAB may, but doesn't necessarily, authorise changes. Not all changes go to the CAB; usually the higher-risk and higher-impact changes require involvement from the CAB.

✔ **Emergency change advisory board (ECAB):** According to ITIL criteria this is 'a subgroup of the CAB that makes decisions about emergency changes. Membership may be decided when a meeting is called, and depends on the nature of the emergency change'. Where possible, emergency changes should be authorised in the normal way; however in some situations a smaller body must be established. The ECAB is likely to consist of the change manager plus one or two others.

Imagine something goes wrong overnight and the IT operations shift manager appreciates the need to fix it before the morning. In a phone call at 3 o'clock in the morning, the shift manager explains the issue to the change manager, describes the solution and gets authorisation to make the change. The change manager then goes back to sleep. In many cases, the authority to make such decisions in the twilight hours can be delegated to the shift manager.

Deciding the scope of your change management process

You need to define the *scope* of the change management process: which changes go through change management and which don't. In particular, consider:

- ✔ When it's a business change, not an IT change; examples include departmental reorganisations
- ✔ Situations such as swapping out a network card in a workstation to resolve an incident
- ✔ What the relationship is between your change management process and your project management process
- ✔ What the relationship is with any supplier's change management processes

I have no definitive answers to these situations: you must decide how they will be handled in your organisation, and document the decisions in your change policy and process.

Looking at the activities of change management

The following sections explore the main activities of the change management process.

Creating and recording the RFC

Changes are initiated by an RFC. Anybody in your organisation should have access to requesting a change, including business people. The change should be recorded by the IT department, normally in the *configuration management system* (CMS). This usually involves the creation of a change record that provides a historical record of the change.

In some cases where the change is large or complex, more information may be required. In this case a change proposal should be created. Change proposals are often used to gain initial authorisation for new services or major changes to services initiated by service portfolio management (for more information about change proposals and service portfolio management take a look at Chapter 4).

Reviewing the RFC

This is an initial review of the RFC. Imagine a change manager entering his office one morning and discovering that a pile of new RFCs has landed in the in-tray. I'm sure this is not an unfamiliar situation for many of you. The first thing he does is give each request a quick read and look for the following:

✔ The form has been filled in correctly.

✔ The mandatory fields are complete.

✔ It's not a duplicate of another request.

✔ It's not a ridiculous request that is outside of the scope of the change management process.

Assessing and evaluating the change

Assess and evaluate the change. This can be a major activity and influence the decision whether to authorise the change. Who does this depends on the type and scale of the change. All aspects of the change must be considered, taking into account the business, technical and financial impacts of the change.

Use the seven Rs of change management to remind you of the key questions to ask:

✔ **Raised:** Who raised the RFC?

✔ **Reason:** What is the reason for the change?

✔ **Return:** What is the financial or business return, or what are the benefits required from the change?

✔ **Risks:** What are the risks involved in making, or not making, the change?

✔ **Resources:** What resources will be required to make the change?

✔ **Responsible:** Who will be responsible for making the change?

✔ **Relationship:** What is the relationship with other changes, or what are the dependencies on other changes?

This stage also includes the planning and scheduling of the change. This can include deciding whether to group a number of changes into a release and adding the change to the *change schedule* – a list of changes that have been authorised and have a planning implementation date.

Authorising the change build and test

Based on the assessment (see the last section) you can now authorise the building and testing of the change. The *change authority* – the person who authorises the change! – can be whoever you want it to be.

Establish a policy for how you want to authorise changes and decide on a set of change authorities. Table 7-1 provides an example set of authorities.

Table 7-1	Example Change Authorities
Change Authority	*Level of Risk/Impact*
Business executive board	High cost/risk change – requires decision from executives
IT management board or IT steering group	Change that affects multiple services or organisational divisions
CAB or ECAB	Change that affects local or service group only
Change manager	Low-risk change
Local authorisation	Standard change

© *Crown copyright 2011. Reproduced under licence from the Cabinet Office.*

Coordinating the change build and test

The next activity is to coordinate the build and test of the change. The amount of work here depends on the type of change. If the change is the update of a document, you have a very small amount of build and test work. But if the change is, say, the installation of a new network router, then the router will have to be built or configured and tested, and the whole service may have to be tested to ensure there's no unpredicted impact.

The change manager coordinates the change build and test by coordinating the activities of the individual, team or supplier who will make the change. I don't know what your change manager is like, but in my experience it's unlikely to be the change manager himself who rolls up his sleeves, picks up a screwdriver and builds the change.

The change manager ensures that those responsible for the change have test plans in place and also a back-out plan or other remediation plans. A *back-out plan* ensures that if a failure occurs while the change is being implemented, the service can be restored to a previous, known, stable state. A *remediation plan* states what further action is required to minimise the impact upon the business in the event that the IT service cannot be restored to a stable state.

Authorising change deployment

Once the change has been built and tested (see the previous section), authority is given for deployment. This provides an opportunity to check the test results, review the remediation plans and check the scheduled deployment date for the change. Many changes will be deployed using the process and procedures of release and deployment management – see the later section 'Getting the Change Out There: Release and Deployment Management').

Coordinating change deployment

This activity is similar to *Coordinating the change build and test* that I describe in a previous section. It is very unlikely that the change manager actually deploys the change. If the change is part of a release, then the release and deployment process coordinate the deployment. If it's a simple change then it will be deployed under the control of change management.

Reviewing and closing the change record

The final activity in the change management process is to review and close the change. All changes should be reviewed after implementation, although where there are a high volume of changes, spot checks are acceptable. The review isn't just to check that the change did not fail, but to ensure that the change achieved the aims and benefits that were intended. This review is often referred to as a *post implementation review*.

Scheduling change reviews

Sometimes the review is difficult to schedule because it isn't clear how long you have to wait to be sure that the change has had the intended effects. I recall a case where I investigated an incident that caused the financial software application's year-end routine to fail. I was monitoring the service via remote access, and luckily I was able to restart the routine and the year-end figures were produced on time. Subsequently, the associated problem was investigated, the cause identified and an RFC raised to correct a programming error. The change was made and tested and then implemented into the live environment. However, it wasn't possible to establish for certain that the change had resolved the issue until the same routine was run the following year. So the change record remained open and the review wasn't completed until the following year.

Knowing What You've Got: Service Asset and Configuration Management

Described simply, *service asset and configuration management* (SACM) is the process that ensures you maintain up-to-date information about all your assets and the component parts of the IT services you manage. It aims to maintain a repository of information about these components – one or more databases of information. Theoretically, this means recording every PC, software application, document, network component, server and so on that's part of your IT environment.

I'm sure, like me, you've experienced the flush of enthusiasm when you decide to record details of every PC, every server and every piece of software you possess and store it in a spreadsheet or database. Having completed this piece of work, you proudly produce reports of all your IT stuff, sliced and diced in every way possible. The trouble is that the enthusiasm wanes a few weeks later when the database falls out of date. Because it's a process, SACM consists of activities that not only ensure you capture and record this information, but also keep it up to date.

Understanding the asset and configuration aspects

ITIL states that 'the purpose of the SACM process is to ensure that the assets required to deliver services are properly controlled, and that accurate and reliable information about those assets is available when and where it's needed. This information includes details of how the assets have been configured and the relationship between the assets'. (Chapter 2 explains assets.)

Asset management, as distinct from configuration management, is generally described as the process responsible for tracking and reporting the value and ownership of financial assets throughout their lifecycle. This sort of asset management is sometimes known as *fixed* asset management or *financial* asset management. In some organisations, SACM will be used to do some or all fixed asset management on behalf of other parts of the business.

The majority of the advice in the SACM section of the ITIL service transition book relates to *configuration management*. Configuration management is different from asset management in two main ways:

- It's concerned with all assets required to deliver an IT service, not just financially valuable ones.
- It maintains information about the relationships between assets.

This second point is the most important because it enables you to create a logical configuration model of the infrastructure and the services. The main use of the logical model is to be able to control the infrastructure and provide information to all other service management processes. For example:

✔ To improve the impact assessment of changes

✔ To improve the diagnosis of incidents and problems

✔ To provide processes such as availability management and capacity management with a view of the services and their components in order to identify weaknesses and areas for improvement

Defining some service asset and configuration management terms

There are quite a few abbreviations and bits of jargon in SACM, so here I define a few of them:

✔ **Configuration item (CI):** The ITIL definition of this term is 'any component or other service asset that needs to be managed in order to deliver an IT service'. You record information about each CI (called *attributes* – things like unique identifier, name, status, owner, location, make, specification) in a configuration record within the CMS, and maintain the record throughout its lifecycle. CIs are under the control of change management. Typically, CIs include IT services, hardware, software, buildings, people and formal documentation such as process documentation and *service level agreements* (SLAs).

✔ **CMS:** According to its ITIL definition, this is 'a set of tools, data and information that is used to support service asset and configuration management'. Figure 7-1 provides a pictorial view of a CMS. ITIL goes on to explain that 'the CMS is part of an overall service knowledge management system and includes tools for collecting, storing, managing, updating, analysing and presenting data about all configuration items and their relationships. The CMS may also include information about incidents, problems, known errors, changes and releases. The CMS is maintained by service asset and configuration management, and is used by all IT service management processes'.

A CMS is not a single database, but as you can see from the figure, the CMS takes data from many sources. One or many *configuration management databases* (CMDBs) contain information about CIs. There may be one for each of your sites: say one for the London office and another for the New York office. The CMS is the set of software tools or applications that relates the CIs recorded in the CMDB with the relevant incidents, problems, changes and other records that are stored in other places.

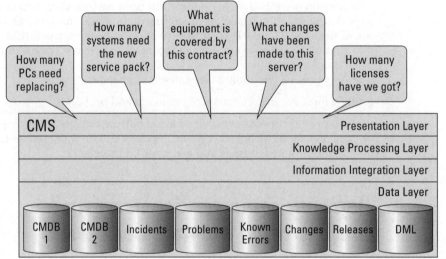

Figure 7-1:
Example
pictorial
view of a
CMS.

© Crown copyright 2011. Reproduced under licence from the Cabinet Office.

✔ **Configuration baseline:** ITIL defines this as 'a baseline of a configuration that has been formally agreed and is managed through the change management process. A configuration baseline is used as a basis for future builds, releases and changes'. A configuration baseline serves as the basis for further activities and can be changed only through formal change procedures. A good example is a standard build of a PC, where it's agreed that every PC should be built and configured in the same way. In any case, it's wise to document this as a CI in its own right.

✔ **Snapshot:** According to ITIL, this is 'the current state of a configuration item, process or any other set of data, recorded at a specific point in time. Snapshots can be captured by discovery tools or by a manual technique such as an assessment'. A snapshot records the configuration of one or many components at a given point in time and doesn't necessarily reflect the intended, authorised state of the components. A baseline can be said to indicate the 'intended' configuration of one or many CIs, whereas a snapshot is the 'actual' configuration – intended or otherwise.

As the names suggests, a snapshot is the equivalent to taking a photograph of an IT component at a point in time. I'm sure you recall the children's puzzle 'spot the difference' where you are required to identify differences between two seemingly identical pictures. It's usually the man's tie that is spotted instead of striped! In the same way, you can compare a snapshot with an authorised baseline and attempt to spot the difference. Any differences you discover may mean an unauthorised change has taken place, for example the user has downloaded and installed a software application from the Internet without permission.

✔ **Definitive media library (DML):** ITIL states that this is 'one or more locations in which the definitive and authorised versions of all software configuration items are securely stored. The DML may also contain associated configuration items such as licences and documentation. It's a single logical storage area even if there are multiple locations'. The DML is controlled by SACM, although it forms the foundation of much release and deployment management activity. A 'list' of what is in the DML will be in the CMS, and there will be defined procedures for the addition, copying and removal of CIs stored here.

The DML is where you store the controlled and authorised master copies of all versions of software, along with any relevant documents. It may be physical or a file-storage area. A physical DML can be a locked cupboard: shelves containing tapes, CDs, DVDs and other media that contain master copies of software and documents such as licence agreements and purchase orders that prove ownership. The DML must be carefully controlled, managed and backed up, and separate from any other environments such as your development, test or live environments.

Looking at the activities of SACM

The following sections take you through the activities of the service asset and configuration management process.

Management and planning

Though you need to plan all service management processes, the activity doesn't appear in every ITIL process, so why is SACM special? Because managing and planning is critical to get the design of the CMS correct, such that it supports all service management activities and is scalable for future needs.

You need to document an SACM plan. The plan contains things such as:

✔ Scope and requirements of SACM for your organisation

✔ Applicable policies, standards and organisation for SACM

✔ Processes, procedures and tools for SACM.

The combination of SACM policies and a configuration management plan drives the remainder of the SACM activities.

Configuration identification

Configuration identification includes all those activities required to decide how the service assets will be recorded in the CMS and how they will be identified and labelled. This includes:

✔ Defining and documenting how CIs will be selected and grouped

✔ Assigning unique identifiers

✔ Specifying the other attributes of each CI and their relationships

A common issue is deciding how many CIs you should record in your CMS to represent assets from your IT environment. For example, would you record a desktop PC as a single CI or several CIs? You may choose to have a separate CI for any or all of the components such as the monitor, mouse, keyboard, base unit, hard disc, DVD/CD drive, network card and so on. You must bear in mind that for each of these that you decide is a separate CI, you are committing to track it by its serial number or other unique identifier throughout its lifecycle. This can be represented by parent–child relationships as shown in Figure 7-2. For each CI you record a set of attributes.

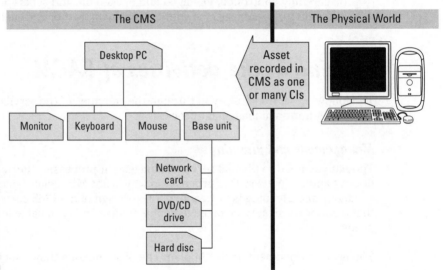

Figure 7-2: Example of CIs and their relationships for a desktop PC.

© Crown copyright 2011. Reproduced under licence from the Cabinet Office.

The example used here is that of a PC; however, the principle is just the same whether you are considering hardware, software or any other type of asset. So how do you decide which CIs to record? Well the answer is, it depends.

Here are some general rules of thumb for deciding what CIs to record in your CMS:

✔ Go down to the level of independent change, in other words decide which level is most appropriate for controlling changes to the asset.

✔ Consider the balance between level of detail and the effort and cost of keeping up to date.

✔ Don't record the asset in your CMS if you have no intention of keeping the record up to date.

Configuration control

Configuration control is the term for the activities that help you decide the appropriate level of control for each CI. The basic question to ask here is: 'How do we control changes to CIs?' The simplest answer is: 'With the change management process.' SACM and change management are inextricably linked. At a very basic level, change management authorises changes to CIs while SACM updates the configuration record. In practical terms, this is an over-simplification. The best way to start is to look at each CI type (for example, software application, PC) and decide whether changes must go through the full change management process or some other mechanism with delegated authority. The important point is to ensure that there is at least some audit trail of changes.

Status accounting and reporting

Status accounting accounts for the status of each CI. Wander into any IT department and you will see a monitor on the floor with a sticky note stating 'does not work – do not use', and a laptop with another label stating 'awaiting upgrade', or a server with a label saying 'under test'. All these bits of paper tell you the current state of the asset, or CI. Status accounting is the equivalent of putting a piece of sticky paper on every CI to denote what state it's in, or its status. However, in reality, the status of the CI is recorded as an attribute in the CMS.

The power of status accounting is the ability to query or report on the status of CIs recorded in the CMS. By using status accounting you can answer such questions as:

✔ How many PCs need replacing?

✔ How many systems need the new service pack?

✔ What equipment is covered by this contract?

✔ What changes have been made to this server?

✔ How many licences have we got?

Verification and audit

The *verification and audit* activity prompts you to check whether your CMS is an accurate representation of your actual assets, infrastructure and services. Surely you don't need to do this! With configuration control and change management in place, all your records are up to date – aren't they? Well, as soon as people get involved, things don't always go as planned. So it's common sense to check that the processes and procedures are followed by performing regular or occasional audits.

Audits can be performed physically by using staff to check the IT equipment, noting down the details, and comparing the details with, and updating, the CMS. Often software discovery tools can be used to electronically collect details of components. Such tools are enormously useful, but don't assume that they're a substitute for a well designed, documented and communicated SACM process. Think about when you perform audits: maybe before you make changes, before releases are deployed, and at planned and random intervals.

Getting the Release Out There: Release and Deployment Management

Release and deployment management is much more than just the last steps of change management: it's an additional set of activities that are triggered once you decide to group a number of changes together into a release.

The purpose of the release and deployment management process is to plan, schedule and control the build, test and deployment of releases, and to deliver new functionality required by the business while protecting the integrity of existing services.

Not all changes go through release and deployment management. However, it's likely that, over time, a large proportion of changes will be introduced into the live environment using procedures and methods developed by release and deployment management.

Not only does release and deployment management implement new and changed services, but it also deals with requests for additional components. Once changes and releases have been implemented, requests for repeat deployments are easily fulfilled using a deployment model. The success of the request fulfilment process (see Chapter 8) is reliant on good deployment models.

For example, a request for a new PC is received by the service desk through the request fulfilment process. The service desk follows the standard change process model in order to log and obtain approval for the request. It then passes it to the technical team responsible for implementing the request, who follow the pre-agreed deployment model. It's just like cranking the handle on a machine, and another one pops out of the end.

Defining some release and deployment management terms

The process is called release and deployment management, but is there any difference between the words *release* and *deployment?* Yes: a *release* is the thing – the object or the noun. The *deployment* is what you're doing to the thing – the verb. So when you perform a deployment, you're deploying a release into the live environment. Figure 7-3 shows a pictorial overview of this.

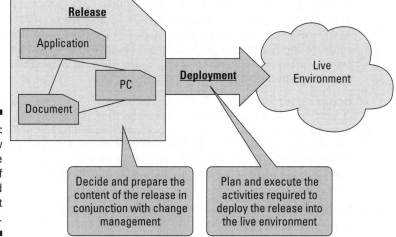

Figure 7-3:
Overview
of the
elements of
release and
deployment
management.

Based on ITIL® material. Reproduced under licence from The Cabinet Office.

An example of a release

Suppose you take the example of going to work, on the assumption that you have to go into the office and you're not working at home. You can consider yourself to be the release. I'm sure you prepare yourself, or the release, before you leave the house. You ensure you are dressed, you have your briefcase with you, and you have also planned the means of travelling to work. You may even check for traffic or transport problems before you leave: you check the means of deployment. All this is done before you get to your doorstep and leave your home. This is the equivalent of planning, building and testing the release. Now you are at the doorstep, you deploy yourself into the big wide world, using the travel method and objectives that you have already set. So this is equivalent to deploying a release into the live environment.

To understand the release and deployment management process, you need to understand some terminology:

✔ **Release:** ITIL says that this is 'one or more changes to an IT service that are built, tested and deployed together. A single release may include changes to hardware, software, documentation, processes and other components'. Many of the activities of release and deployment management are concerned with the preparation of the release. For example, deciding which changes will be grouped together into a release, and how the release will be built and tested.

✔ **Deployment:** According to ITIL, this is 'the activity responsible for movement of new or changed hardware, software, documentation, process and so on to the live environment'. Deployments vary in size and complexity. They may range from installing a single PC in accordance with a deployment model to fully implementing a new service consisting of multiple software and hardware components across many target workstations, servers or users. Deployment also includes the handover of the service to service operation.

✔ **Release unit:** The ITIL definition of this term is 'the components of an IT service that are normally released together. A release unit typically includes sufficient components to perform a useful function. For example, one release unit may be a desktop PC, including hardware, software, licences, documentation, and so on. A different release unit may be the complete payroll application, including IT operations procedures and user training'.

Imagine that the sales department of your organisation uses a sales IT service consisting of a suite of applications such as the *customer relationship management* (CRM) system, the sales order system and the after-sales system. There's a policy decision to be made here. If, say, a software module of the sales order system has a change made to it, should you deploy just the single module, all the sales order system, or the entire sales service? The answer is, inevitably, 'it depends'. But you must now consider whether it would improve the overall quality of your IT services to put a general rule in place to guide all future deployments of the sales service. So if you decide that a change to a module of the sales order system will result in the deployment of the whole sales order system, you have chosen the sales order system as your release unit. This is now the policy for the sales software suite.

Release units are useful in allowing you to break your live environment into bite-sized chunks, especially when it comes to deploying repeat standard installations and changes such as those initiated through the request fulfilment process.

✔ **Release package:** ITIL's definition states that this is 'a set of configuration items that will be built, tested and deployed together as a single release. Each release package usually includes one or more release units'.

In order to minimise the impact of deployments on users, it's often convenient to deploy many release units at one time. When you move into a new house, you don't move each possession separately, you pop things into boxes, usually organised by the destination room such as bedroom or kitchen. A release package is rather like the cardboard box that you put your possessions in.

✔ **Deployment options:** When a new or changed service is designed, the method of deployment should be considered at the same time. This happens in the service design stage of the service lifecycle. Thus much of the approach to release and deployment is decided during design. Here are some possible deployment options:

- **Big bang versus phased approach:** *Big bang* refers to deploying the release to all the target areas at one time. For example, an upgrade to the sales office software application may need to be distributed to all sales staff in one go, because it contains new product data. On the other hand, a *phased approach* is when the release is deployed to different areas at different times, possibly the London office this week followed by the Paris office the week after. This is a less risky approach and allows resources to be managed more efficiently.

- **Push versus pull:** *Push* refers to when a release is deployed from a central point. This often involves the use of automatic software distribution tools that despatch a new release from a central server and install the updated software on all the target workstations. Users normally don't get a choice about when to receive the update. On the other hand, *pulling* a release allows a user to obtain the new release by clicking on a hyperlink and installing the software at a convenient time.

- **Manual versus automatic:** The push and pull methods (see the previous bullet) are usually achieved by using automatic tools to distribute and install the release. In some cases, automatic deployment may not be possible and manual deployment is the appropriate method. Sometimes sending an engineer out with a box full of CDs and a screwdriver in his pocket may be the only way.

✔ **Release policy:** Many of the elements of release and deployment management should be agreed in advance and documented in a release policy. A *policy* is a set of decisions – rules if you like – that provide high-level guidance on how the process should be performed. It saves people reinventing the wheel each time they do something. The release policy should contain:

- Definition of the allowed types of release, for example major, minor and emergency

- Naming and numbering conventions for releases

- Expected frequency of each type of release

> • Roles and responsibilities for the release and deployment management process
>
> The release policy is usually created and agreed with the change manager and also includes the chosen approach to grouping changes into releases.

Looking at the activities of release and deployment management

The following sections give you the low-down on the activities you undertake in this process.

Release and deployment planning

Release and deployment planning involves high-level planning of the release, including planning the subsequent activities, deciding or confirming the changes that are to be included in the release, and the selection of a pre-defined release and deployment model.

Release build and test

Build and test refers to the build and test of the release and the deployment mechanism. So this not only includes tests that assure that the new or changed service will fulfil its objectives, but testing of the means of deploying the release, such as the use of an automatic software distribution tool to ensure that, once distributed, the new software release will install itself on the target workstation and be available to the user.

Building includes taking the individual components that have been subject to change and building them into a single unit, or release. In the case of a desktop PC, this may be the assembly of the hardware components and the installation of the software applications. This, of course, should now be tested.

Service testing ensures that the changed components still operate correctly as part of the overall IT service. If necessary, a pilot may also be performed. A *pilot deployment* is the installation of the release to a representative number and type of targets or users to prove that both the release works as required and the deployment methods are also successful.

Deployment

Some of the planning for deployment is done as part of the overall release and deployment planning. However, at this stage you need to add more detail.

Deployment may include deployment, retirement or transfer; the term refers to performing the appropriate action on the assets. It may be the deployment of the components that make up the release into the live environment. In some cases, the project may be to retire or replace a service, therefore the relevant assets such as hardware and software will be removed from the live environment and records updated. Transfer refers to the case where the ownership of the assets is being changed. Perhaps you are outsourcing a service that you used to provide yourself, and ownership of some hardware, software or even people is to be transferred to a different organisation.

The deployment activity includes not only the deployment of the new or changed service but can involve many other tasks, some financial and commercial, and some administrative such as purchasing software licences and transferring intellectual property.

Early life support

Early life support is the set of activities that ensure that the new or changed service is not just 'thrown over the wall' into service operation. You need to ensure that the staff involved in service transition liaise with service operation staff to ensure that everything appropriate that was learned during the build, test and deployment is handed over to the staff responsible for looking after the service when it's live.

Early life support should only be withdrawn when certain criteria have been met. These may include the following:

- ✔ Users can use the service as intended.

- ✔ SLAs are finalised and signed off. (More on SLAs in Chapter 5.)

- ✔ Service targets are achieved consistently for an agreed period.

- ✔ Unexpected variations in performance are reported and managed.

- ✔ Service releases are signed off by the business.

Review and close

I suspect that most of your deployments or service transitions are carried out as projects, therefore when it comes to closing down the deployment or service transition, many of the tasks are those that you perform at the end of any project. There will, of course, be some that are specific to the service or the release.

For closing each deployment:

- ✔ Capture feedback from users and IT staff.
- ✔ Review open changes, problems and known errors.

✔ Review performance targets and achievements.

✔ Document lessons learned.

For closing the service transition:

✔ Carry out a formal review.

✔ Check that all activities are complete and records updated.

✔ Evaluate the service.

Making Better Decisions: Knowledge Management

Knowledge management, of course, concerns the management of knowledge – but what knowledge? In short, the knowledge required to manage your IT services throughout the service lifecycle. Do you know where all the data, information and knowledge is stored in your organisation? Is it written down, in a database or in someone's head? When you do find it, do you know that it's accurate, up to date and not duplicated elsewhere? Data, information and knowledge include such things as service measurement data and targets, SLAs, operational level agreements and contracts, technical manuals, documents of past experiences, project documentation and references to Internet resources. The list is endless.

The purpose of the knowledge management process is to:

✔ Share perspectives, ideas, experience and information, and ensure that these are available in the right place at the right time to enable informed decisions

✔ Improve efficiency by reducing the need to rediscover knowledge

So, what informed decisions do you make? Here are some possibilities:

✔ Should we invest in this service?

✔ Should we retire or replace this service?

✔ What are the risks to delivering the service in accordance with the service level requirements?

✔ What are the common problems with the service?

> ✔ Who has the skills to resolve certain types of problem?
>
> ✔ Who are the customers and users of this service?
>
> ✔ What resources do we have available?
>
> ✔ Are our SLA targets being met?

Defining some knowledge management terms

Here's an explanation of some key terminology:

✔ **Data:** A set of discrete facts.

✔ **Information:** Comes from providing context to data.

✔ **Knowledge:** Composed of the tacit experiences, ideas, insights, values and judgement of individuals.

✔ **Wisdom:** Makes use of knowledge to create value through correct and well-informed decisions. Wisdom involves having the application and contextual awareness to provide a strong common-sense judgement.

Figure 7-4 illustrates the relationship between data, information, knowledge and wisdom (this is the DIKW model).

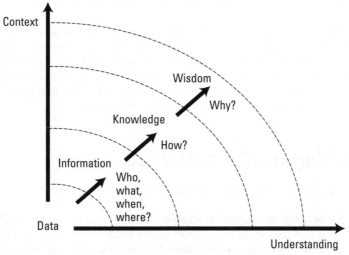

Figure 7-4:
The flow of data to wisdom.

© Crown copyright 2011. Reproduced under licence from the Cabinet Office.

Example of data to wisdom

If I told you that my service desk had logged 1,000 calls on Monday, what would you think? Are you impressed? Well you shouldn't be. All I have given you is a single piece of data. Without more data you have no idea whether this is good or bad.

Suppose I now told you that in addition to the 1,000 calls on Monday, we received 2,000 calls on Tuesday. Are we any further forward? Well in its most simplest form, you now have a piece of information. You know that we logged twice as many calls on Tuesday as we did on Monday. Admittedly, this is not very exciting.

Next, I'll spill the beans. Actually, we logged 3,000 calls on Wednesday, 4,000 on Thursday and 5,000 on Friday. Further, I have been measuring this for three months and I can tell you that this is a trend and is repeated every week. What's more, I have been using these trends to manage the shift rota for my service desk. Hopefully, you will now conclude that I have knowledge with which I have been making decisions – perhaps wise decisions.

✔ **Service knowledge management system (SKMS):** ITIL defines this as 'a set of tools and databases used to manage knowledge, information and data. The SKMS includes the CMS as well as other databases and information systems. The SKMS includes tools for collecting, storing, managing, updating, analysing and presenting all the knowledge, information and data that an IT service provider needs to manage the full lifecycle of IT services'.

The SKMS contains the CMS, and the CMS contains one or many CMDBs.

The DIKW model and the SKMS are related. First you must decide what decisions you want to make and which services you want to make them about. Then you can start to describe the knowledge that will be stored in your SKMS. But where does the knowledge come from? It comes from the way you combine and organise the information. Finally, you have to decide what data you need in order to create the information.

Looking at the activities

The activities of knowledge management are:

✔ **Knowledge management strategy:** The decisions that are made regarding your services are only as good as the data, information and knowledge provided to the decision maker. So before you design and set up an SKMS, you must decide on a strategy. As with all service management processes, the required strategy must start from an understanding the needs of stakeholders. So you identify who'll use the knowledge and what sort of decisions they want to make about the IT services. From this you can define a strategy and policy for knowledge management.

✔ **Knowledge transfer:** How knowledge is transferred to, or shared with, the appropriate people in the organisation. Knowledge can be transferred in many ways. It's important to vary the method of transfer and, in particular, to take audience into account. Examples of knowledge transfer methods include training, hands-on experience, attendance at seminars and webinars, and distributing journals and newsletters.

✔ **Managing data, information and knowledge:** I'm sure you've heard the expression 'garbage in, garbage out'. The knowledge provided by the SKMS is only as good as the data and information that is collected and stored. So now you've decided what knowledge is required to make decisions, you identify the information and data that is required to provide it. The amount of data concerned is potentially huge, thus careful consideration must be given to the collection, maintenance and manipulation of the data and information that is stored in the SKMS.

✔ **Using the SKMS:** It's important to ensure that, once established, the SKMS is used by the appropriate people and that the goal of improving the quality of decision-making is achieved. Consider:

- Controlling access to the SKMS

- Providing knowledge materials in the appropriate format, for example as reports, manuals or websites

- Monitoring the use, accuracy and usefulness of the SKMS

Transition Planning and Support

Do you have a programme or project office in your organisation? If you do, you may be familiar with its role in the high-level planning and coordination of projects. Transition planning and support performs similar activities for your transition projects. Service transition activities are often carried out as projects, or are part of other projects. When you consider all the processes of service transition, there are potentially a large number of activities that need coordination.

'The purpose of the *transition planning and support process* is to provide overall planning for service transitions and to coordinate the resources they require'.

The input to the service transition phase is the SDP (see the earlier section 'Understanding the Purpose of the Service Transition Lifecycle Phase'). This should contain all the information required to plan and manage a transition project, including high-level plans and resource estimates. Many of the activities of the transition planning and support process take information from the SDP and use it to create detailed plans.

Here's a brief look at the activities of transition planning and support:

- ✔ **Transition strategy:** You outline the overall approach to service transition and maintain a set of service transition policies.

- ✔ **Prepare for service transition:** You take the SDP and perform some of the following:

    - • Review the SDP and the service acceptance criteria.

    - • Identify, raise and schedule RFCs.

    - • Check or establish baselines.

- ✔ **Planning and coordinating service transition:** You do the following:

    - • Create the detailed plans and timescales.

    - • Allocate resources.

    - • Manage issues and risks logs.

    - • Coordinate the project.

- ✔ **Provide transition process support:** Throughout the transition project, you carry out activities including the following:

    - • Offer advice and guidance.

    - • Provide administration support.

    - • Monitor and report on progress.

Identifying Service Transition Roles

Each service management process should have a process owner and a process manager. I explain these two roles in Chapter 2. For the service transition processes, the relevant process manager roles are:

- ✔ Change management process manager

- ✔ Service asset and configuration management process manager

- ✔ Release and deployment management process manager

- ✔ Knowledge management process manager

Each role is responsible for the activities described in the appropriate section of this chapter.

Using technology for service transition

Here are some tools you can use in the service transition stage to support the service transition processes:

✔ The CMS for storing information about configuration items and associated records

✔ The SKMS

✔ Discovery tools that automatically identify components attached to a network

✔ Software distribution tools for automatically distributing software releases

✔ Testing tools that automate test practices

Chapter 8

Making Services Work Every Day: Service Operation

In This Chapter

▶ Managing events

▶ Dealing with things that go wrong

▶ Helping the user

▶ Handling access to services

▶ Solving problems

*W*hat do you think happens in the *service operation* stage of the service lifecycle? Hurrah! Yes – you operate the IT services. This is where your IT services are live. Terms like *live environment, production environment* or *operational environment* all mean the same thing: the services are live and in use by your customers. So, guess what? – the services have to work as expected; they have to provide value.

When you buy a new mobile phone, what do you expect? I'm sure you expect it to work. You expect the provider to help you get connected to the phone network. You also expect it to provide help and support as and when you need it. What do you suppose the phone network provider is doing behind the scenes to ensure that you and all its other customers are getting the service they've paid for? I sometimes think of service operation as the beautiful swan gliding majestically across a pond. If you look under the surface of the pond, you find the swan paddling like mad. Do you think your service operations are like this? Beautiful IT service, but a madhouse of an IT organisation trying to keep it going? I'd like to think you're a little more organised than that.

The service operation stage is the only point where the customer can see and measure the value that is obtained from the service. It's in this stage that you put your money where your mouth is. If your plans are accurate and your deployment went without a hitch, you should be delivering a service that meets the agreed requirements of your customer.

This chapter provides a description of the service operation stage and the processes associated with it. The service operation stage includes all the activities necessary to keep the service going on a day-to-day basis and provide support when required. I introduce five processes: event management, incident management, request fulfilment, access management and problem management.

If your services aren't available and working as expected on a day-to-day basis, your customers complain, or worse, they go elsewhere for their IT services. Can you be sure that you and your colleagues are doing the right things at the right time to ensure that this doesn't happen?

Understanding the Purpose of the Service Operation Lifecycle Stage

Service operation is sometimes described as the *realisation of your strategic objectives*. Basically, you realise the strategy you laid down at the start of the service lifecycle. (I explain the lifecycle in Chapter 3, and strategy in Chapter 4.)

ITIL says that the purpose of service operation is to coordinate and carry out the activities and processes required to deliver services to business users and customers and manage the services at agreed levels. Service operation is also responsible for the ongoing management of the technology that is used to deliver and support services.

So, all you do is make sure the services are working in the way you have agreed with your customers. Sounds very easy, but perhaps not so easy in practice.

The service operation stage is where you deliver and support your IT services. I think of the *deliver* bit of this as ensuring that the service is 'turned on' and ready for use as agreed with the customer. It's a bit like a shop. A staff member arrives early and makes sure the lights are on, the tills are working and the doors are open by the time the customers arrive. In IT terms, this means that the technology must be working properly before the users log on in the morning – and continues to work throughout the day. The *support* bit refers to when things go wrong – like the customer service desk in the shop. Of course, in IT terms I'm referring to the service desk and other support staff.

The ITIL definition of service operation also mentions 'the ongoing management of the technology that is used to deliver and support services'. Much of the activity of service operation is concerned with understanding and managing the technological components such as the servers, mainframes, networks, communications, databases, storage systems, desktop systems and software applications. This involves monitoring and control of the components to check that all is working as intended and to get early warning when things go wrong. To do this, you need to coordinate both processes and functions. I describe the service operation functions in Chapter 3; in this chapter I focus on the processes.

One really important thing about service operation is to encourage your service operation staff to realise that they themselves are part of the service. It's very easy to get to the point where you can't see the wood for the trees. The service operation stage is obviously technical, but the focus should be on everybody working together to provide the IT services that have been agreed with the customer. The opposite of this is staff who concentrate on their own technical areas without an appreciation of the broader IT and business view. This broader view is really just a state of mind, but one that good management can build.

Understanding Some Basic Principles

The service operation stage involves you understanding a couple of basic principles.

Getting the balance right

Delivering and supporting the IT services in the service operation stage isn't easy. A fundamental conflict exists between maintaining a stable infrastructure and adapting to the needs of the business. In order to provide the services, you need a solid, stable live infrastructure and suitably technically focused staff to maintain it. On the other hand, you must focus on the needs of the business; typically these don't remain stable, but your service must be able to change without undue disruption. A real balancing act. In order to address this issue you can break things down into four balances:

- **Internal IT view versus external business view:** Ensuring you have the appropriate balance between a technology focus and understanding that you're part of a service that supports the business activities.

- **Stability versus responsiveness:** Maintaining a suitable balance between keeping a stable infrastructure but at the same time being able to respond to changing business needs.

- **Quality of service versus cost of service:** Establishing where the balance is in your organisation. Are decisions made mainly based on cost or quality? The best answer is, 'it depends': the decision is made on a case-by-case basis.

✔ **Reactive versus proactive:** Getting ahead of the game. 'We never get time to be proactive; we're too busy being reactive!' I hear this a lot. Do you spend more time reacting to stuff and fixing things than you do on planned work that is intended to improve your IT services? You have to try to get a balance. Break the vicious circle – make time to make time.

Communicating well

One of the keys to providing a good service on a day-to-day basis is communication. Communication is highlighted here in service operation but it is, of course, vital to all stages of the lifecycle. A lot of your staff get involved with delivering and supporting the services, and in many cases service operation involves staff working in shifts or staff working in multiple locations. So this brings the need for rapid and accurate communication with support teams and suppliers. You must ensure that all communication has an intended purpose or resultant action.

Here are some examples of the sort of communications that are needed in service operation:

✔ Routine operational communication

✔ Communication between shifts

✔ Performance reporting

✔ Communication in projects

✔ Changes, exceptions and emergencies

Listening to the Technology: Event Management

Many of your bits of technical equipment attempt to talk to you: they send you little electronic messages, sometimes just to let you know they're there and still working, and on other occasions to let you know that something's wrong. Servers, workstations, network equipment, software applications can all log messages about what's happening to them, or can be configured to do so. The technology is talking to you, and the clever bit for you is to decide what to listen to.

It's critical to the smooth day-to-day running of your services to detect anything unusual and do something about it before it leads to an outage that affects your users. Your infrastructure may be creating thousands, if not millions, of messages or notifications every day. You need to decide what to listen to, what to record and how to respond.

The purpose of the *event management* process is to manage events throughout their lifecycle. This lifecycle includes the activities that detect events, make sense of them and determine the appropriate control action.

I really like the part of this definition that says *make sense of them;* this speaks volumes to me. When you consider the events that you can detect, you start to ask questions like: 'Do I want to know about this?' 'Why should I care?' 'What should I do about it when it happens?' I'm sure you can add many more questions.

So, *making sense of events* involves deciding what to do about them. Some of the options include to log and ignore, alert someone, or raise an incident, problem or change. Your event management process should be designed so that the appropriate response is taken.

Some events may result in you logging an incident; however, not all events result in incidents, and not all incidents are the result of events.

The scope of event management extends beyond checking whether components are working correctly. It can also be used to monitor and control software licence usage to ensure that utilisation doesn't exceed agreed limits. It can also help support your security controls by logging possible intrusion or other security-related events.

Defining some event management terminology

Here are some key terms you need to understand:

- **Event:** ITIL defines this as 'a change of state which has significance for the management of an IT service or other configuration item'. Basically, an *event* is a significant thing that happens in your IT infrastructure. The tricky thing here is knowing whether the thing *has significance* for you or not. You can only start from the assumption that it is significant until you know better.

  Generally speaking, there are three types of events:

  - **Informational:** An event that signifies something expected and normal has happened, and which does not require any action. For example, a scheduled backup has completed normally or a user has logged on to a system. You have to develop a policy for how long you keep records of these. At the time they occur, you don't always know how useful they will be. It may be months later when you realise you need to analyse the trends of certain activity over that period.

- **Warning:** A notification that a pre-defined threshold has been reached. Action may or may not be required. The notification of such an event allows checks to be made that may prevent a potential failure; for example, the notification may be that the used volume of a disc is within 5 per cent of its allowable maximum capacity.

- **Exception:** A notification that a service or component is operating abnormally. Action is usually required. Examples are a router failing or the number of concurrent users on a system exceeding the maximum.

✔ **Alert:** ITIL calls this 'a notification that a threshold has been reached, something has changed, or a failure has occurred'. An alert is a means of acquiring human intervention – when you want a technical engineer to get involved and investigate the event. Usually this involves sending a message to the engineer's screen, phone or pager.

✔ **Tools:** Bits of IT equipment (hardware and software) that help you do a job, like monitoring tools, network management tools and event management tools. Tools are essential for effective event management. Some pieces of IT equipment arrive out of the box ready to send you notifications. Others require specialised software agents to be installed to allow them to communicate. Network management tools can communicate with a large number of components scattered across your IT environment. These tools must be carefully configured to automatically respond to events in the appropriate way. This can sometimes take a lot of time and effort – and trial and error!

Looking at the activities of event management

The following sections consider each of the activities of the event management process in turn. In many cases, the decision about how these activities are performed for specific IT services is made in the service design stage of the service lifecycle, which I explore in Chapters 5 and 6.

Event notification; event detection; event logging

Events occur all the time: your infrastructure components create messages. Many of them go unnoticed or are ignored. You must decide which notifications you want to know about. Some components generate events; others have to be interrogated by monitoring or management tools. Some of these tools are proprietary and are designed to be compatible only with a given manufacturer's equipment.

Here's a brief description of these activities:

- ✔ **Event notification:** Deciding what messages you want your components to generate and what information the message will contain.

- ✔ **Event detection:** Deciding which notifications will be detected and identifying the tools that will do the detecting. In addition, you must decide whether, or how, the event will be logged.

- ✔ **Event logging:** Recording the data in the tools that detected the event, or creating an event record in your own event-logging tool.

Event filtered; event correlation

Filtering allows you to decide whether you want to progress the event further or simply log it and ignore it. In some cases, it isn't possible to turn off the generation of events, so filtering is necessary to separate unwanted events from the rest of the process. In this activity you also start to decide whether the event is informational, a warning or an exception.

Simply put, event *correlation* relates similar events together so that you can understand their combined impact. For example, one warning event in a day informing you that your network bandwidth has reached its threshold may not be important; however, if you receive and relate together a hundred events in a day informing you that your network bandwidth has reached its threshold then you may want to take action. The result of correlating similar events together is likely to be the creation of an exception event or the creation of an alert.

Response selection

Where possible, it would be great to automate as much of the event management process as possible. With this is mind, you might be able to predict how you will respond to specific types of event. The following is a brief outline of some of the possibilities:

- ✔ **Auto response:** In some cases, you can automatically request that a device – a server for example – restarts itself or one of its functions.

- ✔ **Alert:** The response is to raise an alert to attract the attention of a person.

- ✔ **Incident, problem, change:** Event management systems can be configured to automatically raise one of these three record types. In each case, the record alerts the appropriate process to the existence of an issue; it does not necessarily mean that, for instance, the change will be approved. It's important to define the criteria for the creation of each record type.

Review actions; close event

Reviews of events should be carried out to ensure that the correct action has been taken and that it was effective. Given the number of events generated every day, you can't review every event. So you carry out spot checks, especially for significant events, to provide confidence that the process is working in the required way. This review may also allow you to identify trends.

Once actions are complete, events should be closed. Many events are closed automatically, such as informational events that are simply logged then closed. Where events have initiated other events or other records such as incidents or problems, the original event should be closed and the event record updated with the appropriate references.

Stuff Happens: Incident Management

What do your users find the most annoying thing about your IT services? When the service fails or they can't use the service for some reason. Don't forget that you provide the services that enable the business to do its job. Remember, a *service* is a means of providing value to the customer to help the customer achieve its business outcomes. So, when the service fails or is unusable, you must do your best to restore it in the way you have agreed. Stuff happens and you must be ready to deal with it.

The purpose of the *incident management* process is to restore normal service operation as quickly as possible and minimise the adverse impact on business operations, thus ensuring that agreed levels of service quality are maintained.

Balancing incident management and problem management

The important part of incident management is to restore normal service operation as quickly as possible. Concentrate on getting users up and running so they can continue their business. In fact, I often repeat this definition and whisper an extra bit on the end: restore normal service operation as quickly as possible *without necessarily understanding what went wrong*. The incident management process concentrates on dealing with the *symptoms* of an outage or issue and not the *cause*. It's the responsibility of the problem management process to identify and deal with the cause of the incident, as I explain later in the section 'Getting to the Bottom of an Issue: Problem Management'.

Imagine an incident in your own home. Suppose a pipe bursts and floods your house. What do you do first? Do you investigate the pipe to identify the cause of the burst while the pipe is still leaking? No, you turn the water supply off to prevent further damage. You deal with the symptom first.

Some IT organisations don't distinguish between incidents and problems. One of the effects of this is to have users who can't work because of an IT outage doing nothing while a conscientious IT support engineer tries to identify the cause of the failure. In fact, some technical staff consider it their devout duty to identify the cause of anything they come into contact with without first considering whether users can continue to work!

The opposite result of not distinguishing between incidents and problems is to treat everything as an incident and deal only with the symptoms and not investigate the underlying cause. You may have heard technical staff tell you they don't have time to investigate the cause because they're too busy fixing incidents. In this case, the cause is never identified and fixed, and so the users are inconvenienced every time the incident recurs.

What you need is a balanced approach. The incident management and problem management processes help you organise your resources to meet the needs of the business and prevent incidents recurring in the future.

Defining some incident management terms

Before you dive into incident management activities, you need a good grounding in some terms:

- ✔ **Incident:** According to ITIL, an incident can be:
    - 'An unplanned interruption to an IT service'
    - 'A reduction in the quality of an IT service; for example an Internet page is slow to refresh, or an email message is taking longer than usual to reach its destination'
    - 'Failure of a component that has not yet had an impact on service: issues that IT staff spot'

Your *service level agreement* (SLA), which I explain in Chapter 5, defines normal service operation. So if you stated that your finance management IT service is available from 8 o'clock in the morning until 6 o'clock in the evening, and a user cannot access it for some reason between these times, then this is an incident.

✔ **Major incident:** ITIL calls this 'the highest category of impact for an incident. A major incident results in significant disruption to the business'. You have to generate the exact definition of a major incident for your organisation, but it's definitely one that has a severe impact on your users or the business as a whole, for example a total network failure affecting 5,000 users. Having created your definition of a major incident then you create a special procedure for how you deal with major incidents. The procedure defines the timescales and staff involved in dealing with incidents.

✔ **Incident model:** A pre-agreed outline procedure for dealing with a particular type of incident, maybe one that occurs frequently. For example, you may decide that all printer issues are dealt with by Brian from the technical team. You can create a procedure that documents the preferred category for printer incidents, provides advice to help the selection of the priority, and states that the incident should be escalated to Brian.

Incident models are great when you want to automate a procedure. You may be able to configure your service desk software application to automatically populate the incident record when the incident model is selected. The tool may also be able to automatically assign the incident to Brian.

✔ **Service desk:** A function (that is as an organisational unit – a team or group of people) whose role includes performing many of the activities of the incident management process. It receives, logs, categorises, prioritises and closes incidents. I describe the service desk in more detail in Chapter 3.

Looking at the activities of incident management

Read the following sections to get a picture of the activities of the incident management process.

Incident identification and logging

You identify incidents in many ways. Incidents may be:

✔ Reported by a user to the service desk

✔ Reported via an email

✔ Logged by a user on a web interface

✔ Identified from events detected by the event management process (see the earlier section 'Listening to the Technology: Event Management')

Regardless of how the incident is identified, it must be logged. Many service desks have incident management software applications. These are often part of what are known as *integrated IT service management toolsets.* The incident is logged using an incident record. This record holds the details of the incident and is updated as the incident is investigated, resolved and closed. As part of logging the incident, you record the category and priority of the incident (see the following sections).

Categorising incidents

Categorisation of the incident gets you to describe the incident in a specific way that helps later. Typically, you record the IT service and the component that is affected. You often do this using a hierarchical set of drop-down lists in your incident logging tool. Figure 8-1 provides an example. You create a set of categories that match your needs.

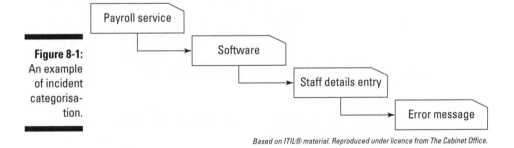

Figure 8-1: An example of incident categorisation.

Based on ITIL® material. Reproduced under licence from The Cabinet Office.

The category of the incident can help many other subsequent activities like:

✔ Deciding who to escalate the incident to for further support

✔ Providing an input to deciding the priority of the incident

✔ Providing an input to trend analysis

Prioritising incidents

Prioritising is a way of identifying the relative importance of an incident. The priority of incidents dictates the order in which they should be dealt with. Priority is based on:

✔ **Impact:** You can judge impact in many ways – maybe the potential cost of lost revenue and/or the number of users affected.

✔ **Urgency:** How quickly does the business need a resolution; how long can it wait?

Have a clear set of rules for establishing the impact and urgency and hence the priority of an incident. Without such rules, IT could fix incidents in any order without consideration of business needs.

During the prioritisation activity, you allocate a priority code to each incident, usually 1, 2, 3, 4 and so on. Each priority code has a timescale associated with it; for example, a priority 2 incident is resolved within eight hours. Basically, the priority puts all incidents in order, thus telling IT teams which incidents to resolve first. Table 8-1 shows a simple example of some priorities.

Table 8-1	An Example of Incident Priorities	
Priority Code	*Description*	*Target Resolution Time*
1	Critical	1 hour
2	High	8 hours
3	Medium	24 hours
4	Low	48 hours
5	Planning	Planned

© Crown copyright 2011. Reproduced under licence from the Cabinet Office.

The definitions and timescales must be agreed with the business and documented in an SLA (see Chapter 5).

A user contacts the service desk to inform it that the benefit claims IT service isn't working. When the service desk agent selects the category using the service desk logging software, the priority is automatically set to priority 3. (When the SLA was agreed, the business decided that the starting priority for all incidents relating to the benefit claims IT service was priority 3.) As the service desk agent discusses the incident with the user, it becomes apparent that 30 users are affected and can't use the IT service, thus increasing the business impact. When the agent enters this into the service desk logging software, it triggers another pre-agreed setting and the priority is automatically raised to priority 2. Finally, through further discussion, it turns out that the team of users must achieve a business deadline which lapses in three hours. The agent accepts this as a justified level of urgency and raises the priority to priority 1, meaning that the incident will now be resolved within 1 hour as agreed in the SLA.

Initial diagnosis

In the *initial diagnosis,* the service desk agent attempts to resolve the incident without escalation to a technical team. The agent gathers information from the user, including a full description of the activities leading up to the incident and all the symptoms. The agent then seeks a resolution. To achieve this, the agent must have access to good information. This is usually access to the *known error database (KEDB),* which I explain in the later section 'Defining some problem management terms'.

Investigation and diagnosis; resolution and recovery

If the service desk agent either knows or is able to identify a suitable resolution, then she now applies the resolution or workaround (I explain workarounds in the later section 'Defining some problem management terms'). If the agent is unable to identify a resolution, the incident is escalated to a support group. This group is usually another function or team, hence this action is often referred to as a *functional escalation.* The support group seeks a resolution or workaround and applies it. In this activity, *investigation* and *diagnosis* refer to identifying what the resolution is; *resolution* and *recovery* refer to applying the resolution.

Although the incident has been escalated to a second-line support team, it's not a problem (as defined by ITIL). The aim is still to restore the service to the user, and the support engineer should be limited to resolving the incident and not encouraged to seek the underlying cause.

Sometimes the service desk or support engineer identifies that the incident cannot be resolved in the target resolution time for the allocated priority, or some other issue has arisen that is making resolution difficult. In this case someone should be informed. *Hierarchical escalation* means communicating the issue up the management chain to raise awareness of the issue and to try to identify a solution. Hierarchical escalation can also be instigated by the users or customers if they think that further action is justified.

Incident closure

After the incident is resolved, the service desk should confirm with the user that the service is restored and the user is happy with the resolution and will agree to the closure of the incident. The best way to do this is to contact the user by phone.

Service desks often use email to contact users, and ask them to reply if the incident isn't resolved. Be careful to be proactive in gaining the approval of the user. The user may be on holiday and unable to respond to your emails.

Dealing with Those Strange Things the User Asks for: Request Fulfilment

Not every call made to the service desk is a true incident, that is an unplanned interruption or reduction in the quality of the service. Your service desk should be a single point of contact for all things IT. I'm sure your service desk receives calls regarding all manner of things, some of them incidents, but others simply requests for advice or guidance.

Request fulfilment is the process responsible for managing the lifecycle of all service requests.

Many organisations don't use a request fulfilment process; instead they manage all requests using their incident management process (see the earlier section 'Stuff Happens: Incident Management') and software tools. This works if service requests are appropriately categorised and prioritised (I cover these two jobs in previous sections). However, if your organisation receives a large number of service requests, the requests can become confused with incidents or changes, with the result that service levels are not met and customer satisfaction becomes poor. In this case, a separate process of request fulfilment is useful.

Request fulfilment is a process: a coordinated set of activities that achieve an objective. Some people believe that introducing request fulfilment requires setting up another function: employing a bunch of people to sit in a room and deal with service requests. In some cases this may be justified, but not always. Often service desk staff deal with service requests in addition to incidents. The request fulfilment process is simply a different way of handling requests so that they don't get confused with incidents and take precedence over incidents when not justified. Just as an example, take a look at Figure 8-2, which shows one of the ways in which the service desk can handle both incidents and requests. In this way, the service desk performs triage: it reviews each call to the service desk and ensures it's handled in the appropriate way.

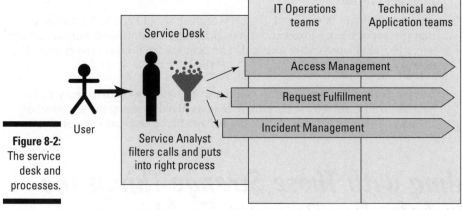

Figure 8-2: The service desk and processes.

Defining some request fulfilment terms

Now I get you up to speed with the lingo of request fulfilment:

- ✔ **Service request:** ITIL defines this as 'a request from a user for information or advice, for a standard change, or for access to an IT service, for example to reset a password or provide standard IT services for a new user'. Service requests are usually handled by a service desk and don't require a *request for change* (RFC) to be submitted. (I cover change management in Chapter 7.) Service requests include:

  - • **Requests for information:** Such as a user wanting to know whether the sales service will be running on Saturday, because she plans to do overtime, or a user wanting to know where to find the 'save as' function on the new version of the word-processing software application.

  - • **Standard changes:** Such as resetting a user's password or installing a copy of a standard software application.

  - • **Compliments or complaints:** Such as a user wanting to inform the service desk supervisor that an incident took longer to resolve that expected.

- ✔ **Request model:** A pre-agreed outline procedure for dealing with a particular type of service request, maybe one that occurs frequently – basically, a template for dealing with certain requests in a consistent manner. For example, all requests to purchase IT consumables will be referred to Eric to raise the purchase order. Eric will check the request and resolve any issues with the requestor before placing the order.

- ✔ **Self-help technology:** Service requests are owned by the service desk, and the service desk is usually responsible for receiving service requests and fulfilling them or referring them to a team that can fulfil them. However, request fulfilment provides an excellent opportunity to use technology to automate the selection and fulfilment of requests by using what is known as *self-help technology*. Self-help technology provides a web-based interface that allows users to select and log their own requests. This often takes the form of a shopping basket experience just like the one provided by your favourite Internet store.

Just because users create their own requests doesn't mean that requests are not logged by IT. The web interface should require users to identify themselves by username and password. The service desk still owns the service request and oversees its fulfilment. The service desk is often required to produce statistics and reports of the use of the self-help system.

Looking at the activities of request fulfilment

The request fulfilment process incorporates these activities:

- **Receive request; request logging and validation:** You must decide how you will receive service requests. You can create special forms for the common types of request such as moving a PC or installing software, or you may be happy to receive some requests via email or formal RFCs. It's important to decide your policy and communicate it clearly. You can use a self-help system (refer to the previous section for details), which allows users to log their own requests. Service requests are usually received by the service desk, and the service desk logs and validates the request. A request record should be created to record the details of the request and its fulfilment.

- **Request categorisation; request prioritisation:** As with incident management, requests can be prioritised using a combination of impact and urgency in order to put them in the appropriate order to be fulfilled. Timescales for the fulfilment of requests should be agreed and documented in SLAs and communicated to service desk staff and users.

- **Request authorisation:** One of the main purposes of the request fulfilment process is to reduce the load on the incident management (see the earlier section 'Stuff Happens: Incident Management') and change management (see Chapter 7) processes. However, this doesn't mean relinquishing control of requests. Some service requests will be fulfilled using standard changes (which I explain in Chapter 7), which means each individual request may have to be authorised by someone before being fulfilled. Many service requests involve spending money. Who authorises this expenditure depends on how budgets are managed in your organisation. The important point is to ensure it's clear who authorises, or signs off, each type of request.

- **Request review; request model execution:** Service desk staff review the request in order to establish the appropriate method of fulfilment. As stated earlier, the service desk will be able to fulfil some requests, for example requests for help on how to use applications and services, for information, and to purchase consumables and standard components. Other requests will be escalated to other teams or groups. Request models should be used to document the fulfilment procedure for common tasks.

> ✔ **Request closure:** The service desk is responsible for ensuring that the completed request has fulfilled the expectations of the user. The warning I give in the 'Stuff Happens: Incident Management' section applies here: if you use email notifications to inform the user that the request has been fulfilled, ensure the user gets the email, and also provide a mechanism for users to respond to the service desk if there are outstanding issues.

Allowing the Right People to Use Your Services: Access Management

Are the right people able to use your IT services, and are the wrong people prevented from using them? Allowing the wrong people to use your systems can lead to accidental or malicious damage. This may be from deliberate hackers or from poorly trained or curious users.

Every organisation should have a policy describing who can use its services and how these people can request access. This policy is agreed in the service design stage of the service cycle and involves the information security management process and the availability management process (see Chapter 6). The access management process implements this policy on a day-to-day basis.

The purpose of the *access management* process is to provide the right for users to be able to use a service or group of services. Access management is therefore the execution of policies and actions defined in information security management.

Put simply, access management is the bunch of activities that provide you with a user profile and password for every application or service that you use – or at least those that are controlled. This is another process centred around the service desk.

Defining some access management terms

Here are some terms you hear and need to understand:

> ✔ **Access request:** The means of requesting access to a service. It can be a service request or an RFC.

✓ **Information security policy:** Provides the rules that the access management process implements. The policy is created and owned by the information security management process (see Chapter 6) and covers many areas of IT security, one of which is access to services. Each time a new service is designed, consideration is given to access controls: who will be allowed access and how this will be administered.

✓ **Access:** The level and extent of a service's functionality, or of data that a user is entitled to use. For a big organisation-wide system, this may mean you can have access to the sales functions but not the financial functions.

✓ **Identity:** The information that tells you the user is who she says she is. It's also used to verify the user's status within an organisation, in other words what she is allowed to access. The identity is unique to a user, and is used to identify who she is when making a request for access to a service.

✓ **Rights or privileges:** The actual settings by which a user is provided with access to a service or to a group of services; for example, can a particular user just read a document or is she able to make changes to it or even delete it?

✓ **Services or service groups:** Similar sets of services required by users performing a similar set of activities. So, if I add a user to the sales department group, she automatically gets access to the customer relationship management system, the sales ordering system and the invoice system.

✓ **Directory services:** A specific type of tool that the service desk or technical team uses to manage access and rights.

Getting the keys: access management

To illustrate some of the terminology of access management, suppose I was to give you the keys to a building. This is a secure building and you can't go everywhere. I'm only going to give you the keys to the rooms you need.

Access – refers to which rooms you're allowed into.

Rights – refers to what you can do once you're in the room. You're not allowed to open the windows!

Groups – because you are allowed access to several rooms, I won't give you each key separately, I'll give you a key ring with the appropriate keys already on it.

Looking at the activities of access management

Here are the activities the IT organisation performs as part of the access management process:

- ✔ **Request access:** Access requests are usually received as a form of service request from the request fulfilment process. In some cases, an RFC (see Chapter 7) may be justified, for example when a new IT service is deployed and access must be provided for all 1,000 users.

- ✔ **Verification:** The access request includes the identity of the user for whom the access is requested. This should be adequate to verify that the user is who she claims she is. Sometimes, verification includes asking the user for information that has also been collected in advance by the human resources department. This is likely to be the usual stuff you're asked when contacting your bank, such as mother's maiden name or the colour of your cat. Verification also includes checking the validity of the request – that the user is allowed access to the requested service as defined in the information security policy.

- ✔ **Providing rights:** Once the user and the request have been validated, the person in the IT department who has the skill and access to your directory service facility provides the rights. This job is sometimes called *system administration* or *network administration*.

- ✔ **Monitoring identity status; removing or restricting rights:** Access management is also responsible for tracking changes to access, so if users leave the organisation, their rights must be removed in a timely fashion. Similarly, if users change their job role, some rights may be restricted and other rights added. There must be a procedure in place to track the status of each user and trigger the appropriate changes to users' rights. This is often done with the help of the human resources department, which notifies the IT department of any new starters or leavers or changes in job role due to promotion or other changes.

- ✔ **Logging and tracking access:** You log and track access to ensure it's not being abused. Most logging and tracking activity is done automatically using monitoring tools. Certain events must be identified, such as unauthorised attempts to access services, or an excessive number of mistakes when entering passwords. Any unusual activity should be logged as an incident and investigated appropriately.

Getting to the Bottom of an Issue: Problem Management

In the 'Stuff Happens: Incident Management' section, earlier in this chapter, I describe how important it is to distinguish between incidents and problems. Incident management deals with the symptoms, and problem management deals with the cause.

Users get frustrated if an incident continues to recur on a regular basis and the IT department appears to be doing nothing. After the service desk has dealt with the symptoms of the incident and restored the service to the user as part of the incident management process, the IT department now has an important decision to make: close the incident record and do nothing until it happens again, or raise a problem record and start to investigate the underlying cause before further incidents create more business impact? This is all part of the domain of the problem management process.

The purpose of the *problem management* process is to manage the lifecycle of all problems from first identification through further investigation, documentation and eventual removal. Problem management seeks to minimise the adverse impact on the business of incidents and problems that are caused by underlying errors within the IT infrastructure, and to proactively prevent recurrence of incidents related to these errors. In order to achieve this, problem management seeks to get to the root cause of incidents, document and communicate known errors, and initiate actions to improve or correct the situation.

Defining some problem management terms

Here are some bits of terminology you need to know:

- **Problem:** ITIL states that this is 'A cause of one or more incidents. The cause is not usually known at the time a problem record is created.'

   When you decide that the cause of an incident requires investigation, you *create a problem:* you raise a problem record to record its details and history. You may create a problem record after only one occurrence of an incident or after it has occurred a number of times. I like to think of a problem record as an intent: when you raise a problem record you *intend* to get to the bottom of it and identify the cause.

   Problems are created in response to one or many incidents. An incident does not *become* a problem. When you raise a problem record, the incident record does not go away but is linked to the problem record such that anyone investigating the problem can trace a path back to the incidents and review the data captured when the incident was logged.

✔ **Known error:** According to ITIL, this is 'a problem that has a documented root cause and a workaround' (see the next bullet but one). After you identify the root cause of the problem you create a known error record to hold details about the symptoms of the related incidents, the underlying cause, workaround and any permanent resolution. Known error records can be created at any point in the problem lifecycle where it's useful to record information that can help the resolution of the problem.

Known errors are not only identified by your engineers responding to incidents and identifying the underlying cause, they may also be identified by your software developers or by third-party suppliers. I'm sure it's the case that whenever your IT department is ready to launch and deploy the new version of a major software application, the development manager willingly provides information about the *undocumented features* or *characteristics* of the new software, or whatever euphemism you use to describe any outstanding bugs! Such information is of great help to the service desk when dealing with the initial wave of queries that are inevitable when you launch new software.

✔ **Known Error Database (KEDB):** A database of all your recorded known errors that is used by the service desk and support staff to identify workarounds when performing incident management.

✔ **Workaround:** According to ITIL this is 'a way of reducing or eliminating the impact of an incident or problem for which a full resolution is not yet available'. Put a little more simply, a workaround is an agreed and documented way of restoring the service to the user or minimising the impact of the incident. Workarounds are sometimes established by staff involved in the resolution of an incident; however they should be verified as soon as possible by problem management staff and documented as part of a known error record.

✔ **Problem models:** A pre-agreed outline procedure for dealing with a particular type of problem. If you recommend that certain problem types are handled in a specific way, for example always routed to the same support team or always referred to a third-part supplier, the problem model documents this.

✔ **Reactive and proactive problem management:** The two types, or aspects, of the problem management process. *Reactive problem management* refers to reacting to incidents as they occur and raising problems as necessary to identify and resolve the underlying cause. *Proactive problem management* is the identification and resolution of problems and their cause *before* any incidents occur. This is achieved through trend analysis, that is by investigating the patterns and frequency of the incidents that have occurred and using the information to provide clues of where undiscovered problems lie.

From incidents to problems to changes

The following figure shows the path from incident to problem to change. Keep this figure in mind as you read an example of this journey.

© Crown copyright 2011. Reproduced under licence from the Cabinet Office.

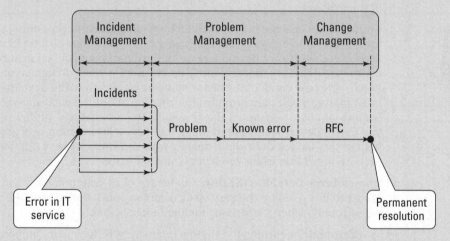

A user is innocently using her desktop system one day, and all of a sudden one of those dialog boxes pops up on the screen informing her she has a message. The message tells her that the spreadsheet software application has encountered error 3479 and can't save the current spreadsheet to the user's home folder on the network. It then gives a choice: 'do you want to click on OK or Cancel?' Now, this user lives in the ideal world of ITIL where everyone does things properly. So, what does the user do when faced with this error? She rings up the service desk of course.

The service desk analyst logs the call as an *incident* and goes through the incident management process. The analyst attempts initial diagnosis by searching the KEDB to look for a resolution, but doesn't find one. Next the analyst escalates the incident to second-line support, not to investigate the problem but to search for a way to restore the service to the user. The incident is allocated to an engineer who manages to replicate the incident and advises the service desk analyst to tell the

user to click cancel and save the file to a local folder instead of the network home folder. The service desk analyst contacts the user and the user saves the file locally. The user and service desk analyst agree that, because the service is now restored, the incident can be closed and no further action is required. The analyst tells the user to ring if it happens again. Are you happy with the story so far? It's only happened once – IT systems are like that!

The next day the same error happens to other users and the service desk logs six incidents and links them together. In each case, the user has stored a file locally and gone away happy. However, would you like the IT department to do something more? It's at this point that a *problem* record should be created. The service desk has the ability to do this, so a problem record is raised. The problem must now be allocated to an engineer or technical team to investigate and find the cause of the incidents. After some time, you hear a shout of 'eureka!' as the engineer identifies the root cause. The engineer creates a known error record documenting the cause and confirming that a suitable workaround is to save files locally. This information is passed to the service desk. This will hopefully make it easier for the service desk to deal with other incidents.

Now there is a decision to be made. The engineer who identified the root cause also identified a permanent solution. In this case, the cause was a *change* that had been made to the configuration of a number of servers to accommodate another system. This has had the effect of denying some users access to this server. The permanent solution is to make another change to the server. A decision must be made as to whether an RFC should be raised to implement the solution. Not all known errors will result in changes being made. Some will be too costly, some will be negated by new version updates. In this case, I'll assume that the RFC is raised. It is now the role of the change management process (see Chapter 7) to manage the change through to conclusion.

When the change is implemented and reviewed, the change manager will close the change record. This will set off a game of *knock down dominoes:* the known error record and problem record will be closed, and if any incident records are open, these will be closed. The problem is resolved and no related incidents will happen again. And they all live happily ever after.

This is just one example, and I'm sure you can think of many more. It's the principle that's important: you must have a balanced approach to the sequence of activities.

Looking at the problem management activities

Here's the low-down on the activities that problem management involves:

Problem detection; problem logging

Problems can be detected from many sources: service desk, event management, incident management, proactive problem management, third-party suppliers.

The tricky issue here is to provide clear guidance on when to raise a problem record. Problems may be raised by service desk staff. When service desk agents close incidents they may be directed to decide whether an investigation into the cause is justified and therefore create a problem record. This may be considered inappropriate in some cases, so often the service desk manager and problem manager review the day's incidents and choose which problems to raise – if any. Some organisations leave it to problem management staff to review incident trends and decide what problems to raise. It's also possible to define a set of rules that can be configured into your service desk software tool that automatically create problem records; for example, if an incident of a given type and priority occurs ten times in one day, this triggers the automatic creation of a problem record.

The ITIL guidance suggests the following ways of detecting problems:

✔ The service desk suspecting a problem or detecting an unknown cause of one or more incidents

✔ Analysis of incidents by technical support groups

✔ Notification from a supplier that a problem exists that has yet to be resolved

✔ As a result of analysis of incidents as part of proactive problem management

Once detected, the problem is logged as a problem record created in your IT service management toolset. This tool may be part of your configuration management system, which I describe in detail in Chapter 7. The problem record links to all relevant incident records and records as much information as possible to aid resolution.

Problem categorisation; problem prioritisation

Problems are categorised in a very similar way to incidents (see the earlier section Stuff Happens: Incident Management). In fact, you can use the same categories for incidents and problems. Problem management staff are often responsible for deriving these categories to ensure they are consistent and conducive to good problem investigation.

Hopefully your incident management process is mature enough to apply workarounds or resolutions to a large number of your incidents, thus when the problem record is created the immediate impact on the business is reduced. That is not to say that the incident won't recur very soon. But it does mean that many of your problems will be prioritised based on the *potential* impact of the incident recurring fairly soon. This may prompt you to take into account the frequency of related incidents as well as their impact on the business.

Problem investigation and diagnosis

This is the point at which the appropriate technical team, individual or third-party supplier investigates and identifies the root cause of the problem (referred to in some organisations as root cause analysis). In some cases, this may involve a coordinated investigation by several people or parties who possess varied skill or experience. These can become little projects, and in such cases must be carefully managed to focus on the problem under investigation and not get diverted to unrelated matters.

Raising a known error record

Theoretically, a known error record is created when the diagnosis is complete, the root cause identified and a workaround found. However, in reality, a known error record can be raised at any point in the process when it's considered advantageous to record workaround or resolution data.

Problem resolution

Once the cause is identified, you can consider the resolution of the problem. If a workaround has been identified, it should be documented in the known error record and the service desk advised. If a suitable permanent solution has been identified that requires a change in functionality then an RFC must be raised and dealt with by the change management process (see Chapter 7).

Not all known errors result in permanent solutions being implemented. In some cases, the solution may not be cost-effective and on balance it will be acceptable to live with the workaround. In some cases, future upgrades or releases negate the need to raise a change.

Problem closure

Once the problem has been resolved, the known error record and problem records will be closed. This means they will be marked with the status of closed; the record will not be deleted and can be used in the future for reference, if necessary. Remember to document a historic record of events.

Major problem reviews

You occasionally have *major* problems, as defined by your organisation. It's important to hold a major problem review in these cases. The review identifies the following:

- ✔ Those things that were done correctly
- ✔ Those things that were done wrongly
- ✔ What can be done better in the future
- ✔ How to prevent recurrence
- ✔ What follow-up actions are needed

Identifying Service Operation Roles

In Chapter 2, I explain ITIL roles. As well as the process owner role, which I outline in Chapter 2, service operation encompasses the following roles.

Service desk roles

The service desk is an important function because it provides a single point of contact for your users. The roles are:

- **Service desk manager:**
  - Manages the service desk staff
  - Takes overall responsibility for dealing with incidents and service requests at the service desk
  - Acts as the escalation point for difficult calls

  A large organisation may add a service desk supervisor role to share some of the duties.

- **Service desk analysts:** Provide first-line support for all incidents and service requests. Service desk analysts are key to providing a good perception of your IT organisation, so their role should be clear, and appropriate training must be provided. Service desk analysts are likely to play a major part in the incident management, request fulfilment and access management processes, so their involvement must be made clear, either by assigning additional roles or combining the roles with the service desk analyst role.

Incident management, request fulfilment and access management roles

I have grouped these processes together because of certain similarities. In each case, the initial activities of the processes are carried out by the service desk. However, many incidents and service requests are escalated to other functional teams as required.

Many of the service operation processes use different levels of support provided by your staff. Common terminology is *first-line, second-line* and *third-line* support. In fact, you can have as many lines of support as you like. 'Line of support' usually refers to your technical teams. First-line is usually the service desk, and then each level of support is more technical, or specialised, than the last.

- **Incident management:** Involves first-line (service desk), second-line and third-line support. These teams may form part of the IT operations management, technical management and applications management functions.

✔ **Request fulfilment:** Once initiated by the service desk, service requests are often referred to other IT operations management teams as required. These teams must be aware of their responsibilities for dealing with service requests. In some cases, service requests are referred to a procurement team or direct to a third-party supplier.

✔ **Access management:** Access requests are a type of service request, so the initial activities are carried out by the service desk. Fulfilment of access requests requires knowledge of directory services tools, a skill that is often found in the IT operations management function.

Problem management roles

Allocate these problem management roles to members of your technical teams:

✔ **Problem manager:** Responsible for the management of problems. When problem records are raised, they must be allocated to the appropriate technical staff or teams for investigation. In addition, the problem manager is responsible for the known error database (see the section 'Defining some problem management terms') and ensures that it becomes a reliable source of information about problems and known errors.

✔ **Problem-solving groups:** The technical staff who investigate problems. These staff are drawn from your service operation functions and must be aware of the problem management process and the timescales involved in problem resolution. Some problem investigations may include third-party suppliers.

Event management roles

Event management is usually focused around your IT operations management function. Some organisations have an operations bridge or network operations centre which monitors and controls the IT infrastructure on a day-to-day basis. Those involved in event management need to be clear of how events of different types will be dealt with and any rules that exist for raising incidents in response to events.

Using technology for service operation

Many service operation activities are repetitive and therefore lend themselves to automation. The activities benefit from an integrated service management toolset. These are sometimes initially perceived as service desk logging tools, but most have a much broader role in supporting many of the ITIL processes. The scope of your tools often depends on the willingness of your organisation to purchase the necessary additional modules to support other processes. What follows is a brief overview of the generic requirements of such a toolset:

✓ **Self-help:** The functionality that allows users to log on to a website and get access to IT information, log service requests, or possibly log incidents.

✓ **Workflow or process engine:** The ability to automate a process by, for example, referring or escalating incidents, service requests and changes to staff members.

✓ **Integrated configuration management system (CMS):** A CMS is a set of tools and databases that contains information about your services and their assets and components. It allows asset information to be linked to incidents, problems, and known error and change records. The CMS is owned by the service asset and configuration management process. You can find more information about the CMS in chapter 7.

✓ **Discovery/deployment/licensing technology:** Discovery tools electronically 'discover' components in your infrastructure and collect information about them. Deployment tools automatically distribute and deploy software to target PCs and workstations. Licensing tools record and keep track of the usage of licensed software.

✓ **Remote control:** The ability to take control of a user's desktop PC or workstation. This is really useful for service desk and support staff.

✓ **Diagnostic tools:** Tools that allow service desk and support staff to diagnose faults. Can also be used to provide guidance to service desk staff to allow them to deal with a greater number of incidents without huge amounts of technical knowledge.

✓ **Reporting and dashboards:** The ability to provide reports and display statistics and measurements about the IT service and service management processes.

Chapter 9

Striving to Do Better: Continual Service Improvement

In This Chapter

▶ Understanding why improvement matters

▶ Justifying improvement

▶ Looking at some approaches to improvement

▶ Measuring improvement

▶ Thinking about governance and risk

Do you have time to improve your IT services or improve the way you manage your IT services? Often the organisation's response to this question is, 'Sorry, we're too busy fixing things to have time to improve.' This organisation needs improving.

People often think of *continual service improvement* (CSI) as a state of mind, a philosophy or a nice-to-have. In fact, the ITIL service lifecycle stage includes an established set of activities and methods for the continual measurement, reporting and improvement of both the IT services and the service management processes. CSI also provides you with the tools necessary to implement the service management processes and lifecycle in your organisation. I outline the service management processes in Chapters 4–8.

This chapter provides a description of the CSI stage of the service lifecycle and the activities and methods associated with it. The preceding chapters describe the other four stages of the service lifecycle; for an overview of the lifecycle, take a look at Chapter 3.

As you read through this chapter, keep in mind that the point of this service lifecycle stage of ITIL is that you and your organisation want to gradually improve the way you do things. Improvement is better all round. You either improve customer satisfaction or reduce your costs; hopefully you do both and much more besides.

Understanding the Purpose of the CSI Lifecycle Stage

Why does any organisation want to improve? How many reasons can you think of? Here are some ideas:

- ✔ To identify and make efficiencies
- ✔ To reduce costs
- ✔ To improve your support of the business
- ✔ To meet service levels
- ✔ To help create competitive advantage

You may have heard the expression 'running to stand still'. Basically, this means if you don't start moving now, everyone else overtakes you. I'm sure you're familiar with many fast-moving commercial organisations. Take the mobile phone industry, for example. Almost weekly, a new phone or a different tariff or incentive is advertised. When one phone organisation launches a new model, it's not long before the competitor companies launch their own versions. No organisation wants to be left behind. These companies must improve so that they remain successful.

You may be thinking that concern for improvement only applies to a commercial organisation (what ITIL calls a *type 3 provider*), one that provides IT services to other companies in exchange for money, but that's wrong. Improvement is equally important for organisations that provide IT services internally to other parts of the same organisation. 'But our users don't have a choice,' I hear you cry. 'Our internal users have to use the services we provide.' But they do have a choice. If you don't do the job, they can find someone else. The most common response in this case is to outsource the IT department. So all organisations, regardless of type or size, should focus effort on improvement.

The purpose of the CSI stage of the service lifecycle is to align IT services with changing business needs by identifying and implementing improvements to IT services that support business processes. These improvement activities support the lifecycle approach through service strategy, service design, service transition and service operation. CSI is always seeking ways to improve service effectiveness, process effectiveness and cost effectiveness.

The purpose of service management is to deliver value to customers in the form of services that enable them to achieve their business goals and outcomes. So CSI has to ensure that the IT services align to the changing business needs and continue to provide value. Value, here, means value as defined by utility and warranty. In Chapter 2, I explain more about value.

You may be impressed by this ITIL stuff and decide to implement a project in your organisation to improve the service management processes. To do this, you engage with customers, identify their needs and set the project in progress. So, you think you've gathered all you need from the business, and you concentrate solely on the project. But what does the business do after your back is turned? The pesky business picks up the goalposts and runs off with them.

Improvement isn't a one-time-only activity, it should be continual. This means continually checking with customers to see what's changed.

Perhaps you're wondering why this stage is called *continual* service improvement and not *continuous* service improvement? Well, *continuous* means unbroken or uninterrupted. So in terms of improvement, this implies one long, unending project. I'm sure you've encountered these sorts of projects from time to time! However, *continual* means frequently recurring, which reflects the ITIL view of improvement. View CSI as a number of initiatives or projects, each aimed at improving an aspect of IT services.

So, the activities of CSI are primarily:

- ✔ Identify or help others identify opportunities for improvement.
- ✔ Prioritise improvement activities.
- ✔ Set up and run (or help others set up and run) improvement projects.

Understanding Some Basic Principles

What is it that you're seeking to improve? The answer to this question is the IT services *and* the service management processes: the service *and* the way you manage the service. These can, of course, be separate initiatives. For example, you may set up one improvement project to increase the availability of the organisation's financial management system because of complaints regarding a number of inconvenient outages, and thus improve the service. You may set up a second project, this time to improve your release and deployment process in order to provide better support to users during new software deployments. This will be a process improvement.

The following sections help you get to grips with a few basics.

Looking at the activities

The main activities of CSI are those associated with fulfilling the following objectives:

✔ **Review, analyse and make recommendations on improvement opportunities in each lifecycle stage: service strategy (see Chapter 4), service design (see Chapters 5 and 6), service transition (see Chapter 7) and service operation (see Chapter 8).** CSI seeks improvements in all stages of the lifecycle (including seeking to improve how you perform CSI). Figure 9-1 illustrates the relationships between the CSI stage of the lifecycle and the other stages.

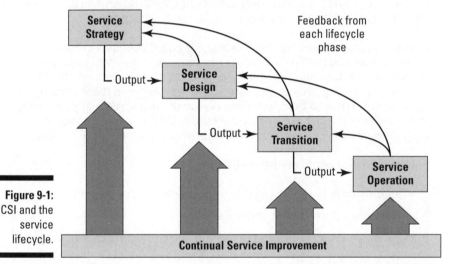

Figure 9-1: CSI and the service lifecycle.

© Crown copyright 2011. Reproduced under licence from the Cabinet Office.

As part of improvement, all stages communicate and provide feedback to one another. You can see the main relationships in the diagram; for example, service operation staff feed back to service transition staff the success and failures of any recent deployments, so that this can be improved next time. Similarly, service transition may provide feedback to service design staff on the quality of the designs and design documentation.

✔ **Review and analyse service level achievement results.** A very strong link exists between CSI and *service level management* (SLM), which I look at in Chapter 5. SLM is often the starting point for improvements. One of the responsibilities of the SLM process is to maintain a good relationship with the customer regarding the services you provide. Regular service reviews with the customer are an excellent opportunity to identify possible areas for improvement. During such reviews, both parties can review the reports of recent service achievements and compare them with service level targets. The customer may point out where there have been breaches, or near breaches, of service levels and suggest to the service level manager that further investigation is a good idea. The service level manager can then agree to set up a *service improvement plan* (SIP) to investigate the issues, with the aim of identifying the causes and making improvements. The service level manager sets up this SIP with the help of CSI staff.

✔ **Identify and implement individual activities to improve service quality and improve the efficiency and effectiveness of the enabling service management processes.** Through measurement, reporting, review and communication, CSI helps you identify many opportunities for improving your IT services or your service management processes. As part of CSI you review all opportunities, record them in the CSI register (coming up later in this chapter) and create a business case for each one that you want to take further. CSI helps you prioritise and recommend which ones to initiate.

✔ **Improve the cost-effectiveness of delivering IT services, without sacrificing customer satisfaction.** After IT services have been running in the live environment for some time, you can review them and often optimise the resources needed to deliver and support the services.

Be warned. You mustn't streamline or cut back too much at one time. You must have a clear understanding of how the customer derives value from the service (flick to Chapter 2 for details of value) and ensure that you don't sacrifice customer service in exchange for saving a bit of money.

✔ **Ensure applicable quality management methods are used to support continual improvement activities.** Don't reinvent the wheel. Organisations have used many quality management approaches and techniques over the years. The main relevant method is the Deming plan–do–check–act cycle that I describe later in this chapter, in the section 'The Deming Cycle'.

Creating a business case for improvement

CSI is, of course, all about improvements, but how do you justify the effort and expense that goes into an improvement initiative or improvement project? Justifying the cost of an improvement project is often difficult. Some managers simply say, 'Things are okay as they are; we don't need to spend money on improvement.' Is it enough to state what the improvement is? For example, if I say I want a better car, you'll ask me why and expect me to justify it, maybe in terms of the benefits it will bring me. I'm sure you will also ask me what the better car would cost. You must take into account four factors:

✔ **Improvement:** The measurable improvement you want to achieve; for example, a 1 per cent improvement in availability.

✔ **Benefit:** The financial benefit you hope to gain from the improvement; for example, £10,000 per year cost saving from reducing the number of IT changes that fail and get reworked.

✔ **Return on investment (ROI):** Takes into account what it costs to gain the improvement, and compares it with the financial benefit. ROI is similar to the interest you gain when investing money in a bank. For example, by spending £8,000 on a new service desk logging tool you generate £10,000 of cost savings in a year – an ROI of 25 per cent over one year.

✔ **Value of investment (VOI):** The more-intangible, non-financial benefits you receive from the improvement, for example improved customer satisfaction.

Suppose I run a project that successfully increases the first-time-fix rate at my service desk by 10 per cent. That is, I increase the number of incidents that the service desk staff resolves without escalation to an engineer. If I go to my boss and tell him I achieved the improvement, is he impressed and does he immediately award me a bonus? I hope not! A good boss wants to know more. Hopefully, he wants to know the benefit gained from the 10 per cent increase in first-time-fix rate. In response to this, I can tell him that the benefit to the organisation is £30,000, made up of cost savings from better-utilised IT staff and increased revenue from more productive business staff. Do you think my boss is any more impressed? Well, he's that sort of boss, so he now asks another question: what did it cost and what's the return on my investment? So I tell him I invested £20,000 on a new staff member and some new service desk software. I then calculate that the ROI is 50 per cent. I hear you ask, 'Surely now your boss is impressed and gives you that bonus?' Well, nearly. He asks one final question: what is the value of the investment? By this he means what additional, non-financial benefit did we gain? I tell him that staff morale in the service desk has improved and so has my customer's satisfaction with the service desk. Now my bonus looks promising.

Identifying baselines

A *baseline* is a benchmark (a measurement taken at a point in time) that you use as a reference point. How do you know you've improved? By measuring your start and finish points. The starting point is often called the baseline. A baseline is essential for measuring the incremental improvement that you've made. Without a baseline, you have no evidence that you've improved your service or process.

Suppose your project is to improve the effectiveness of your change management processes (head over to Chapter 7 for details of change management). A suitable baseline is the number or percentage of your changes that fail when implemented. On the other hand, your project may be to improve the availability of your sales office IT service. In this case, you take a baseline of the number of outages to the service last month. After you implement your improvement, you can use the baselines for comparison and measure the success of your improvement.

Keeping a register of improvements

A *CSI register* is a log of all your improvement opportunities. Often you end up with a long list of improvement suggestions, some more viable than others. Therefore it's important that you record them, assess their priority and track them through their lifecycle. For each opportunity, you should record: the description, priority, predicted benefits and justification. You should also categorise the initiatives in terms of the size of the undertaking (perhaps small, medium or large) and the timescale needed to achieve the benefit (maybe short-term or long-term).

Knowing Where to Start

Most improvement initiatives are run as projects, but you can't just set off on the project without careful planning. To be successful, you must carefully plan an improvement initiative. In the following sections, I describe two complementary ideas.

The Deming Cycle

One of the objectives of CSI is to ensure applicable quality management methods are used to support continual improvement activities. *The Deming Cycle* is a well-known quality management approach to improvement. It provides an outline structure for your improvement project or initiative. The cycle consists of four phases:

✔ **Plan:** Identify what the improvement is and how you hope to achieve it.

✔ **Do:** Assign the resources and carry out the project.

✔ **Check:** Use measurements to identify whether you've achieved the objective of the project.

✔ **Act:** Review what you've done and identify where further improvement can be made. The output of this step provides the input to the next improvement initiative and hence the next revolution of the plan–do–check–act cycle.

If you follow this simple approach to any improvement, you can hope to improve the maturity of your operations over time and improve the alignment of IT with the business.

Figure 9-2 illustrates the Deming Cycle by showing the circle rolling up a hill, which reminds you that to improve you should do many small improvements rather than one big one. To move up the slope, you do several small rotations of the plan–do–check–act cycle and consolidate each one before aiming for the next objective.

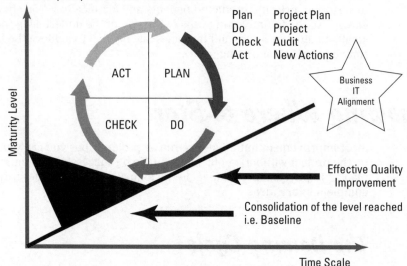

Figure 9-2:
The Deming
Cycle.

The CSI approach

The CSI approach provides a more detailed model for planning and carrying out an improvement project. It has six steps, as you can see in Figure 9-3.

1. **What's the vision?** No project is successful if you don't understand its context. You need to know why you want to do something and how it fits in with the goals of the business or the IT department. Decide which goals you want to achieve first.

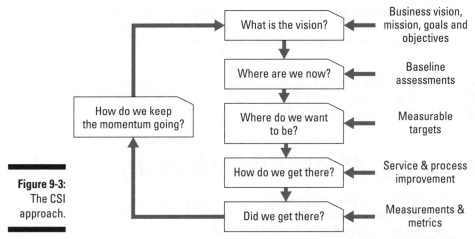

Figure 9-3:
The CSI
approach.

2. **Where are we now?** This is where you take an assessment of the current situation and create a baseline. If the project is to improve the service then you can use service achievement data supplied by the service level management process (see Chapter 5) to provide the baseline.

   Ensure that the measurement is representative. For example, if you are taking a baseline of the number of calls received by the service desk, don't take the measurement during the holiday period when a large number of users aren't at work.

3. **Where do we want to be?** This step sets the targets for what you want your project to achieve. The difference between 'Where are we now?' and 'Where do we want to be?' is often referred to as a *gap*. The study of this gap is often referred to as *gap analysis*. It is this gap that you bridge by carrying out the improvement initiative or project. Make sure the targets are measurable so that you know when you've hit them.

4. **How do we get there?** This step refers to the action the project will take to bridge the gap between 'Where are we now?' and 'Where do we want to be?' This is the actual doing bit of the project – the service improvement or the process improvement.

5. **Did we get there?** This is where you measure the improvements to see whether you've hit the targets. You must decide how to measure the improvement that you want. If you're improving the service desk, you can measure the percentage of calls fixed at first line. Or if you're improving the availability of an IT service, you can measure the percentage increase in the number of hours for which the service is available each week. The measurements must link to the targets set in step 3.

6. **How do we keep the momentum going?** Don't let your improvement slip backwards. You must consolidate the changes you've made, with regular reviews and audits of the service or process.

When implementing your improvement, involve everyone who's affected by it. Involving people throughout a project is a great way of gaining commitment. When staff have been involved, they're less likely to slip back to the old ways of doing things.

Measuring, Measuring, Measuring

How do you know you've improved something? Hopefully, your answer incorporates the word measurement. You only know you've improved something by measuring it to start with and then again after a period of time. So a lot of CSI is to do with measurement.

You can easily get caught out. One colleague relates the story of making improvements at the service desk. When he was asked by his manager to prove his improvements, he couldn't. He had forgotten to take a baseline (see the earlier section 'Identifying baselines'): he had forgotten to take an initial measurement before embarking on the improvement project.

Identifying what to measure

How do you know what to measure? CSI aims to improve the service *and* the service management processes. Three types of metrics are most useful to CSI:

✔ **Technology metrics:** The measurement of individual components; for example, the availability of a server or the performance speed of a network segment.

✔ **Service metrics:** These measure the end-to-end view of the service and best represent the point of view of the user; for example, the refresh speed of a web page, or the end-to-end availability of the email service. Sometimes, measuring end-to-end performance isn't technically possible, so you have to calculate or estimate it from the individual technology metrics.

✔ **Process metrics:** These tell you how well you're managing the service. These are usually critical success factors and key performance indicators (which I explain in the following section) relevant to each service management process. For example, a percentage decrease in the number of failed changes in the last month will measure the effectiveness of your change management process (more on this process in Chapter 7).

You don't use these metrics only when you want to improve something. They form a framework of measurement you can use to measure the achievement of your SLA targets. The clever bit is to choose the right metrics for each situation.

Deciding what to measure and how

Many types and methods of measurement exist. ITIL suggests a cascade of measurements starting at the top: you start with a clear objective of what you want to improve and then break it into bite-sized chunks. The objectives must be consistent with the organisation's higher-level vision and goals. Exactly what you measure depends on whether you're measuring a service or a service management process.

The following sections help you determine what to measure and how.

Determining the critical success factors and key performance indicators

A *critical success factor* (CSF) is something that must happen if a process, project, plan or IT service is to succeed. A critical success factor is a *factor* that is *critical* to the *success* of your process, service or project. So for incident management this may be things such as 'quickly resolve incidents' or 'maintain customer satisfaction'.

You use *key performance indicators* (KPIs) to measure the achievement of each CSF. A key performance indicator is a *key* measurement that *indicates* your *performance* towards meeting a target or CSF. So a sense of direction or comparison is very important. For example, if I was measuring my service desk, a KPI may be a percentage increase in the number of incidents resolved at first line.

When used to measure service management processes, KPIs often focus on one or many of the following aspects of the process:

- **Compliance:** Do the staff who carry out the process activities stick to the procedures?
- **Quality:** How well is the process performed? Often measured by effectiveness and efficiency.
- **Performance:** The speed and accuracy of the process activities.
- **Value:** Does the process make a difference? Is it contributing to the organisation's goals?

Deciding on metrics and measurements

After you set the CSFs and KPIs that you need to measure an objective, the next step is to decide what metrics and measurements to collect:

- A *metric* is a scale of measurement: a collection of related measurements. Examples of metrics are a customer satisfaction score and the cost of implementing a change.

✔ A *measurement* refers to individual measurements. For example, to calculate the cost of implementing a change, you have to add up and calculate the time spent building, testing and deploying the change, and the cost of the engineers involved.

For example, if your CSF is to improve the customer satisfaction provided by the service desk, and your KPI is to increase the percentage first-time-fix rate by 10 per cent, your metrics may be the number of incidents fixed first time as a percentage of all incidents, both at the start of the measurement period and at the end of the measurement period. And your measurements may be the total number of incidents logged during the measurement period, and the number of incidents fixed first time during the measurement period.

Working out how to use measurements

Monitoring and collecting lots of data is all very well, but you must know what you intend to do with it. The use of the data can influence what data you collect. On many occasions, I've discovered that my technical staff were producing irrelevant reports that nobody read, and no one questioned why they were produced. Here are the four main reasons for monitoring and measuring, all of which benefit from the use of factual evidence:

✔ **Direct an action towards a target.** This is critical for the success of an improvement initiative. For example, for my service desk, the baseline measurement of the current first-time-fix rate and a suggested achievable target helps to focus staff on the CSF I set to improve customer satisfaction with the service desk.

✔ **Intervene when something slips off target and you want to take corrective action.** Suppose the first-time-fix rate at your service desk decreases inexplicably. You must investigate. For example, measurements may show that more users than expected are ringing the service desk because of problems with a new release.

✔ **Justify a future or intended action.** Justifying a course of action is easier if you can provide factual evidence. You obtain this evidence through measurement. If the service desk improvement needs another staff member to be employed, you must be able to provide the factual evidence necessary to support your request.

✔ **Validate a previous decision or past action.** After you achieve an improvement, say a 10 per cent improvement in first-time-fix rate at the service desk, you can produce the factual evidence to show that your target has been met, and your course of action is validated.

Understanding the seven-step improvement process

The seven-step improvement process provides a model for establishing what you need to measure and how to go about measuring it. Have a look at Figure 9-4.

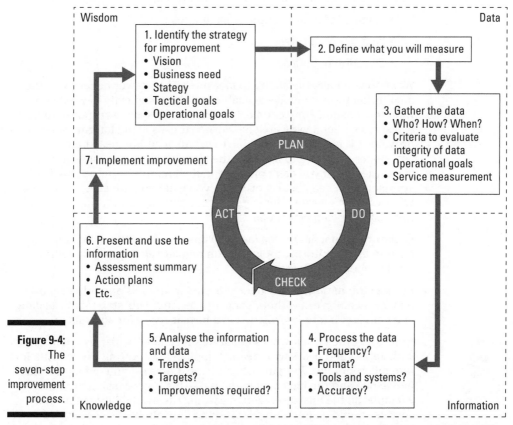

Figure 9-4: The seven-step improvement process.

1. **Identify the strategy for improvement.** As with all projects, the first thing you must do is establish the context for what you plan to improve. You identify and assess your vision and your strategic, tactical and operational goals. The focus here is on what the IT provider can do to improve the IT services and enable the achievement of the business vision.

2. **Define what you will measure.** This will relate to the goals you set in the previous step. You need to consider what you *should* measure and what you *can* measure. A good starting point is what you've promised to your customer: the service targets you are committed to. This is documented in the *service level agreement* (SLA; see Chapter 5).

The SLA with the production department states that the manufacturing IT service must be available 24/7, unplanned outages must be recovered within one hour, and only three outages per week are permitted. What should you measure? How about the following:

- Number of hours of uptime each week

- Number of outages

- Duration of outages

What do you have the ability to measure? The answer depends on the monitoring tools you have available and the complexity of what you want to measure. For example, to measure the system response time of a service over a wide area network that uses many Internet service providers, it is often not possible to get an accurate measurement. Sometimes you have to measure the bits you have control over and guess the rest. If you can't measure it, it shouldn't be in the SLA! Looking at existing or even past reports tells you what you are able to measure. What you can measure depends on your existing monitoring tools and the cost of buying new tools.

3. **Gather the data.** Set up the mechanisms to collect the data. You may need to use monitoring tools and run regular reports, which your service operation staff can do.

4. **Process the data.** The raw data gathered from tools and other reports may be meaningless without some processing. This step takes the data and converts it into information in a format ready for analysis.

Processing the data involves collating the data – that is, grouping apples with apples and pears with pears. I think of it as putting like information into different piles. Perhaps when the post arrives, you put all the bills in one pile and the junk mail in the bin – this is processing the data. For example, all the measurements regarding the availability of the email service should go into one pile, and the data about the effectiveness of the change management process in another pile.

5. **Analyse the information and data.** My definition of *analysis* is 'stare at it and see what it tells you'. Now you've sorted the data and started to create information, you can stare at it and see what it tells you. You're looking for trends, changes, comparisons with targets – in fact anything that tells you whether, or how well, your targets are being met. By analysing the data and information, you are putting it into a context that you can learn from – in other words, you are creating knowledge.

6. **Present and use the information.** Put the information and knowledge in an appropriate format for the audience who use it. If it's a technical report, there will be lots of technical jargon, possibly a lot of supporting data. If it's a management report, you concentrate of comparing performance with targets. Exception reports are a great idea – just document the cases where targets were missed.

Use pictures or graphical representations. Busy senior management or customers often find it quicker and easier to digest and understand reports in this format.

7. **Implement improvement.** At last, the time has come to make a decision. Presentation of the data, information and knowledge allows decisions to be made. The knowledge derived from this process, along with previous experience, allows you to decide which services and service management processes to correct, optimise or improve.

The seven-step process is an *improvement* process. It's included in CSI to help you focus on what you must measure in order to achieve the objective of a specific improvement project. In addition to this, the seven-step process is an excellent approach for setting up monitoring and measuring of service level targets on a more day-to-day basis, and can help you ensure that in the service operation (see Chapter 8) stage you have the right tools in place and are collecting the right data and information.

Buying a car using the seven-step improvement process

Suppose I want to buy a new car and I'm not quite sure what I want. I use the seven-step process:

1. I start by considering why I want a new car and what I hope to achieve. Is it a family car or a high-performance sports car?

2. I know that I should measure: customer satisfaction of all users of the make of car I want; performance data for the models I like; running costs. I can also measure: experiences of my friends; performance and cost data from car magazines; opinions from the Internet.

3. I gather data by taking my friends to the pub and asking them questions, buying some magazines and downloading data from the Internet.

4. To process the data and turn it into information, I write down what my friends tell me about each make and model, tear out pages from the magazines (or rewrite the data to compare the performance and cost data), and combine all relevant data together.

5. To analyse the data, I make comparisons, finding the cars with the best and worst performance characteristics.

6. I summarise the information in a simple-to-read format and strip out all irrelevant stuff.

7. I decide which car to buy.

Linking Governance and CSI

In Chapter 2, I describe governance and its relevance to service management. But how does governance fit with CSI? Governance is simply one of the many drivers for improving your service management processes. If a new regulation comes along that affects IT, how will you respond to it? Who'll check the IT department practice to see whether you're affected? It's likely that if action is required, it becomes a project that improves your service management processes or the services themselves.

A good example is the Sarbanes–Oxley Act of 2002, often referred to as SOXA. This is a US law that was implemented as a response to well-publicised corporate fraud cases. In order to comply, a company has to implement processes and procedures to demonstrate that its business is performed fairly and transparently. The influence of SOXA has reached far beyond the USA. Those IT departments that have implemented ITIL processes have found it easier to comply with the act.

Getting to Grips with Risk

Risk is a possible event that may cause harm or loss, or affect the ability to achieve objectives. A risk is measured by the probability of a threat, the vulnerability of the asset to that threat, and the impact the event would have if it occurred. Risk can also be defined as uncertainty of outcome, and can be used in the context of measuring the probability of positive outcomes as well as negative outcomes.

Risk is something that *may* happen. Usually, we think of risk as something bad, but something that may happen can just as easily be good. For example, there may be a risk that the availability of your email service exceeds the agreed targets. You must agree an approach to predicting and managing all those things that *may* happen that can influence the quality of your IT services. Good risk management can support better decision-making through a good understanding of risks and their likely impact.

You address risk throughout the service lifecycle. Many processes perform risk assessments, and sometimes each process uses a different approach. Because risk is relevant to many areas of service management, it's something that gets put in the melting pot of CSI. So CSI is often an appropriate place to get advice on a single approach to risk to ensure that all risks to your IT services are identified, and mitigation activities are coordinated.

Risk management consists of:

- **Risk analysis:** Gathering information about risks, and identifying and assessing risks. You can assess risk in many ways. Generally, all risk-assessment methods put some relative value or score on each risk, so that you can put them in order of ranking. Those risks with the highest score are the ones you must deal with first. Project management methodologies suggest scoring two things:

  - The likelihood (or probability) that the risk will happen

  - When the risk happens, what the impact will be

  Another method suggested by ITIL is to value the assets that may be at risk, and for each asset score the threat to the asset and the asset's vulnerability to the threat.

- **Risk management:** Monitoring risks and identifying, selecting and adopting justified countermeasures. When you identify and assess a risk, you measure it throughout your project, or throughout the life of the service, to see whether the level of risk changes. If the risk increases, you decide whether action is necessary. When you assess a risk, you can decide straight away what action to take. In some cases, you can implement actions to reduce the risk. For example, if you think your house is at risk from burglary, you put additional security in place on the doors and windows. In other cases, you can put a plan in place to deal with the risk as and when it happens. For example, if you think your house is at risk from fire, you buy some fire extinguishers and place them around your house.

Risk management is important to all service management processes. However, three processes regularly perform risk analyses: availability management, information security management and IT service continuity management (Chapter 6 outlines these processes).

Risk management is also relevant to each stage of the service lifecycle. Here are a few examples:

- **Service strategy:** A customer asks for a new call centre IT service but can't provide a reliable prediction of the volume of usage of the system. The service provider must evaluate the risk of acquiring resources to support the service that may not be used. Unused resources cost money.

- **Service design:** A new data centre is to be built, and the architecture is currently being designed. Availability management, security management and IT service continuity management perform a risk assessment on the service and its components.

✔ **Service transition:** Testing a new or changed service reduces the risk of not having the right resources in place to provide the service.

✔ **Service operation:** Monitoring and event management proactively identify things that may precipitate a service failure and ensure they are dealt with before any business impact occurs.

Identifying CSI Roles

Many roles are associated with CSI. Some roles are dedicated; other roles are general ones or roles associated with other processes. However, all the roles I cover in this section have some involvement with CSI. (For the low-down on roles, take a look at Chapter 2.)

ITIL describes two roles that are dedicated to CSI:

✔ **CSI manager:** Ultimately responsible for the success of your improvement initiatives and the point of contact for all things to do with improvement. Here are some responsibilities of the role:

- Communicates the vision and need for CSI across the organisation.

- Initiates activities and SIPs to improve the services and service management processes.

- Works with service owners, process owners and the service level manager to identify opportunities for improvement.

- Gets involved in monitoring, reporting and the use of related tools, to make sure these all support improvement.

✔ **Reporting analyst:** Monitoring, reporting and measurement are essential to effective improvement, so it makes sense to allocate the role of reporting analyst to one of your staff. The following are just a few of the relevant responsibilities:

- Works with the CSI manager and service level manager to review performance data.

- Reviews and analyses data from components and services to ensure that an end-to-end view is taken of service achievements.

- Identifies and analyses trends.

The following roles have a close relationship with CSI:

- ✔ **Service level manager:** Responsible for managing the service levels, and so has a first-hand view of how well the service level targets are met. During regular reviews with the customer, the service level manager identifies opportunities for improvement. The service level manager works with the CSI manager to set up a SIP.

- ✔ **Service owner:** The role provides a point of contact for a given service. The person to whom the role is allocated doesn't necessarily know everything about the service, but does know someone who does. Here are a few of the relevant responsibilities of the role:

  - Represents the service across the organisation

  - Represents the service in change advisory board meetings

  - Participates in internal service review meetings

  - Provides input to CSI and works with the CSI manager to identify and prioritise service improvements

- ✔ **Process owner:** The process owner owns a process. So for example, if the incident management process doesn't achieve its aim of restoring the service to the user, the process owner gets shouted at. I don't mean this literally (although I'm sure it happens). The process owner is accountable for the process and is responsible for identifying improvements to ensure that the process continues to be effective and efficient. Here are a few responsibilities of this role:

  - Ensuring that the process is performed in accordance with the agreed and documented process

  - Documenting and publicising the process

  - Working with the CSI manager to identify and prioritise process improvements

Using technology for CSI

The technology and tools used by CSI include the tools needed to process and analyse data and information and then report it in an appropriate form. These tools may already be in place in your organisation, but it's useful to review all IT tools because there may be some functionality that's not currently used that could support CSI.

Further, CSI also takes an interest in the tools used by all other service management processes with a view to improving them and ensuring they are used in the best way possible. So one of the things that CSI can aim to improve is how tools are used throughout the lifecycle to improve the IT service and the service management processes. This may include helping with the identification, evaluation and selection of new or proposed tools.

Part III
Getting Practical

In this part . . .

When you understand the basics of the processes and the lifecycle (and Parts I and II give you that), you move on to the practical concerns of using all this ITIL stuff for the benefit of your organisation. This part takes a practical view of how you can implement and use the service management processes and practices in situations in which you actually use them.

Chapter 10

Implementing ITIL

In This Chapter

▶ Making plans to implement ITIL

▶ Working through your implementation project

▶ Designing your service management processes

▶ Seeing an implementation project in action

▶ Getting help and support from the people involved

Sometimes the core ITIL guidance can seem a bit dry. After you have an understanding of the basics of the processes and the service lifecycle, which I cover in Parts I and II, you can consider the more practical concerns of how all this ITIL stuff applies to your organisation. ITIL may look prescriptive, but it isn't. The ITIL books provide guidance that applies to any organisation of any size. That is the power of best practice guidance that recommends processes. Not every organisation can employ lots of staff, but every organisation can adopt processes to make better use of what they've got. The clever bit is making ITIL work for you.

If you're enthused by ITIL and the framework of service management processes and want to use them in your organisation, how do you go about it? This chapter uses the ITIL guidance to give you advice on implementing processes.

Before you start, be aware that when you implement an ITIL process you're telling people how to do their jobs. By providing a procedure for them to follow, you're messing about with how they do things. Implementing ITIL creates organisational change, so tread carefully and make sure you address the soft 'people' issues. At the end of this chapter, I include some ideas on how to address these issues.

This chapter is all about implementing the ITIL service management processes that I describe in Part II of this book. In this chapter I assume you have some knowledge of the processes and are thinking about how to implement or improve them in your organisation. If you're not sure of some of the details of the processes, refer back to Part II as you go through this chapter.

Planning to Implement ITIL

How do you implement ITIL in your organisation? For example, if your boss told you to implement the ITIL change management process (which I cover in Chapter 7), what would you do? How would you organise that piece of work? Hopefully, you said to yourself 'as a project'. Yep, sounds like a good idea. So to implement ITIL you set up a project to implement one or many service management processes. The following sections elaborate.

Seeing how projects fit with implementing ITIL

What is a *project*? Well, this is a book about ITIL, so I'm not about to tell you how to do project management. But here are some basic things you should know about projects:

✔ They have a beginning, a middle and an end (yes, honestly they do!).

✔ They utilise a defined amount of time and resources.

✔ They have a defined set of deliverables or products.

The key thing to consider is the deliverable. If you set up a project to implement a change management process, what's the main deliverable of the project? The answer is: a change management process and everything that goes with it.

If the deliverable of your project is a process, what does this mean? For every process, you must design and document the process flow and the procedures for each activity. This also includes deciding the process owner, process objective, trigger, metrics and so on.

For each process that you implement, you must do many things including the following:

✔ Design the process flow and create the procedures for each activity.

✔ Create other artefacts such as records, forms, reports and so on.

✔ Document the process.

✔ Train the staff who will be involved in the process.

✔ Create awareness of the process for all stakeholders.

✔ Agree how you will audit the process and how often you will audit it.

When you consider all of the above you can see that your project includes the design, transition and operation of the ITIL processes. Your project needs structure, and a project management methodology helps to provide structure but it won't tell you what the phases of your project cover. For this, you should take a look at the service lifecycle (see the following section).

Using the service lifecycle to implement the ITIL processes

You don't just use the service lifecycle for the planning and implementation of your *IT* services. You apply the same approach to planning and implementing your *service management* processes. The service lifecycle helps you plan the structure of the phases of your process implementation project.

Here are some thoughts on how you use the lifecycle:

✔ **Service strategy:** In this stage you first seek to understand how managing your IT services supports the business. Then you decide which processes to introduce, and create a business case for introducing them. This forces you to perform a cost–benefit analysis and calculate *return on investment* (ROI). You also get approval and funding at this stage. The output of this phase is a high-level plan of which service management processes you want to implement, in which order, along with rough timescales. Flick to Chapter 4 for more on the service strategy stage.

✔ **Service design:** You establish the detailed requirements of the processes you want to implement and design the processes to meet the requirements. The basic requirement is for your service management processes to help you manage your IT services so that the services provide value to the business (value as defined by utility and warranty). Therefore the processes focus on these needs. If your organisation is in a fast-moving industry and constantly has to update its products in order to compete, this results in a lot of IT change. So the change management process in this case will be designed to meet the volume of change requests and the speed of response to requests needed by the business. For each process, you design and document the process flow, the procedures, identify tool requirements and so on. Check out Chapters 5 and 6 for details of the service design stage.

✔ **Service transition:** This is the build, test and implement phase of your project, which I discuss in Chapter 7. Can you build, test and implement a process? Yes, you can.

• **Build:** Create all the documentation – the process flow, the procedures, any records (such as incident records and problem records) – acquire and/or configure any tools; assign roles and responsibilities.

- **Test:** Try it out. If, for example, you're implementing incident management, you can rehearse what happens when the service desk receives an incident and play out the activities in the process. This is often called a conference room pilot or a walk-through. It gives the chance for everyone to get involved and to point out issues in the process before you go live.

- **Implement:** This is where you implement, or deploy, the process. The day it all goes live. From this day on, you expect all those involved with the process to follow the new process and procedures.

✔ **Service operation:** The implementation of the process marks the end of the project. The new service management process or processes are now live and should be used as the normal way of doing things. However, your processes can't be forgotten or ignored. You must review the outcome, or results, of the process to ensure that it's working the way you planned. So you measure the process. You audit the process regularly to ensure that staff are sticking to the process. This provides an opportunity to look for improvements to the process. Head over to Chapter 8 for more detail on service operation.

✔ **Continual service improvement (CSI):** Chapter 9 is all about CSI, which does what it says on the tin. The book *ITIL Continual Service Improvement* (published by The Stationery Office) provides information on both improving your services and improving how you manage your services. This includes improving your service management processes or, if you are starting from scratch, implementing the processes. This chapter is about *implementing* service management. So how does improvement fit in? Well, the point is that in most cases you aren't starting from scratch. Even the most immature IT organisation is likely to have some activities in place that are vaguely coordinated towards managing IT as a service. So the advice given in the ITIL CSI book is relevant to implementing your processes.

If you're planning to implement the ITIL processes in your organisation, I urge you to read *ITIL Continual Service Improvement.* You will find loads of good concepts and advice in there, some of which I include in this chapter.

Creating a Plan for Your Implementation Project

You use the service lifecycle as a structure for your service management implementation project, so the first stage is to determine your strategy (Chapter 4 focuses on the strategy stage). In other words – start planning your project.

Developing a strategy for implementing ITIL basically means deciding which processes to implement and in what order to implement them.

In the next few sections I outline a few things that help you plan your project.

Using the CSI approach

I describe the CSI approach in Chapter 9. When you implement the service management processes in your organisation, this model provides an approach to planning your project, in other words for thinking about what you intend to do.

Here are some thoughts on how to use the CSI approach to help you plan your service management implementation project:

1. **What's the vision?** You must understand how your service management project fits into the bigger business picture. How will your service management processes help you to better manage the IT services you provide to the business and therefore help the business achieve what it wants to achieve? You need to set the goals of your project.

2. **Where are we now?** Set your starting point or baseline: assess your current processes. It is common to assess the maturity of your service management processes; I say more about this in the section 'Assessing the maturity of processes' later in this chapter.

3. **Where do we want to be?** Now set the targets for what you want to achieve. This is the decision about which processes you want to implement. Your decision depends upon the results of the process assessment carried out in step 2. The combination of steps 2 and 3 provides you with a gap. This is the gap you hope to bridge by implementing the service management processes.

4. **How do we get there?** Address how you'll implement the processes and in which order. Create your project plan for implementing or improving your processes.

5. **Did we get there?** After you set the targets for what your project must achieve you need to set the measurements that you can use to check whether you've met your targets. All processes must be measurable, and you will identify the appropriate metrics as part of designing your processes.

6. **How do we keep the momentum going?** For your project, this step will be a review at the end of the project and the agreement of any further steps.

Grouping ITIL processes for implementation

Do you have to implement all the ITIL processes? Well, the real power of ITIL comes from its synergy. *Synergy* refers to a situation where the whole is greater than the sum of its parts.

Your organisation gets the greatest benefit from ITIL if you can implement all the processes. If you and your organisation truly want to manage your IT services in the best possible way then you implement all the processes. However, the best approach is to have a vision that you'll eventually implement all the processes, but break this into a number of projects and concentrate initially on the processes that give your organisation most benefit.

The ITIL books describe over 20 processes, but they vary in size and complexity. Some processes are closely related to one another, and for the purposes of implementation may be considered as one and implemented together. One example of this is incident management and request fulfilment (see Chapter 8). Both these processes have an impact on the service desk and your support teams, so you're best combining the deployment of these processes.

When planning your ITIL implementation, it makes sense to group closely related processes. These groups won't be the same for everyone. The main logical groups of processes are generally those as divided by the stages of the service lifecycle, but certain processes do have closer links.

In the following sections I describe some possible groups of processes. Some of these are related because they require similar skills or resources to implement. These aren't hard-and-fast rules; this information is given as guidance to help give you ideas and help you plan your project. You must then decide which processes to implement in your organisation.

Change management, service asset and configuration management, release and deployment management

The change management, service asset and configuration management (SACM), release and deployment management processes (which I explain in Chapter 7) are more or less inextricably linked. You can, of course, implement them separately, but the effect will be stronger if they are kept together. Many organisations implement these as a single function, or department, thus strengthening the identity of the processes. This approach ensures the integrity of the *configuration management system* (CMS) and makes it easier to ensure that all parts of the IT services and infrastructure are carefully controlled. Almost all the other service management processes rely upon good SACM and the CMS, so it's helpful to implement it early in the project if possible.

In my experience, SACM is a process that is left to later in the implementation of service management. This is often due to the difficultly of collecting configuration data and the cost of the tools to collect and store the data, as well as the overhead of keeping it up to date. Bear in mind that you don't have to implement an all-singing, all-dancing CMS on day one of your project. What you're seeking is control. So implementing some form of change management and SACM processes simultaneously helps to drive your service management implementation. It's unusual for an IT organisation to have no form of asset recording or record keeping, so take a look at what you already have and build on it. It's essential to plan the structure of your CMS, but once the structure is defined then the most rudimentary tools (such as spreadsheets) can be used to gradually build up a repository of data and information. Further, make best use of existing tools, attempting to build interfaces between them where possible.

Service desk, incident management and request fulfilment

If a service desk doesn't exist, create one as soon as possible. The combination of the service desk (Chapter 3) and incident management (Chapter 8) is a good one for a quick win. Users respond well to a warm, friendly customer care approach, which helps you gain support for the rest of the project. You can implement a request fulfilment (Chapter 8) process at the same time.

Incident management and problem management

The incident management and problem management processes (see Chapter 8) are a logical pair, so if possible implement them at the same time. Users often complain about recurring faults, so committing time to identifying the cause will be well received. Both processes often use similar resources, so it is a good idea to train support teams in both processes at the same time.

Capacity management and financial management for IT services

One of the main responsibilities of the capacity management process (see Chapter 6) is to perform the balancing act of capacity versus cost. This will be made very much easier if the process for financial management for IT services (see Chapter 4) is in place. The data collection needs of each process are similar, so the CMS can be populated for both processes at the same time.

Availability management and IT service continuity management

Think of the availability management and IT service continuity management processes (which I explore in Chapter 6) as opposite ends of the same piece of string. Both are concerned with the risk of failure of the service. These processes share many of the same techniques which are used to identify weaknesses and risks in the services and infrastructure which may lead to loss of a service. While it isn't essential to implement both at the same time, it is wise to plan to implement IT service continuity management shortly after availability management.

Service level management and financial management for IT services

These two processes are often carried out by similar staff. It's useful for the person who negotiates with the customer (service level management; see Chapter 5) to understand the cost of delivering the IT services in accordance with the business requirements. Your financial management for IT services process (see Chapter 4) is influenced by the main finance or accounting department in your organisation. In smaller organisations, IT financial management is performed by the IT manager with access to the organisation's financial management system, along with a few spreadsheets. The point here is that if you are an internal IT provider, financial management for IT services doesn't have to be very complicated to start with. On the other hand if you're a commercial IT supplier (providing IT services in exchange for money), your financial management for IT services process is more rigorous.

Warranty processes

It makes sense to implement the warranty processes of availability management, capacity management, IT service continuity management and information security management (flick to Chapter 6 for details) together because they share similar triggers and similar resources. For example, a trigger may be a request from a customer for a new or changed service which involves a review of the requirements and possibly the design of the service. All four processes are involved in these activities. In some cases the same staff consider all four aspects within their technical domains. For example, your server experts consider the availability, capacity, continuity and security of the servers in one go, not as four separate investigations. Therefore, if you want to organise their activities a little better, you implement all four processes at the same time.

Implementing the service lifecycle

In this chapter I refer to the service lifecycle in two contexts. In the earlier section 'Using the service lifecycle to implement the ITIL processes' I describe how you can use the stages of the service lifecycle to help you plan your service management process implementation project. In this section I discuss using the service lifecycle for its original intention: as a structure for the lifecycle of your services.

In Part II of this book I describe the ITIL service management processes. ITIL encourages you not only to adopt and implement the service management processes but also to organise them around the service lifecycle. So, when you come to implement these processes, the question arises – how do you implement the service lifecycle? Well, it is, without a doubt, the processes that you're implementing. For the service lifecycle, it's a question of triggers.

The processes don't move around from stage to stage of the service lifecycle like some strange beast. The lifecycle structure makes you realise that some process activities are triggered in different ways.

Implementing the service lifecycle means ensuring that the right activities are triggered at the right time during the development or change of your IT services.

The structure and timing of the activities are important. The emphasis is on ensuring that when developing a new IT service or changing an existing one, you follow the sequence and don't rush to deploy the service without proper planning.

For example, the availability management process consists of many activities, some of which you carry out in the service design stage and some in the service operation stage. So, when designing and implementing your availability management process, you must identify how the various activities are triggered. The proactive activities in the service design stage will be triggered by the receipt of new requirements via service level management. The reactive activities of the service operation stage may be triggered by events detected by the event management process.

Assessing the maturity of processes

One of the important steps in your project is to decide which processes to implement or improve, and by how much to improve them. This is achieved through assessing the maturity of your service management processes. A *mature* process is one that's adequate for the purpose. The ITIL books provide what is called a process maturity framework, which you can see in Figure 10-1.

The assessment involves someone (an internal or external assessor) talking to the staff who perform the process activities and asking a series of questions. The answers to these questions provide the assessor with an understanding of how well the process is understood and how well it achieves its aims. The result is to give each process a score between 1 and 5, relating to the levels shown in Figure 10-1. Level 1 is lowest and 5 is highest. Here's a quick explanation of each maturity level:

- ✔ **Level 1 – initial:** This level means that the organisation recognises that a process exists, just, but it is not managed. Therefore no importance, resource or focus is allocated to or associated with the process. Sometimes this level is described as *ad-hoc* or *chaotic*.

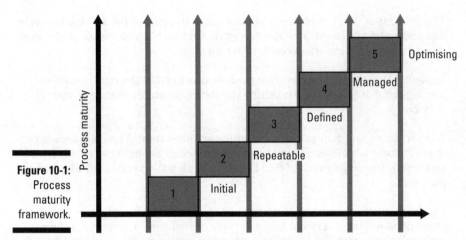

Figure 10-1:
Process
maturity
framework.

- ✔ **Level 2 – repeatable:** This level means that the process is recognised and that some importance, resource or focus is allocated to or associated with the process. The activities tend to be uncoordinated, irregular and lack direction.

- ✔ **Level 3 – defined:** A process at this level is recognised and documented, but there is no formal agreement, acceptance or recognition of its role in IT. The process is likely to have an owner, objectives and targets are set, and resources are allocated.

- ✔ **Level 4 – managed:** This level means the process is fully recognised and accepted in the IT department, is service focused and has objectives and targets that are based on business goals. The process is fully defined, documented and managed, and is proactive with established interfaces to other service management processes.

- ✔ **Level 5 – optimising:** A process at this level is all singing and dancing! It is fully recognised and has strategic objectives that are aligned with strategic business and IT goals. The process is institutionalised: part of the everyday activities. The process has a self-contained continual process of improvement.

Deciding which processes and in what order

The result of all the planning activity that I outline in the preceding sections is an outline project plan telling you which processes you intend to implement and in which order. Now you can move on to the next stage of the lifecycle: design. The following section takes you through designing your processes.

Designing Your Processes

You use the service design stage, which Chapters 5 and 6 explain, in the life-cycle to help you design the service management processes that you planned in the previous stage (the strategy stage; see the earlier section 'Creating a Plan for Your Implementation Project'). Designing the process means you must design and document the process flow and the procedures for each activity. This also includes deciding the process owner, process goal, trigger, metrics and so on. Figure 10-2 shows a theoretical picture of a process and its constituent parts. The figure may look a little complicated but it shows you all the elements of a process that must be considered and documented in order for the process to achieve its aim.

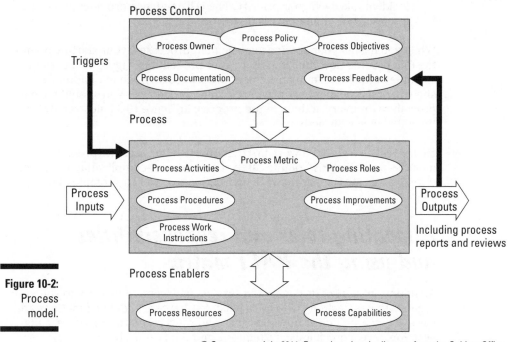

Figure 10-2: Process model.

© Crown copyright 2011. Reproduced under licence from the Cabinet Office.

Knowing what to adopt and what to adapt

'You must adopt ITIL and adapt it to suit your organisation' is a phrase I've heard too many times to count. What does this really mean? The ITIL guidance doesn't clearly answer the question, but I believe you must do the following:

✔ **Adopt the basic process flow, relatively unchanged.** So, for example, the incident management process starts with the logging, categorisation, prioritisation and initial diagnosis of an incident, and continues through several more activities (see Figure 10-3). If I was auditing your processes for conformance to the ITIL guidance, I'd expect to see documentary evidence that those activities are in place and the appropriate staff perform them.

✔ **Adapt your procedures.** For each activity in the process, you require a procedure that tells your staff how you want the activity to be performed. This can be a written document or sometimes a software application such as a service desk tool that guides the staff member automatically through the procedure. It's this procedure that allows you to adapt the process to suit your organisation. For example, in the prioritise activity of incident management, I have no idea how you will define your priorities. It's up to you to agree with the business which type of incident takes a higher priority. The ITIL guidance provides some suggestions, but ultimately it's up to you.

When you design your service management processes, your starting point is the ITIL process flow then you write your procedures. Figure 10-3 uses the example of the incident management process (described in Chapter 8) to show the relationship between process and procedure. You should have a procedure for every activity in the process; in Figure 10-3 I illustrate this for the initial diagnosis activity.

Figure 10-3 also shows a work instruction. In some cases the procedure includes a particularly complex step. To avoid over-complicating the procedure, you create a separate work instruction to cover the complex bit.

Allocating roles and responsibilities and using the RACI matrix

An important part of designing the service management process to suit your organisation is deciding who does what. In Chapter 2, I define functions and roles. If you aren't clear how functions and roles relate to processes, I suggest you have a quick look at Chapter 2 and then return here.

Deciding who does what

It's very easy to fail because you do not get the support of your IT staff for your process implementation project. One cause of this is staff who don't understand what you want and are not clear about their responsibilities. Of course, you can't tell them who's responsible for what if you don't know yourself. Involving your staff at this stage helps you gain their support.

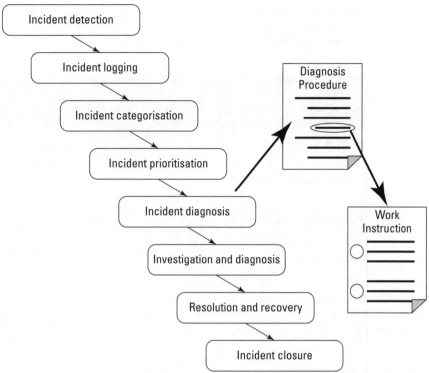

Figure 10-3:
Process and
procedures.

Creating a RACI matrix for each process is an excellent way of deciding and communicating who does what for each process. RACI is an acronym and represents:

- ✔ **Responsible.** The people who perform the activities. The ones who get the job done.

- ✔ **Accountable.** Where the buck stops! The person who takes ultimate ownership and gets her wrists slapped when the process or activity goes wrong. There should only ever be one person accountable for an activity or process.

- ✔ **Consulted.** The people whose advice or opinions are sought.

- ✔ **Informed.** The people who should be told or kept informed about the process, the activity and its outcome.

Take a look at Figure 10-4, which is a partial RACI for the incident management process. It's partial because much of the detail depends on how you choose to do things in your organisation. This is only an example.

	User	Service Desk agent	Second line support teams	Incident Management Process Owner
Incident logging	C/I	R		A
Incident categorisation	C	R		A
Incident prioritisation	C	R		A
Initial diagnosis	C	R		A
Investigation & diagnosis	I	C/I	R	A
Resolution & recovery	I	C/I	R	A
Incident closure	I	R		A

Figure 10-4: Example RACI matrix for incident management.

© Crown copyright 2011. Reproduced under licence from the Cabinet Office.

Creating the process flow

After you create a RACI matrix for a process (see the previous section), you're just a small step from creating a flow diagram for the process. A *process flow diagram* does what it says on the tin: it shows the flow of the process. In fact, it shows the flow of the activities that make up the process.

Have a look at Figure 10-5. This shows the incident management process from the RACI example as a process flow. This sort of picture is known as a *swimlane diagram* and is a very common method used by business analysts to depict process flows. It is so called because each function or role is shown like a lane in a swimming pool. My example shows the swimlanes vertically, but it's just as common to show them horizontally across the page. This is an example only and isn't complete.

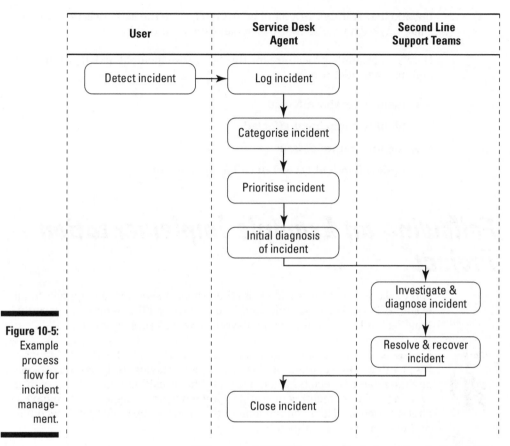

Figure 10-5:
Example
process
flow for
incident
manage-
ment.

© Crown copyright 2011. Reproduced under licence from the Cabinet Office.

Writing the procedures

Having designed the process flow (see the previous section), you must decide how you want each of the activities in the process to be carried out. This means writing a procedure for each. Procedures are often perceived as being the folder on the bookshelf that collects dust until the next time the auditors come. You need to overcome this perception. *Procedures* should be living, breathing documents that reflect the agreed way of doing things.

I've often heard people say that procedures are pointless because nobody sticks to them. On the other hand, in some cases procedures are adhered to too closely, for example turning a call centre assistant into a script-reading robot. You need to strike a balance. Get staff involved in helping to write the procedures. The ideal is simply to reflect what your staff do at the moment but add in that little extra bit of control to ensure the activity is done in the same way each time so that you achieve the right result.

Here's an example procedure for the categorise incident activity of the incident management process:

1. **Identify service affected.**

2. **Identify component affected.**

3. **Identify nature of issue.**

4. **Update incident record in call-logging system.**

Following an Example Implementation Project

I now take some of the advice from the previous sections and apply it to an example. It's only an example, and I won't cover all the details that I would in real life, but I hope to give you a flavour of what a project involves.

In these sections I describe an implementation example. Please remember, it's just that – an example – and isn't complete. Having designed the process and the related artefacts, you move on to the transition phase. This involves creating and documenting everything you have just designed – if you haven't already done so. Then you implement the process, meaning that it becomes part of everyday use (hopefully).

The scenario

Dummy Co. is an organisation that has grown rapidly and now relies on the internal IT department in order to do its business. The IT department recognises the need to improve the way it manages the IT services in order to better support the business. In fact, the department embraced ITIL six months ago and already has some basic processes in place. Figure 10-6 shows the organisation diagram for the IT department of Dummy Co.

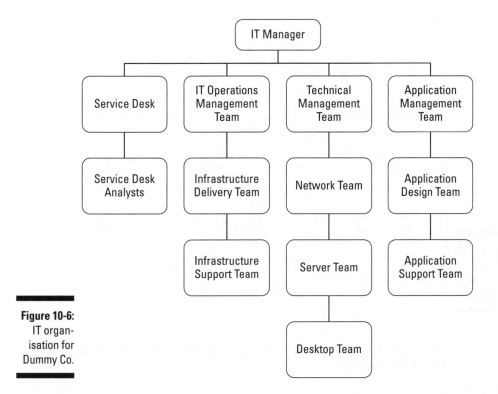

Figure 10-6:
IT organ-
isation for
Dummy Co.

The planning phase

The IT manager of Dummy Co. has established a strategy for IT that supports the business goals and strategy. It has been agreed that a formal project is required to review and improve the IT service management processes.

Deciding which processes to improve

The first thing the IT manager did was to engage an external service management consultant to perform a maturity assessment of the existing processes (see the earlier section 'Assessing the maturity of processes'). The result of the maturity assessment was to allocate a score to each process indicating its level of maturity. A score of 1 is very low and indicates a process that barely exists. A score of 5 is very high and indicates an excellent process. Take a look at Figure 10-7, which shows the results of the assessment in a spider diagram. Each radial arm of the web represents a service management process.

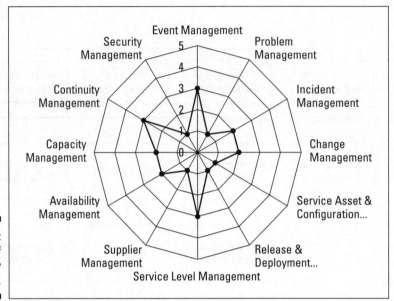

Figure 10-7:
Results of
a maturity
assessment.

The diagram shows some strengths in some areas and weaknesses in others. This is fairly normal.

Creating a project plan

As a result of the assessment (see the previous section) and much discussion with all those involved, a high-level plan is put in place. Part of the overall plan is shown in Figure 10-8. This is a typical project plan showing the tasks to be performed and the time period over which they should be carried out. This sort of diagram is often called a Gantt chart.

Dummy Co. decides that the initial improvement project should focus on the service operation processes of incident management and problem management. For the sake of this example I shall focus on problem management.

The design phase

Now the plan is in place, Dummy Co. moves on to designing the problem management process. The elements of a process are shown in Figure 10-2, a few pages back. The following sections look at some of the aspects Dummy Co. needs to consider when designing the process.

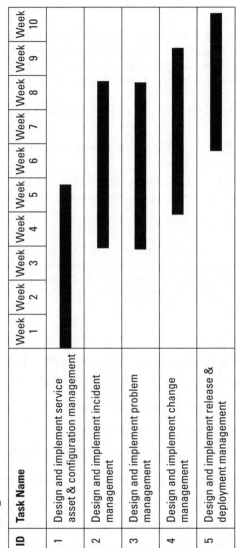

Figure 10-8:
Project plan.

ID	Task Name	Week 1	Week 2	Week 3	Week 4	Week 5	Week 6	Week 7	Week 8	Week 9	Week 10
1	Design and implement service asset & configuration management	█									
2	Design and implement incident management				█						
3	Design and implement problem management				█						
4	Design and implement change management					█					
5	Design and implement release & deployment management							█			

Objectives/outcomes

A *process* is defined as a structured set of activities designed to accomplish a specific objective. This specific objective is sometimes referred to as the *outcome* of the process. This objective must be absolutely clear and drives the policy and the rest of the process.

Policy

Every process should have a written policy. This policy records and communicates a few basic rules that apply to the process. You use the policy to help guide the design of the process. Here are some examples of policy statements that may be in Dummy Co.'s problem management policy:

✔ Problem management will identify and resolve problems that create recurring incidents.

✔ Problems will be recorded as problem records and will be stored separately from incidents.

✔ Problem resolutions will be implemented by raising a *request for change* (RFC) and submitting it to the change management process.

Triggers

Defining the triggers answers the question 'When will the process be used?' In other words, what will trigger the first activity in the process? In the case of problem management, the trigger will be the detection of a new problem and the decision to log it and create a problem record.

Metrics

All processes must be measured to ensure that the outcomes and objectives are achieved. Here are some *key performance indicators* (KPIs) for Dummy Co. that relate to process control and measure the effectiveness of the process:

✔ Percentage reduction in repeat incidents/problems

✔ Percentage increase in documented known errors

✔ Percentage increase in positive customer satisfaction survey responses

And here are some KPIs that relate to process enablers and measure the efficiency of the process:

✔ Percentage reduction in average time to resolve problems

✔ Percentage reduction in the IT problem management budget

✔ Percentage of reports produced on time

Designing the process

Dummy Co. uses a basic process flow for the problem management process, modelled on the process flow found in the ITIL service operation book. I describe the problem management process activities in Chapter 8. Dummy Co.'s version of the process flow is shown in Figure 10-11.

Deciding who does what

Now Dummy Co. must decide who will do what. Dummy Co. looks at the organisation chart and allocates responsibilities to roles for the main activities of the problem management process using a RACI matrix – see Figure 10-9 and 'Deciding who does what' earlier in the chapter.

	User	Service Desk Analyst	Problem Manager	Problem Solver	Problem Management Process Owner
Problem detection		R	R	R	A
Problem logging			R		A
Problem categorisation			R		A
Problem prioritisation			R		A
Problem investigation and diagnosis	C	C	C/I	R	A
Create known error record		I	C/I	R	A
Problem resolution		I	C/I	R	A
Problem closure	I		R	C	A

Figure 10-9: Example RACI matrix for problem management.

© Crown copyright 2011. Reproduced under licence from the Cabinet Office.

Roles and responsibilities

Having decided who'll do what (see the previous section), Dummy Co. must document the roles. In this case, the process involves creating and documenting the role description for three roles:

✔ **Problem manager:**

- Oversee the management of the problem management process.
- Assign problems to problem solvers.

- Take ownership of the *known error database* (KEDB).
- Liaise with all problem-solving groups and third parties to ensure timely resolution of problems.

✔ **Problem solver:**

- Investigate problems within agreed timescales as assigned by problem manager.
- Liaise with other problem solvers and third parties as required to resolve problems.

✔ **Problem management process owner:**

- Own the process and be accountable for the process working as required.
- Ensure that the process is performed in accordance with the agreed and documented process.
- Document and publicise the process.

The role of a process owner is described in more detail in Chapter 2.

Now Dummy Co. allocates the roles to real people; see Figure 10-10, which shows how you might do this for the problem management example.

Designing the process flow

Dummy Co. maps those responsible for each activity to the process flow. Take a look at Figure 10-11.

Note that I have added an extra activity into the flow of 'assign problem'. This step allows the problem manager to decide which individual or group within the other functions should be involved in the investigation. This also indicates that the ITIL process activities are outlines only and need adapting to suit your needs.

Writing the procedures

The next step is to write a procedure for each activity in the process. This allows you to provide instructions to the staff who do the activity, to ensure that it is completed accurately and consistently. The procedure should not be too prescriptive but give just the right amount of control.

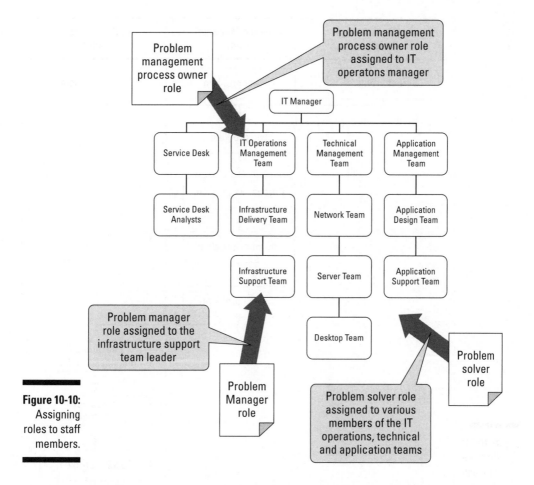

Figure 10-10:
Assigning roles to staff members.

Here's Dummy Co.'s procedure for the investigation and diagnosis step of problem management:

1. **Select next problem in queue.**

2. **Update problem status to 'investigate'.**

3. **Carry out investigation.**

4. **Document findings.**

5. **Update problem status to 'investigation complete'.**

You write a procedure for each activity. If the activity has any particularly complex steps, you create a work instruction document for these.

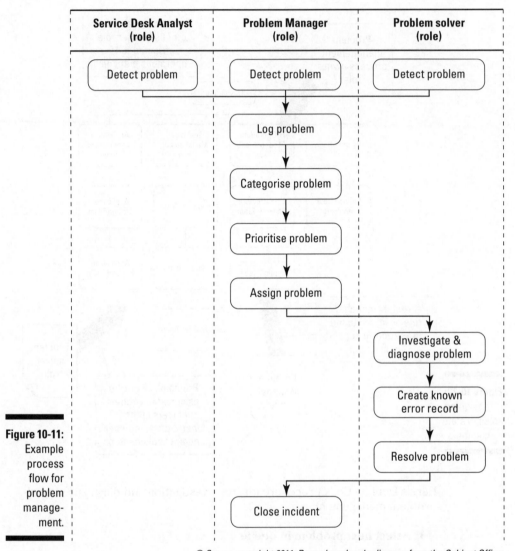

Service Desk Analyst (role)	Problem Manager (role)	Problem solver (role)
Detect problem	Detect problem	Detect problem
	Log problem	
	Categorise problem	
	Prioritise problem	
	Assign problem	
		Investigate & diagnose problem
		Create known error record
		Resolve problem
	Close incident	

Figure 10-11: Example process flow for problem management.

Other documents and records

Dummy Co. must create other documents and records. For the problem management process these include: problem record, known error record, and any report formats. As an example, here's the typical content of a *problem record* – the record that documents the details of the problem and is maintained as a record of the actions required to resolve the problem:

- ✔ Unique identifier
- ✔ Date/time recorded
- ✔ Name/ID of person/group recording the problem
- ✔ Description of problem
- ✔ Problem category and priority
- ✔ Problem status
- ✔ Service and components affected
- ✔ Related incidents
- ✔ Resolution details, date and time
- ✔ Closure category, date and time

You must decide the structure and format of each of these items and make sure they are documented and created.

Tools

Dummy Co.'s process doesn't need to be manual. Many software application tools automate some or all of your processes. For problem management, the best solution is to look for an integrated service management toolset. This is a software application that supports many of your service management processes. Sometimes these are perceived as being service desk tools, but often, with a little bit more expenditure, they can be extended to support multiple processes.

In my example, the IT department at Dummy Co. invests in upgrading its service desk tool so that it can log and assign problem records separately from incident records. The tool also provides most of the problem management reports that are needed.

Dealing with the People Stuff: Organisational Change

Why do projects fail? Many reasons exist; however, a surprising number of projects fail not because of a technical issue but because of a lack of consideration of the 'people' issues, or what are sometimes called the 'soft' issues. When you implement ITIL, you inevitably change your IT staff's activities and roles. Any organisational change causes disruption. So you need to be prepared and manage it.

Planning to involve people

John P. Kotter, a professor at the Harvard Business School, is well known for investigating why projects sometimes fail. He developed an approach called Eight Steps to Transforming Your Organisation. It provides advice on change projects and how to ensure you address the people issues. The eight steps are based on the eight reasons why projects fail. Turn this around and you get a list of the eight important things you must do if you want your project to succeed. Here's a quick overview of the eight steps:

- ✔ **Creating a sense of urgency:** Can you answer the question 'What if we do nothing?' You don't want your project to be ignored, so you need to create a sense of urgency. Make sure you understand the urgency of what needs to be done.

- ✔ **Forming a guiding coalition:** Assemble a team with the power to lead the change effort, and work as a team. Identify and include people in your project who'll support your changes.

- ✔ **Creating a vision:** Make the time and effort to decide and document what the project will achieve. It's all very well having a vision, but you must tell people and get them to act on it.

- ✔ **Communicating the vision:** Imagine you suddenly bump into a key stakeholder in the corridor – this is someone whose support you really need. Can you get your point across quickly and clearly and gain the person's backing? If the answer is 'no', you must return to your vision and make sure you can describe it – with a sense of urgency.

- ✔ **Empowering others to act on the vision:** Enable others to make change. So, if someone offers to get involved, don't put barriers in her way – let her get on with it. Your job is to give others a sense of direction.

- ✔ **Planning for and creating quick wins:** Plan for quick wins then make sure you achieve them! Successful quick wins help to gain support for the more difficult stuff.

- ✔ **Consolidating improvements and producing more change:** Change breeds change. Follow up successes with plans for the next stage. Mix quick wins with longer-term plans.

- ✔ **Institutionalising the change:** Make sure that the new way of doing things becomes the norm.

Identifying stakeholders

A *stakeholder* is someone who has an interest in, or is affected by, whatever you're doing. It's important to identify anyone who is involved with or affected by the implementation of your service management processes. These are the people whose support you need. When you know who the stakeholders are, you can decide how best, and how often, to communicate with them. The ITIL service transition book contains many techniques for indentifying and engaging with stakeholders.

One approach is to identify your stakeholders then identify their particular interests. You can now target your communication or involvement with the stakeholders, focused on their interests and needs.

Don't forget that your stakeholders include people both within the IT organisation and outside it: the customers and the business.

Communicating effectively

Communication is a two-way thing. To truly communicate with someone, you must send a message *and* receive a reply – even if it's simply a nod or a grunt. People want to know what is going on, and to fail to communicate with them can be seen as deliberately excluding them. However, it's possible to overdo it. I'm sure you've experienced communication overload or fatigue when the TV tells you for the squillienth time of the return of a popular programme. So, the trick here is to mix up the format and methods of communication.

Here are some suggestions:

- ✔ **Email:** Okay for short messages, but I know people who've set up rules on their email accounts to send messages from certain people straight to the recycle bin! Keep it short and sweet.

- ✔ **Internet:** Having a website for your project is a good idea, but there is no guarantee that people will visit it.

- ✔ **Meetings/briefs:** Nothing is better than talking face to face. But the message must be focused – don't bore people. There are many types of meeting, both formal and informal. Providing food tends to go down well: a breakfast meeting with bacon rolls – yum!

✔ **Social networking:** Adopting the same methods that are used outside the workplace is a good idea. You can set up the equivalent of a social networking site for your project and encourage people to contribute their thoughts and comments.

✔ **Workshops/training sessions:** Workshops are great for getting involvement. Get the staff who will be involved in the process together and ask them to design the process and procedures.

The result of all of the activities must be the creation of a communication plan. This is the plan that documents when and how you communicate at the beginning of your project and all the way through.

Chapter 11

Getting Carried Away: Using Service Management as a Strategic Asset

In This Chapter

▶ Having a strategy for your services

▶ Understanding what the customer wants

▶ Defining and managing your entire collection of services

▶ Defining services

▶ Knowing where the demand for your services comes from

*1*TIL service management is often perceived as a set of processes that can improve the consistency of what your IT provider does. However, it can be much more than this and can be used by your organisation to help it achieve business objectives. For those who have the stomach and want to take service management further, this chapter contains more discussion and examples about bringing the parts of ITIL together and creating competitive advantage through service management. I cover two main areas: how to create a strategy for your IT services and how to define your services. The chapter draws on many concepts from the ITIL service strategy book and expands on some of the things that I explain in Chapter 4.

I describe another process from the ITIL service strategy book – strategy management for IT services – and I also add more detail about the demand management process.

Defining a Strategic Asset

An *asset* is something of value. So, a *strategic asset* is something of value that you can use to the advantage of your organisation. For a commercial provider a strategic asset may provide a competitive advantage; for an internal IT provider it may provide a clear benefit that helps the organisation achieve its business goals.

A roadside vehicle recovery company advertises that all its mechanics have certain skills, have been trained to a recognised standard, and have at least five years' experience. As a motorist, this may persuade you to take out a policy with the company.

Can service management be a strategic asset? Yes, it can. Managing your IT services in a way that ensures you provide what you've agreed to the customers and meet their expectations can provide competitive advantage. If you can demonstrate that you can do what you say you can do, you improve your organisation's chances of success. So to identify a strategic asset, you must be clear what the strategy is that your organisation wants to achieve.

A commercial Internet provider may use service management to its strategic advantage by promoting the fact that it has reliable processes for managing the availability of its service; further, it can commit to restoring services within stringent targets. If you are a potential customer of that Internet service, you may be tempted – but only if this is what you want from an Internet provider. You may have different expectations.

If an IT provider is to use service management as a strategic asset, it must understand what its customers want or need, and then provide a service that meets those needs. However, the level of service agreed must be achievable, so it must be carefully planned. In other words: you need a strategy.

Creating a Strategy for Your Services: Strategy Management for IT Services

Many IT organisations gleefully carry on providing the same services to their customers day by day, month by month, year by year, without considering whether they're doing the right thing. Are you providing the right services? Are you providing them in the best way? What are the alternatives? Why do customers want the services? Do your customers really think they get value from your services? I wonder whether you or the managers of your IT organisation can answer these questions – truthfully.

You may be thinking: 'Well, our users and customers never complain.' But does this necessarily mean that you and your organisation are doing the right thing? Does it mean there's no room for improvement? I doubt it.

One way of ensuring that you're providing the right services to the right people is to have a *strategy:* a high-level plan to achieve something (or, in ITIL speak, a plan designed to achieve defined objectives). To get a strategy you have to investigate your customer's needs, understand whether you can provide services to meet those needs, and then put the necessary plans and resources in place to provide the service that meets your customer's needs. Simple.

ITIL describes a process called strategy management for IT services, which provides details of how to go about developing a strategy. I don't have room to explain all the details of the strategy management for IT services process here, but I highlight a few points in the following sections to give you a flavour of what is involved.

Carrying out a strategic assessment

The first thing you should do when developing a strategy is to carry out an assessment of the current situation. This can include the assessment of many things:

- ✔ **Assessing the internal environment:** Assess your organisation as an IT provider, identifying the organisation's strengths and weaknesses and reviewing existing services, their cost and *return on investment* (ROI).

  One important area is to identify those things that are distinctive about your organisation: things that can be used as differentiators. These may be capabilities, resources or core competencies. This is where you start to understand what your organisation is good at. For example, your organisation may be good at providing highly reliable systems or good quality applications. On the other hand, you may have expert staff who can design specialist services to suit customers' needs. You're looking for the things that provide a distinctiveness: in other words, the areas in which you exceed your competitors (or the alternatives; if you're an internal IT provider you probably don't have direct competitors, but this doesn't mean you aren't in competition, because internal providers compete with the possibility of being outsourced).

- ✔ **Assessing the external environment:** Assess factors that are outside your organisation: things that may or may not affect you. These can often be constraints such as legislation or regulatory requirements, or can be opportunities such as emerging markets.

- ✔ **Defining market spaces:** Identify opportunities for a service provider to provide value to customers: the matching of customer needs to provider's products. If I want to sell a spade, I need to find someone who wants to dig a hole. Simple. However, in the business of providing IT services, it's a little more complicated. I describe more about market spaces later in this chapter in the section 'Defining Services'.

✔ **Establishing the strategic objectives:** Identify the things you want to achieve. Based on the assessment, you should be able to identify a number of things that the organisation wants to achieve over the next period. After you identify some objectives, you need a strategy for how you're going to achieve them.

Generating strategy

There are two threads to building a strategy; deciding what your organisation should do and understanding how your services support your customer's business. I cover the second of these in the forthcoming section 'Defining Services'. You address the first with a well-established approach to developing strategy, sometimes known as the four Ps of strategy: perspective, position, plans and patterns. This is a general approach and not one that's unique to ITIL. Here's a quick look at the four Ps of service strategy.

Determining perspective

Perspective refers to your overall vision from the point of view of your organisation. It defines an IT provider's overall direction, values, beliefs and purpose. It can also include a high-level description of how you intend to achieve this vision. It's similar to setting a mission or vision for your organisation describing what you want to achieve.

A good perspective has four main purposes:

✔ Clarify the direction of the service provider.

✔ Motivate people to take action that moves the organisation to make the vision a reality.

✔ Coordinate the actions of different people or groups.

✔ Represent the view of senior management as they direct the organisation towards its overall objectives.

Your perspective can start from a very simple statement. For example, you may want to be 'the IT provider of choice', or 'number one IT services provider in the UK'. This is the starting point for your strategy; all your plans focus on achieving this aim.

Forming a position

Position refers to how you want to be seen as a service provider. It's a bit like deciding what your *unique selling point* (USP) is. You may want to be seen as the cheapest, the fastest, the highest quality. However, your position must be consistent with your perspective.

Your position should be based on the output of your strategic assessment (see the earlier section 'Carrying out a strategic assessment'). It should take advantage of your strengths and any distinctive capabilities that were identified. Your position shows how your organisation can be differentiated from competitors or from the alternative. It should be able to answer the question 'Why should I get services from you?'

Crafting a plan

You need strategic plans that identify how your organisation achieves its objective, vision and position. Of course, your plans must be clearly documented and should describe a deliberate course of action. For example, if you want to be seen as the most friendly service provider, how will you achieve this? This may include training staff or implementing new processes.

Adopting patterns of action

Patterns refer to the patterns of action, or activities, that your organisation carries out, and how you want them to be performed. You must get some sort of structure in place so that things are done the way you want them in order to achieve your strategic objective. This can include creating or changing organisational structures, policies, processes, procedures, budgets, schedules and so on, as necessary.

For example a pattern may be what gives your customers the right impression, the impression that supports your organisation's position. So, if your position is for your organisation to be seen as the most friendly service provider, you need to be sure that your staff habitually behave in a friendly manner.

The service management processes can provide a lot of the guidance required to implement patterns. So you should document plans and policies for all service lifecycle stages that are consistent with the patterns you need to achieve your strategic objectives.

Executing strategy

After you've created your strategy, you must implement it. You often implement strategies as a set of projects grouped as a programme. You should then create a set of tactical plans to introduce into your organisation initiatives and activities that enable your strategy. *Continual service improvement* (CSI; see Chapter 9) will be involved in initiating and managing individual improvements that further your strategy.

To implement your strategy, you must ensure that you have the right assets in place, especially those that will be used to your strategic advantage. You achieve a large part of your service strategy by implementing new or changed services, so the next step is to think harder about the strategic assets required to deliver the services. Here are some examples:

- **Applications:** A set of software applications that can be easily matched to customer needs

- **Knowledge:** Staff with a better understanding of designing specialist storage systems

- **Processes:** Processes that enable a provider to respond more quickly to user issues

You must also think about how the services you provide help the customers make better use of their assets. Assets are usually resources and capabilities, and include things like people, infrastructure, information, knowledge and processes. How will your IT services enable your customers to use less of these, or to use them more efficiently? Maybe you can provide an IT service that allows sales orders to be completed by unskilled staff, thus saving your customers the money associated with maintaining highly skilled staff.

In order to execute your strategy, you must put your strategic plans into action. This may include developing new services, employing new staff, acquiring new infrastructure components. To do this, you may have to acquire the resources to put your strategy into action, or make plans to acquire the resources.

Strategies are often implemented using a programme of activities, usually many projects. In the case of service management, the strategy will be implemented by developing or modifying your IT services. It's unlikely that this happens all in one go, in fact in some cases it can take years. The service portfolio management process (see Chapter 4) is very important to the implementation of your strategy. On the assumption that your strategy involves acquiring a set of services that will fulfil the needs of your customers, these services will be added to the service portfolio. The introduction of the services is then managed by the service portfolio management process: each service is added to the service pipeline, and as services are approved and chartered they move through the service pipeline and make their way to the service catalogue as they approach deployment.

Defining Services

An IT provider can only provide the appropriate IT services to the business if it understands what services are required and why they are needed. Imagine you're starting from scratch, and ask yourself who your customers are and what IT services you can offer them. This allows you to define the complete set of IT services – the service portfolio – that you want to provide to all your customers.

Your strategy provides a framework for defining, analysing, approving and chartering services and changes to services, using the service portfolio management process, which I overview in Chapter 4.

The ITIL service strategy book provides a lot of detail about defining services, and offers eight steps, which I describe briefly in the following sections. You usually do these activities at the same time as generating your strategy; they are complementary activities.

Step 1: Defining the market and identifying customers

The first step to defining the market is deciding what type of service provider your organisation is. I describe the three IT service provider types in Chapter 2.

Types I and II are internal providers, providing IT services to other parts of the same company. You need to establish whether in these cases money changes hands. Your first reaction may be that internal IT departments don't charge money for their IT services, but some do. So you need to find out whether the IT department is there to provide services for free, to recover the costs, or to make a profit. Some organisations start out as internal service providers and then realise that there is a market for them to sell services outside their company; they change from a type I or II provider to a type III provider. Knowing what money is available is essential to understanding who you can sell services to.

Type III providers are commercial organisations that provide services in exchange for money. So in theory the market in this case is anyone or any organisation in the whole wide world. Or possibly not.

So having thought about the type of provider you are, the next thing to do is identify who your customers are – often referred to as *defining the market*. A *market* is a collection of customers or potential customers who have something in common. The thing they have in common is that they may want to obtain services from you. If you sell beer, then your market is everybody who drinks beer. If you sell TVs, then your market is everyone who watches TV. But the scope of both these examples is a bit broad, so perhaps I should narrow things down a bit: for example, everyone who watches TV in my area who has £500 to spare and who wants to buy a new TV.

So in service management terms, an IT service provider must decide what its target market is. If the IT provider is a commercial company providing IT services in exchange for money, it must decide its target market. This may include organisations with similar business outcomes; for example, companies that want to calculate their company finances without owning software.

Step 2: Understanding the customer

To adapt a well-known saying, value is in the eye of the beholder. The value your IT services provide to the customer depends on how well the services support the business objectives or outcomes. These business outcomes should form the basic criteria for measuring the success of your services. They provide a benchmark for providers to use throughout the design, development and deployment of services to ensure they provide the service the customer needs.

Consider the sales department in an organisation, a department that is critical to the success of the business – no sales, no profit! The sales department has asked the IT department to replace its existing IT system – a system that records and tracks sales orders. The sales department states that its main criterion or business outcome for the new system is the ability to create a new sales order in half the time of the current system. For argument's sake, say the new target is to produce a sales order in ten minutes. So, this is the business outcome and the starting point for the identification or design of the service. Are you happy that the success of the IT department as regards this new system should be based on this target? I accept that you need a lot more information and clarity, but I do think this is a good, business-focused objective.

Step 3: Quantifying the outcomes

In this step you consider how the business outcomes that customers need can be achieved. You must get a more detailed view of the value of the service in terms of utility and warranty. (If you want to know more about utility and warranty, have a look in Chapter 2.) Table 11-1 outlines some examples.

Table 11-1	Value in Terms of Utility and Warranty	
Business Outcome	*Utility*	*Warranty*
Create a sales order in ten minutes	Collect and process details of sales orders	Available for use in working hours by a maximum of 100 staff at any one time, securely maintaining records of transactions.
Calculate the company's staff wages	Calculate monthly salary payments for staff, print payslips and maintain records	Available for use from 9 a.m. to 5 p.m. Monday to Friday. Critical period is the third Thursday of each month, when availability must be 99.9%.

Group business outcomes by *critical success factors* (CSFs; I discuss these in Chapter 9). By identifying factors that are critical to a number of potential customers, you can concentrate on developing services that can fulfil these CSFs.

The result of quantifying the outcomes is to gain a better understanding of your customers in order to identify the opportunities that you can fulfil by providing IT services. For example, you may identify a customer's need to improve its decision-making or perform faster business transactions.

Step 4: Classifying and visualising the service

It's much easier to define services if you can group, or classify, them in some way. This helps you understand how you can achieve the required levels of utility and warranty to achieve the business outcome.

For example, if you provide *software as a service* (SaaS), which is providing access for customers to software applications over the Internet on infrastructure that you provide, then you know that your infrastructure must be secure and that performance is very important. You can then define outline levels of utility and warranty for every SaaS you provide.

Step 5: Understanding the opportunities (market spaces)

From the previous steps you gain an understanding of your customers and their business outcomes and an understanding of the IT services you could provide. Now you decide what you are good at. Or, more importantly, what opportunities there are for you to support customers' business outcomes with your IT services. This helps you understand which type of market spaces (groups of customers) to specialise in – in other words, where your organisation's skills and capabilities can be used to best advantage.

Step 6: Defining services based on outcomes

This is where you go into more detail and create a greater understanding of the services needed to fulfil your chosen business outcomes.

For example, you may choose to fulfil business outcomes for customers that require highly available services. High availability means that you need many different reliable infrastructure components to build resilience into the service and therefore add cost. Similarly, you may need specialist skill and knowledge to design such services. So from the understanding of customer needs, you can now build up an understanding of the components and the service required to support them.

Step 7: Defining service models

ITIL defines a *service model* as a model that shows how service assets interact with customer assets to create value. These models describe the structure of a service, that is the components and how they fit together, and the dynamics of the service, in other words the activities and interactions that the service supports. A service model is a bit like a blueprint or a template for the service.

Service models are the starting point for designing services. They provide an insight into how the service can deliver value, and help provide an understanding of the costs and issues associated with delivering the service.

Step 8: Defining service units and packages

The final step in defining services is to decide how to package up various services and present them to the customer. For example, in some cases, rather than provide a customer with three separate software applications, they are bundled into one service that the customer perceives as a single entity. We are all used to word-processing and spreadsheet software being combined into an office suite of applications.

Services can also be packaged differently depending on the level of service required. You may have heard people talk about gold, silver and bronze support packages – customers pay different amounts according to the type of package.

So, once you have an understanding of the services you want to offer your customers, you must decide the most appropriate or perhaps attractive way of forming them into service units and service packages.

Working through Examples

To help you understand the information I provide in the previous sections, here are a couple of examples. One is for an internal IT provider, the second for an external IT provider.

Internal provider example

An internal service provider in Dummies Bank serves many different business units from a single corporate IT organisation. The executive management of Dummies Bank recently stated that as part of the company's aggressive strategy to increase profit and drive down costs, each business unit may acquire IT services from wherever it chooses and is not obliged to use the corporate IT department. This has prompted the IT organisation to assess its strategy.

Assessing

The first thing Dummies Bank does is carry out a SWOT (*strengths, weaknesses, opportunities, threats*) analysis of its IT provider. SWOT is a simple, well-known technique for assessing both the internal and external environment of an organisation. The findings are:

✔ **Strengths:** The IT services are reliable with good availability.

✔ **Weaknesses:** The business customers don't perceive that they get value for money from the IT organisation, and believe they can get IT cheaper by outsourcing.

✔ **Opportunities:** Consolidating services across the business units and creating efficiencies can reduce the cost of providing the services.

✔ **Threats:** The business sees outsourcing as a way of improving the IT services.

This is a very simple SWOT analysis; I expect a real one to have many more points.

As part of the assessment, the IT organisation assesses the type of IT provider that it is. Even though the IT organisation is an internal provider, it can still choose to offer services to customers outside Dummies Bank. However, given the current situation, it decides it will stick to internal provision, and recognises that it is a type II service provider. In doing this, the Dummies Bank IT organisation has also defined its market spaces: it has decided to provide services to its internal customers (business units), and provide them with the sort of services that the bank needs.

The final part of the assessment is for the IT organisation to decide its strategic objectives. Here are some examples:

✔ Create a set of core services to meet the agreed needs of all business units by the end of next year.

✔ Consolidate supporting services and reduce the cost of providing supporting services in nine months.

✔ Increase customer satisfaction with the IT service by 25 per cent by the end of next year.

Generating strategy

Having carried out a strategic assessment, the next step for the IT organisation of Dummies Bank is to create a strategy for how to achieve the strategic objectives. As described in 'Generating strategy', earlier in this chapter, the best way to do this is to use the four Ps of service strategy:

✔ **Perspective:** Dummies Bank's IT organisation decides that its perspective is to be 'the IT provider of choice within Dummies Bank'. It believes it can do this by achieving the strategic objectives it identified in the strategic review.

✓ **Position:** The IT organisation has reviewed the needs of the customer (the business units) and considered the customer's business outcomes. In order to be the IT provider of choice, it recognises the need to provide highly available and highly reliable services. It also recognises the fact that the IT organisation has a good understanding of Dummies Bank's business activities. So these are the areas in which the IT organisation needs to excel.

✓ **Plans:** The plans are to review the portfolio of services and identify those where improving availability is a positive improvement. To compensate, the IT organisation looks for services that are over-achieving and identifies possible efficiency savings. Plans will be introduced to continue IT staff training to increase understanding of the bank's business activities.

✓ **Patterns:** Advantageous behaviours have been identified among specialised service-desk and first-line-support staff who understand the most critical services and are able to respond to incidents in short timescales. Incident and problem management processes, along with service desk procedures, will be reviewed and updated to ensure a consistent approach to support and to aim to increase customer satisfaction.

These are simple examples, and the real strategy would contain much more information.

External provider example

Dummies Outsourcing markets itself as a software as a service (SaaS) IT provider. In this case, the SaaS provider must provide the infrastructure and a means of hosting the software application. In general, Dummies Outsourcing currently only provides software applications; its clients store their own data.

The company has noticed the current trend towards cloud computing. *Cloud computing* takes SaaS a step forward: it enables customers to use an IT service on demand via the Internet or private network. So in this case, the cloud provider provides the software application, stores the data, and provides the infrastructure that runs the application; the customer simply uses an Internet browser to access the service. A simple example is the websites that allow you to upload and store your photographs.

The trend towards cloud computing has prompted Dummies Outsourcing to assess its strategy.

Assessing

Dummies Outsourcing has performed a SWOT analysis. Here are the findings:

- **Strengths:** Good reputation for providing easy-to-use software applications.
- **Weaknesses:** Limited number and scope of software applications.
- **Opportunities:** Increasing demand for complete IT solutions available over the Internet.
- **Threats:** Increase in the number of IT providers that deliver cloud solutions.

This is a simplified SWOT analysis, but you get the idea.

Dummies Outsourcing has assessed its market space and considered who its customers are. It has defined its customers as those that need relatively cheap, easy-to-use software applications and solutions on demand.

The final part of the assessment is to decide Dummies Outsourcing's strategic objectives. Here are some examples:

- Create a set of cloud solutions to meet customer needs by the end of next year.
- Re-launch the company as a cloud solution provider within 12 months.

Generating strategy

Having carried out a strategic assessment, Dummies Outsourcing now creates a strategy in order to achieve the strategic objectives using the four Ps of service strategy (which I introduce in the earlier section 'Generating strategy'):

- **Perspective:** Dummies Outsourcing wants to reposition itself as the cloud solution provider of choice.
- **Position:** In order to achieve this perspective, Dummies Outsourcing will trade on its reputation as a reliable supplier of software applications and provide easy-to-use complete solutions with reliable supporting infrastructure and storage services.
- **Plans:** The company's plan is to create a set of new cloud services based on existing applications as well as new solutions, in order to re-market its services as cloud services.
- **Patterns:** Retraining of staff is necessary to move them away from selling just software usage to complete cloud solutions.

These four Ps are simplistic, and the real strategy would contain much more detail.

Using Service Portfolio Management to Implement Your Strategy

When you have a strategy in place, you must be sure to stick to it. I've heard many stories of organisations spending time and money on developing a strategy only to ignore it when a new, exciting technical development comes along.

The service portfolio management process (which I introduce in Chapter 4) not only provides a way to define your services, but also provides a process for analysing every new proposal or request for a new service or change to a service. Requests can come in many shapes and forms and may include requests for change from business relationship managers. However, imagine that a request has been received from a customer to provide a service. What will you do?

Have you already got a suitable service?

You may already have a suitable service. So you need to define the business outcomes that the customer wants to achieve, and look for a service that can support these outcomes:

- ✔ **Using the service catalogue:** The service catalogue (see Chapter 5) is a great mechanism for matching services to the needs of your customers. It should provide details of all your live services and those available for deployment. When a new request comes along, take a look in your service catalogue to see whether you already have a suitable service.

  You need to have suitable information in the service catalogue. Therefore, make sure your service catalogue contains information about the business outcomes that are supported by each service.

- ✔ **Matching services to outcomes:** If the service isn't in the service catalogue, look in other parts of your service portfolio. There may be a suitable service in the service pipeline – the services that are currently in development. You can also look in the retired services section of the service portfolio. You may have a service that you decommissioned due to lack of demand; maybe the new requirement makes this service financially viable.

Using the activities of service portfolio management

If new work is required to modify or develop a service then you need to follow a few steps. These are basically the activities of service portfolio management described in Chapter 4, that is:

- ✔ **Business case:** Create a business case for the new or changed service that describes the benefits of the service and the costs of developing and delivering the service.

- ✔ **Demand management:** Consider the risks associated with the demand for the service. Consider what the business need for the service is and understand how the business will use the service. If you don't have a clear understanding of the frequency, duration and volume of use of the IT service, you may end up buying pieces of expensive equipment or acquiring specialised resources only to discover that they are not used. Investigating this issue uses the demand management process that I explain in Chapter 4. There is also some more detail coming up in the section 'Getting to Grips with Demand Management'.

- ✔ **Financial management for IT services:** The business case must have a good financial justification. The powers that be review the business case to see whether there is a good ROI; in other words, is it a sound investment financially speaking? Making this decision uses the financial management for IT services process (see Chapter 4).

- ✔ **Making a decision:** The approval step in the service portfolio management process involves senior management making a decision. Usually there is only a limited budget to be spent on making changes to services or developing new services, so the money must be spent wisely. Senior management use the activities of the service portfolio management process to compare investment proposals and choose which to go for. This decision includes the risk involved in meeting demand for the service and the financial viability of the service.

Getting to Grips with Demand Management

I describe demand management in Chapter 4. In this section I go into a little bit more detail and describe how an understanding of demand for your services helps you assess the risks involved in investing in a service.

Demand management identifies and models how the business uses the IT services. You then use the information in the service design (see Chapters 5 and 6) to ensure supply meets demand.

Figure11-1 shows how you can model the business use of a service. The graph shows the sales department activity over one day. This represents the sales department demand for an IT service. You can see that activity peaks mid morning, when the majority of the organisation's external customers ring up to place orders. Things quieten down at lunchtime, and another peak occurs in the afternoon. This represents the amount of activity in the sales department on a typical day. This demand will most likely translate into use of the sales IT service that is used for taking and processing orders from customers. The IT department must ensure that it can match supply to demand: there must be enough processing power, network bandwidth and disk storage to cope with the number of orders processed.

The wiggly line represents a *pattern of business activity* (PBA). I define the PBAs in Chapter 4.

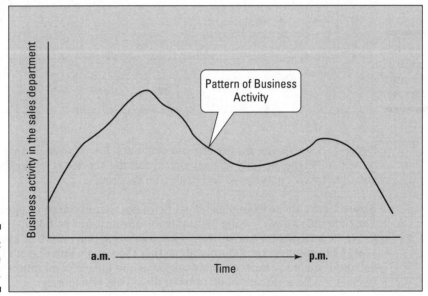

Figure 11-1:
Example
PBA.

So, if the wiggly line represents the demand, where do you put the supply line? The supply line represents the IT capacity needed to fulfil the demand. For argument's sake, please assume that the supply line must be flat and level and can't vary. The next couple of figures show some examples of where you can put the supply line, and the consequence.

Figure 11-2 shows the supply line put at the highest peak. In this case you're left with a lot of unused capacity for most of the day. Unused capacity costs you money, with the consequence that you spend too much and upset your boss.

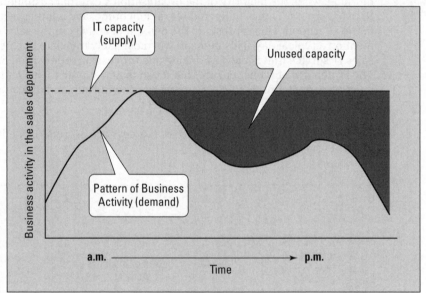

Figure 11-2:
Example of under-used capacity.

Figure 11-3 shows the supply line put at a much lower point. In this case you have insufficient capacity at busy times, and the service runs slowly. Now you upset your customers. You can't win, can you!

Before I leave these examples I must point out that I've kept things simple. The timescale shown on the picture is for one day, but you'd have to perform the same analysis for the patterns over one week, one month or even one year. Also, you may be shouting at me that the supply line doesn't have to be flat and horizontal. Indeed. There are ways and means of adapting the supply to meet the demand, although most of them cost you money.

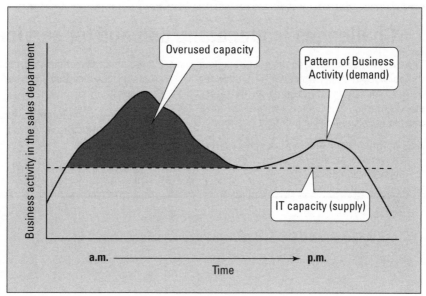

Figure 11-3:
Example of
over-used
capacity.

In conclusion, although I may have oversimplified things, the basic principle remains: you must understand your customer's pattern of usage in order to provide an IT service to meet its needs.

So what has any of this got to do with service strategy? Well, suppose the PBA in Figures 11-1 to 11-3 now represents the *predicted* demand for a new IT service. Senior management must decide whether to invest in this new service. In others words, they want to know whether, once the money has been spent on developing the service, it'll earn enough income to cover their costs. What would your advice be? I think the answer is 'it depends'. It depends on how predictable the PBA is. If I'm told with great certainty that the customer will use the service in the same way every day and their usage is very predictable, I'm inclined to say 'yes, invest'. The risk of spending the money and the service not being used is low. On the other hand, if I'm told that the pattern is only a rough estimate and is highly likely to change, I advise against investing. The risk of spending the money and the service not being used is very high.

An understanding of patterns of business activity is a key input to investment decision-making. The service portfolio management process assesses the business case for major investments in IT services. Through service portfolio management you ensure that all investments are in line with your strategy for maintaining a set of IT services that meet the needs of your customers.

Challenges in managing demand for services

You carry out demand management throughout the service lifecycle. However, ITIL includes demand management in the service strategy stage of the lifecycle because of its importance and the consequences of getting it wrong:

✔ Poorly managed demand is a source of risk for service providers because of uncertainty in demand.

✔ Excess capacity generates cost without creating value that provides a basis for cost recovery.

✔ Customers are reluctant to pay for idle capacity unless it has value for them.

Chapter 12

Going Back to the Drawing Board: Design Projects

....

In This Chapter

▶ Understanding how the service design processes work in practice

▶ Seeing how ITIL fits with service design projects

▶ Seeing a service design project in action

....

Many organisations carry out a lot of the activities of the service design and service transition stages as projects. In this chapter I look at service design projects. (Chapter 13 covers service transition projects.) Here I use examples to show the relationship between the ITIL guidance, projects and the service operation functions.

In this chapter I bring together the concepts of the service design stage in the service lifecycle (which I cover in Chapters 5 and 6) with the ITIL processes that are most relevant at this stage. More often than not, the requirements and design activities of a service are performed as part of a project, or even as a project in its own right. (Chapter 10 gives you the low-down on projects and how you use them to implement the service lifecycle.) This chapter contains advice on how you use the service design processes in practice.

Seeing What Happens in a Service Design Project

As you can see in Chapters 5 and 6, the service design stage includes the activities associated with the requirements and design of the service. I now take a closer look at the core activities you carry out in a service design project. Chapter 3 describes the relationship between the service lifecycle and development projects (Figure 3-2 is particularly useful).

Gathering and analysing requirements

After a service has been chartered or a change requested, you need to get a clear understanding of the requirements. The business case, which I explain in Chapter 4, is a major input to this stage and includes the business requirements. These should be adequate enough to estimate the effort and resource required to develop the new or changed service. It is very unusual for detailed requirements to be established at the business case stage, because it's a costly and time-consuming task to gather and analyse requirements. So now's the time to put flesh on the bones.

The gathering and analysis of requirements is often done by business analysts or requirements engineers. They gather all the requirements of the IT service, including the functional and non-functional requirements. The result is usually a requirements specification which is signed off by the business as a true description of what is required.

Business analysis/requirements engineering

It is important to have a structured approach to identifying requirements. Requirements engineering is a discipline in itself, and many sources of guidance and qualifications are available in this area. The ITIL books briefly cover this area. Here are some important points:

- **Identifying stakeholders:** A *stakeholder* is anyone who has an interest in, or is affected by, the thing that you are doing. So in terms of requirements engineering, you must identify anyone who is associated with the service you're developing. After you identify and list all the stakeholders for the service, you develop a plan of attack for getting their requirements for the service. If you overlook a stakeholder or talk to the wrong stakeholder, you end up with an incorrect or incomplete set of requirements.

- **Gathering requirements:** There are many ways of collecting requirements from stakeholders. Obviously you should go and talk to them; however, there are other ways that may be more appropriate in some situations. This is not the place to go into detail, but methods of gathering requirements include workshops, observation, questionnaires, document gathering and analysis, and prototyping.

- **Documenting requirements:** As requirements are gathered, they must be documented. The most common term you hear is *requirements catalogue:* a catalogue of requirements that is a central repository for all the requirements for a given service or system and is version controlled.

In many cases a spreadsheet is a good way to record the requirements.

Types of requirements

There are many types of requirements, and at the point of gathering requirements all must be treated with equal importance. However, as you move on to the design of the service, it can be helpful to categorise the requirements into groups that are relevant to people who have to design and build the various parts of the service:

- **Functional requirements:** These tell you what the service must do. For example, the basic functional requirement of an email service is to send and receive messages. Without this ability, it would be a fairly useless system. You go into much more detail than this, including a description of what each screen or part of a software application does. For example, the sales service will require a 'customer input screen'. The functional requirements here include a description of the fields that appear on the screen, the calculations or manipulations the application must perform, and the output, in other words what appears on the screen when the user has finished. Roughly speaking, the utility of a service is related to its functionality. These types of requirements are usually of most use to the application developers who create the software application.

- **Management and operational requirements:** Often known as the non-functional requirements of a service, these don't describe what the service does, but they describe how well it will do it. These requirements often put constraints on the system: demands such as how fast the service must operate, who is allowed to use it, and so on. There are many types of management and operational requirements, but the ones that are most relevant to service management are those that equate to service levels: availability, capacity (including performance), continuity and security. These are often known as the *warranty* requirements. (Chapter 6 focuses on warranty.) Generally speaking, these requirements are needed by those that build the physical system hardware as well as the software application developers.

- **Usability requirements:** These refer to ease of use, or what is often called user friendliness. In other words, how easy it is for the user to use the service, whether the software application is intuitive to use, whether lots of training is required, and so on. In general, these requirements, along with the functional requirements, are of most use to the application developers who create the software application.

Designing solutions

Having collected the requirements (see the previous section 'Gathering and analysing requirements'), you need to design a solution to meet these

requirements. Designing IT services is a complex task taking many requirements into account. Specialist staff are required, depending on the technical
needs of the solutions.

In Chapter 5, I describe the many aspects that you consider during the design
phase, including:

✔ Designing the overall service solution including the hardware, software
and support

✔ Determining the need for, and acquiring or developing, service management systems and tools

✔ Ensuring the technology architecture and management systems are in
place to support the design of the infrastructure, data and environments

✔ Designing the service management processes

✔ Designing a structure to collate the right measurements and metrics to
provide the necessary visibility and ability to control the service and the
service management processes

The following sections focus on designing the service solution, considering
service and system architecture, and developing applications.

Designing the service solution

The *service solution* refers to the new or changed service. Designing the solution can include designing some or all of the following:

✔ **Software applications:** The software application that provides the basic
functionality of the service and presents the front end of the service to
the user. Software developers will be involved in creating the detailed
design of the application based on the requirements gathered by business analysts.

✔ **Infrastructure:** For example, the IT hardware and networks, and any
system software such as operating systems. This may include servers,
networks, storage, databases, operating systems, messaging protocols
and software agents.

✔ **Data:** The data and database structure for storing and handling the data
that is collected, manipulated and output by the service. The requirements of data are usually inextricably linked with the functional requirements of the service or software application.

✔ **Support:** The operational requirements such as how the service will be
delivered and supported on a day-to-day basis. Support includes the
skills, processes and resources required to ensure that the service is
operating correctly and can be recovered in the event of a failure.

✔ **Physical environment:** The data centres, computer rooms and so on,
including the air-conditioning systems and the power supplies.

Considering system architecture

There is a growing need for flexible and adaptable solutions, and to provide new systems and services as quickly as possible to customers. One way of achieving this is to adopt a modular approach to the design of your services. This often means that your IT service consists of sub-services that in turn consist of sub-sub-services (if there are such things), and so on.

A service may consist of a network service, a processing service, a storage service and a database service. Each is designed as a service in its own right then, when a new service is required, these building blocks can be joined together to form a service.

An ever-increasing number of technical advancements support this concept and make it easier to be more flexible. However, they come with a greater need for forward planning and good design. Much of this concept has been around for a while and is encapsulated in something known as *service oriented architecture*.

You may be familiar with server or data centre virtualisation. This allows multiple software environments to be created on a single physical hardware server, thus making better use of resources. Computer servers themselves are often built in clusters or using blade servers (servers that are stripped down to their essential components so that many can be fitted into a smaller space, thus using less power and being easier to add and remove), which contributes to more resilient server design and makes more efficient use of resources. In terms of data storage, storage area networks enable storage solutions to be designed independently and are able to be expanded or contracted as necessary to meet changing needs.

All of this contributes to the ever-more-popular concept of cloud computing. A *cloud* is the name given to an invisible IT network and infrastructure, a bit like the Internet. Suppose you store your photographs on an Internet site or back up your data to a virtual file store; you don't know where the physical computer equipment is, you just trust the provider to look after it for you. These are examples of putting things into a cloud. The cloud provider needs to ensure that it has an extremely robust set of systems, and the concepts I describe here are essential to providing such a service.

The point is that you must have a set of architectures that tell you how all these technical bits and bobs join together. In this way, an architecture can act as a long-term plan.

Building an architecture is similar to building a new bookshelf. Perhaps you've taken up a new hobby or interest and you know that over the next few years you'll build up quite a collection of books. You may deliberately build the bookshelf too big with lots of spare space in it. Not only that, but you leave one section the right size for big books and another for small books. Then as you obtain more books you pop them in place. Planning your technical architecture is the same in that you plan the blank spaces for more processor capability or more storage capacity and then fill it up when you need it.

Developing applications

When it comes to designing the software application, there are lots of concepts and methodologies out there. A couple of approaches you may have heard mentioned are *rapid application development* (RAD) and agile methods – these are development methodologies that share the ability to deliver software applications in short timescales. Traditional application development methodologies suggest that you gather *all* the requirements for an application, then design *all* the functionality of the application and then build and deploy *all* the modules of the application. This can take a long time. And in the past, when IT organisations had eventually implemented a new service, the business no longer needed or wanted it because the business had changed!

RAD and agile methods break the development down into bite-size chunks. A certain amount of work is required up front to get the overall business requirements of the application, but then the detailed requirements, design and development are broken down into smaller parts, each of which delivers an amount of functionality to the business. This leads to several releases of the application, deployed at shorter intervals, and each delivering more functionality. This results in the business getting the service more quickly.

Bringing Together ITIL and Service Design Projects

The previous section gave an overview of a service design project and some of the activities involved. You may have noticed that there was very little mention of the ITIL service management processes. Now is the time to explain where these fit in. In this section I show how the ITIL service design processes are coordinated and work together. The processes are not just a disparate bunch of activities; they must work together and complement each other.

Following the design process

Figure 12-1 shows some of the requirements and design activities I describe in the previous section, to which I have added some activities that are performed as part of the service management processes. Please note that this is simply an example, is not prescriptive, and may be different in your organisation.

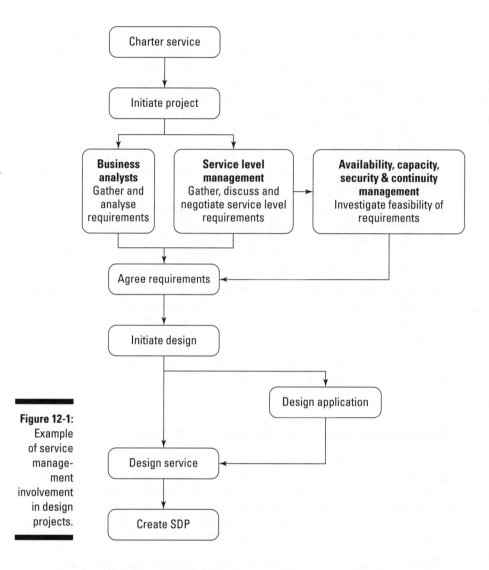

Figure 12-1:
Example
of service
manage-
ment
involvement
in design
projects.

Here's the process broken into steps:

1. **The business relationship manager liaises with the customer and identifies that the customer has a new requirement.** A business case is created (see Chapter 4), service portfolio management (see Chapter 4)
   facilitates the approval of the business case, and then the service is
   chartered. This is when the project is initiated and the design coordination process gets involved to plan the work and coordinate the design
   activities.

2. **The detailed functional requirements are gathered.** The team or individual that does business analysis or requirements engineering in your

organisation performs this step. These analysts often gather the non-functional requirements at the same time as all other requirements.

It is important that there is a trigger to involve the service level management process. The service level manager documents and analyses the service level requirements (SLRs: see Chapter 5) and triggers other service management processes to establish whether the service level requirements are achievable or not. It is often the case that some design work is needed in order to understand what is involved in achieving the SLRs. The technical teams will identify what is required and liaise with the financial management for IT services process to calculate the costs of the new service.

3. **The requirements are agreed and the design work starts.** The software application will be designed by a combination of application management and application development. The infrastructure parts of the service (hardware, networks, system software, databases) will be designed by technical management teams.

4. **The design coordination process produces a *service design package* (SDP).** The package contains all the design documents along with the requirements and the estimates of cost, and is the main output of the service design stage. (See Chapter 5 for more about SDPs.)

Each ITIL process that is involved in these activities has its own flow of activities, as the following sections illustrate.

Coordinating the design processes

There's quite a lot of activity described in the list in the last section, and more detail to come in the next sections. How can you be sure that everything will be done in the way it is intended and nothing will be overlooked or forgotten? Answer: the design coordination process, which I describe in Chapter 5. This process covers all the activities required to ensure that all activities are performed correctly. This will include:

✔ Maintaining policies, standards and guidelines and ensuring they are used

✔ Planning the resources needed for service design activities

✔ Ensuring the production of the SDP from documents and inputs provided by the application and technical teams involved in the design activities

ITIL and requirements

Two processes are especially relevant to the requirements phase of a design project: service level management and supplier management.

Service level management

Service level management, which I explain in Chapter 5, is a key process in the requirements stage of design projects. Figure 12-2 shows an example of a process flow for service level management. Service level management performs many activities and is likely to have several different process flows. This example flow is triggered by the need to gather new requirements.

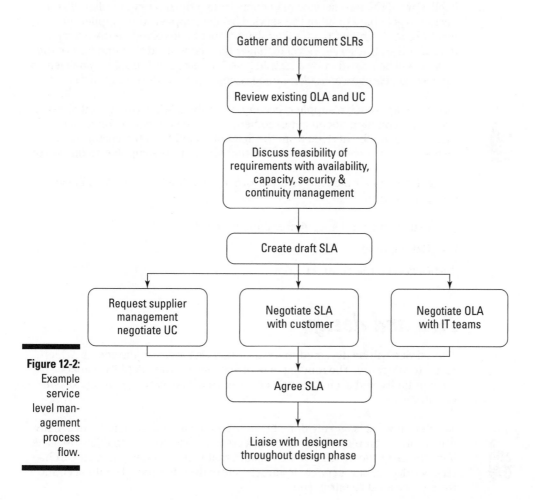

Figure 12-2: Example service level management process flow.

Service level management gathers and negotiates the service levels with the customer. The critical part of this process is to establish whether the service levels are achievable, by liaising with the staff who know.

Once the IT teams have agreed that the service levels are feasible, it's a good idea to get their agreement and create an *operational level agreement* (OLA). Similarly, establish whether your supplier can supply its services to meet the proposed service levels. This involves supplier management (see the next section).

Supplier management

It is often the case that your organisation doesn't provide all of the service itself. Part of the new service may come from a third-party supplier. If you decide to get some or all of the service from a supplier, the supplier management process, which Chapter 5 explains, must be involved. In the example in Figure 12-2, the service level manager has recognised that one part of the service will be provided by a supplier, so has asked the supplier management process to negotiate an *underpinning contract* (UC) with the supplier.

When you approach a supplier, be very clear about what you want it to do or provide. A common document used here is a *statement of requirements* (SOR). The SOR should be derived from the SLRs obtained from the customer, but includes a specification of just the bit that you want the supplier to do for you.

Typically, supplier management performs the following activities in new design projects:

- ✔ Establish whether a suitable supplier exists
- ✔ Get quotations
- ✔ Negotiate the contract

ITIL and design

The service will be designed to meet the service level requirements, which relate to warranty. The four aspects of warranty are availability, capacity, continuity and security, and I cover each of the warranty processes in Chapter 6.

The design work is usually done by your technical management teams. Many organisations employ technical architects and designers to do this work. The importance of the processes is to ensure that when the designers and architects work on a new service or infrastructure design, they take into account the service level requirements.

Figure 12-3 shows an example process flow for the warranty processes responding to a request to review new requirements. You will see that there is much similarity between the processes. This is of course only one example; you must create something to suit your organisation.

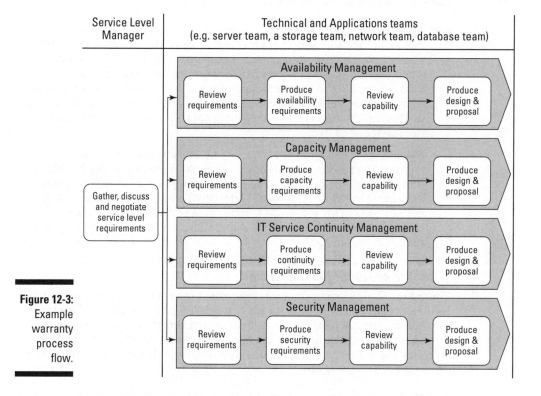

Figure 12-3: Example warranty process flow.

Availability management

In availability management, there are two aspects you take into account when designing the service or infrastructure:

✔ **Design for availability:** Design the service to be available, that is design the service to not fail. Well, perhaps a single component can fail, but you don't want the user to be aware of this. So, designing for availability includes building in resilience such that if one component fails, the service does not fail, and the user is blissfully unaware of any IT problems.

✔ **Design for recovery:** Design the service and your organisation to be able to restore the service as quickly as agreed in the *service level agreement* (SLA). This includes having the processes, spare parts and appropriate people in the right place at the right time so that you can get the service going again.

Capacity management

The role of capacity management in design is to ensure that there are enough IT resources for the number of users intended to use the service, and that the service runs fast enough when those users are using it. Two techniques of capacity management are particularly relevant here:

- ✔ **Application sizing:** Identify the size of the computer that runs the application. In the same way that you need to know the size of the present you have bought for your partner before you buy the box to put it in. So, when your application developers design the software application, they pass information to capacity management, who calculate how much processor power, network bandwidth and storage space are required to run it. This information is used to ensure that these resources exist before the service goes live.

- ✔ **Modelling:** Application sizing can sometimes be inaccurate, and to improve the resource estimates you can do some modelling. Nothing to do with fashion catwalks, *modelling* is testing under various scenarios, like saying 'what if . . .?'. What if I double the number of users: will the system cope? This gives you a better idea of how the application and service will run when it goes live, and therefore improves your application sizing estimates.

IT service continuity management

The role of IT service continuity management in design is to ensure that the business requirements for restoration of service in the event of a disaster are built into the design. This may involve checking that existing recovery arrangements are adequate and the new service can be added to existing recovery plans. On the other hand, a new recovery plan and mechanism may be required. You carry out:

- ✔ **Business impact analysis (BIA):** The analysis of the impact on the business of a disaster or event that prevents the business from operating normally. The IT department will work with the business to identify the business impact and hence the importance of the IT services that the business relies on. For new services, if the business impact is unknown, a BIA must be carried out.

- ✔ **Risk analysis:** The analysis of any risks to the IT service that may cause it to fail in a big way and lead to a major outage or disaster. For new services, if the risks are not known, an assessment must be carried out.

Information security management

Information security management (ISM) must ensure that the requirements of security are built into the design. ISM protects the interests of those relying on the information and data held in the IT services. So the information must not be corrupt, must only be shown to the people that need it, and must be available as and when required. ISM is responsible for assessing any risks to information security and building any new recommendations into the design.

Looking at an Example of a Service Design Project

Dummy Co. is a commercial IT service provider. Dummy Co. has implemented ITIL and allocated many of the service management roles to members of the technical teams, as Figure 12-4 illustrates.

	Dummy Co organisation					
	Commercial team		Service team		Technical management team	
ITIL roles	Account manager **(Henry)**	Finance manager	Service delivery manager **(Charlie)**	Supplier manager	Technical architect **(Fred)**	Technical engineers
Business relationship manager	✘					
Design coordination manager			✘			
Service level manager			✘			
Availablility manager					✘	
Capacity manager					✘	
Continuity manager					✘	
Security manager					✘	

Figure 12-4: Dummy Co. organisation.

An account manager has found a new customer. The account manager is Henry, and one of his roles is to act as the business relationship manager. The customer requires an invoicing service and doesn't want to acquire and run the system itself. It wants to utilise it as part of a cloud (see the earlier section 'Considering system architecture' for an explanation of a cloud) from a *software as a service* (SaaS) provider. This means that the users will access the invoicing service from their Internet browsers over a private Internet connection, and use Dummy Co's software application and hardware.

Henry has established the customer's business requirements. These have been reviewed using the service portfolio management process (see Chapter 4). Dummy Co. has an existing application that can be used to deliver the service, and this will fulfil most of the utility requirements. However, the warranty requirements are quite demanding and exceed any service levels offered to existing customers. A business case has been established and approved via service portfolio management with a little help from the financial management and demand management processes (see Chapter 4). There is a considerable *return on investment* (ROI) to be gained from the venture. The design project is initiated. Charlie is the service delivery manager, and she has been allocated the role of design coordination manager, so she takes charge of the project.

Henry has invited Charlie, who also acts as the service level manager, to a meeting with the customer to identify the service level requirements. The service level requirements are as follows:

✔ The service will be used at several locations worldwide, so it must be available 24/7, five days a week. Any single failure leading to loss of service at a site must be fixed within 30 minutes, and it will not break more than twice in any one week.

✔ The maximum number of people using the service at any one time is likely to be around 3,000. Because the users are spread across various sites, demand will not fluctuate much throughout the day. The response time of the system must be less than two seconds.

✔ As the service provider, you need to have appropriate disaster recovery facilities in place in the event that you have a disaster. As the customer, in the event that we have a disaster and want to relocate our staff, we require the ability for the service to be accessible at alternative locations in less than one hour.

✔ The data protection act requires us to protect our client's information. All invoice data must be protected and must be restorable in the event of a cyber-attack. Our data must be backed up and recoverable in the event that you suffer a security breach.

Charlie takes these requirements and documents them as the SLRs. She follows a process flow like the one in Figure 12-2. Charlie reviews the new requirements and compares them with the targets in the existing OLA and UC to see whether there are other services that are delivered to these service levels. If it turns out that these service levels have not been offered before, or there is doubt as to whether they can be achieved, then the technical designers must be consulted.

Well, Dummy Co.'s IT department has just one technical architect, and he is called Fred. Fred does what he always does when he has a new design project to get to grips with: he looks at the architecture of the infrastructure. He looks to see whether there is enough network equipment to cope with the additional load that the new service will need. He looks at the servers in the data centre to see whether there are enough of the right type. He looks at the data storage to see how much is in use. Pretty much what any technical architect would do.

However, Fred has many roles. For the projects that he undertakes, he performs the roles of availability manager, capacity manager, security manager and IT service continuity manager. So when he is reviewing the infrastructure, he takes the SLRs and looks at the requirements from the four warranty points of view. In fact, Fred takes the SLRs and converts them into detailed requirements for availability, capacity, continuity and security, and then considers the requirements in his musings. The work that Fred is doing is sometimes called a *capability review*. The results of this are that Fred produces an outline design and proposal of how the new requirements will be met. This of course comes at a cost, so Fred will obtain costs and quotes for any additional resources that are needed.

The main content of Fred's proposal is as follows:

- To fulfil the 24/7 availability requirement, additional server equipment will be required to provide the necessary resilience. The network currently operates at this level, and no additional resilience is required.

- To meet the capacity and performance requirement, additional data storage will be added to the existing storage area network. This will also contribute towards the security requirement.

- In addition, to meet the security requirement, additional data backups are required, and an additional off-site storage facility is needed.

- The continuity requirement can be met with the existing recovery facility, but the recovery plans must be updated to ensure that the new service is recovered within the target time.

Fred sends the proposal back to Charlie. The next step is for Dummy Co. to decide whether it wants to spend the money required by Fred's proposal in order to upgrade the infrastructure, agree to the customer's requirements and win the business. This involves Charlie, Henry and Dummy Co. senior management. The decision is made to go ahead. Hurrah!

Henry and Charlie arrange to see the customer, and get into negotiation about the finer points of the SLA and, of course, the commercial stuff. Once the SLA is agreed, the detailed design work is started and Charlie liaises with Fred and others in the technical management team to help with any issues as they arise. When the design work is complete, Fred creates an SDP. This marks the end of the design project. Of course the next step is to build, test and implement the solution – but that's another story that comes under service transition, which I cover in Chapters 7 and 13.

Figure 12-5 provides an overview of the example in this section. It is not complete as I need a much bigger piece of paper than a page of this book to show it all, but hopefully it gives you an idea.

A swimlane flow diagram like the one in Figure 12-5 is a really good way to visualise how the processes will work in your organisation.

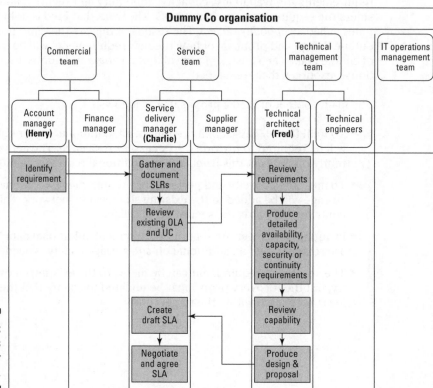

Figure 12-5:
Process
flow for
Dummy Co.

Chapter 13

Organising the Troops: Transition Projects

· ·

In This Chapter

▶ Finding out what a service transition project is

▶ Understanding how the transition processes work in practice

▶ Seeing how ITIL fits with transition projects

▶ Working through an example service transition project

· ·

*I*n Chapter 7, I introduce the service transition stage. Now, in this chapter, I bring together the concepts of the service transition stage with the ITIL processes that are most relevant at this stage. More often than not the build, test and implement activities of a service are performed as part of a project, or even as a project in its own right. This chapter contains advice on how you use the service transition processes in practice, and shows how the service transition processes work together.

Service transition is part of the service lifecycle that I explain in Chapter 3. Chapters 4 and 11 look at having a strategy for deciding which services your organisation will provide to your customers. The result is using the service portfolio management process (see Chapter 4) to help with your investment appraisal and deciding where to spend your money or this year's budget. This results in a charter – communicating the decision to develop a new service, retire an existing service, or modify a service. Once a service has been chartered, it starts its journey through the service design (Chapters 5 and 6) and service transition (Chapter 7) stages of the service lifecycle and into service operation (Chapter 8).

Introducing Service Transition Projects

As I explain in Chapter 7, the service transition stage of the service lifecycle is the bit where you take the paper-based design of a service and turn it into a living and breathing service that delivers value (in the form of utility and warranty) to your customers.

The service transition stage includes all the activities required to build, test and implement an IT service into the live, or operational, environment. Now I don't know how the service transition activities work in your IT organisation. Maybe you have a dedicated team of engineers who do the work every time a new service or major change comes along. Perhaps certain members of staff get seconded to the build and test activities and are told to do them at the same time as their normal work. But, what I'm fairly sure of is that the work is coordinated as some sort of project. To take the design of a service and create the actual hardware and software and any other related bits and bobs requires coordination, and that coordination normally comes from using a project management methodology. Therefore, in this chapter I talk about service transition *projects*. (You can find a bit more information about using projects to coordinate activities in Chapter 12. In this chapter I assume you use a similar approach to projects as the one I describe in Chapter 12.)

Now, I don't believe that the service transition activities are the only bit of an IT service development that is done as a project. In Chapter 12, I describe service design projects and outline how you need a project structure in which to control the requirements and design activities that form part of the service design stage. Often a project is set up for all of the service development activities from the inception up until the service is handed over to the IT operations staff and the business signs off the project.

In some cases there is one single project; in other cases there are many projects, one for each stage in the lifecycle. Whichever is the case in your organisation, there is one important point to note: there must be some form of approval to allow your project to move from the design stage to the service transition stage.

There are many ways in which that approval can be given:

- ✔ The project management methodology ensures that senior management give their authority.
- ✔ The service portfolio management process (see Chapter 4) ensures that authority is sought
- ✔ The change management process (see Chapter 7) gains approval from the change authority.

In some cases all three methods are used and are coordinated. What must be true is that a *service design package* (SDP) is created as the last activity of the service design stage or project. The SDP contains all the aspects of the requirements and design for a service and, once approval is given, the SDP forms the main input to the service transition stage. If you want to know more about an SDP, have a look in Chapters 5 and 12.

Seeing What Happens in a Service Transition Project

As I explain in Chapter 7, the key activities of service transition are build, test, and implement or deploy. The following sections look at how you carry out each step as part of a project.

Getting started

You need to have a trigger or instruction to get your service transition project started. After someone has fired the starting gun then you can get started.

One important decision to be made is whether you make or buy. In other words, is your organisation going to build, test and implement the service or are you going to get another organisation to do some or all of the work for you? This decision may well have been made during the service design stage, but having a clear understanding of that decision is key to knowing who does what.

The SDP includes the *service acceptance criteria* (SAC). Just as it sounds, the SAC tell you what the service must do in order for the business to accept the service once it has been deployed into the live environment. Well, you must start with the end in mind. The SAC along with the business requirements are the starting point for the design of the service. Similarly, once you start to build and test the service, you must ensure that nothing happens that may affect the ability of the service to meet these requirements. Therefore the SAC represent the starting point when it comes to planning your testing.

Building services

You build whatever has been designed. Building the service involves building each of the component parts. Once the component parts have been built, they have to be assembled as a complete service. Therefore there may be several phases of building going on.

Building the solution can include building some or all the following:

✔ **Software applications:** The front-end bits that provide the functionality of the service to the user. These are designed by one or many software developers. Building an application is carried out by software programmers, who write and create the software code required to make up the application. In theory the programmers code whatever they are told to by the designers. Of course this all depends on how organised you are.

In smaller organisations the design and development of software are not always separate phases of a project and are often done all at once. In other organisations, especially those that provide our well-known software applications, there will be hundreds of programmers working on a new release at any one time.

There are many methodologies for software development which include both the design and building of software applications. I describe these briefly in Chapter 12.

✔ **Infrastructure:** The IT hardware and networks, and any system software such as operating systems. Infrastructure may include servers, networks, storage, databases, operating systems, messaging protocols and software agents. So, clearly, 'building' here is getting physical: this is where you get your screwdriver out. The equipment must be purchased, delivered and assembled in accordance with the plans and designs created in the design stage. Detailed plans may be needed to ensure that the equipment is built in the right way.

✔ **Data:** 'Building' here refers to the building of the database systems. This may include the gathering or migration of the data that will be held in the database.

✔ **Support:** The operational requirements such as how the service will be delivered and supported on a day-to-day basis. Support will include the skills, process and resources required to ensure that the service is operating correctly and can be recovered in the event of a failure. 'Building' here refers to the creation or modification of any processes and procedures that are required to support the service. The new service may require new skills. In this case, staff will be recruited, and this must be timed carefully to ensure that the skills are available when the service goes live.

✔ **Physical environment:** The data centres, computer rooms and so on, including the air-conditioning systems and the power supplies. The new or changed service that is part of your service transition project may require additions or changes to the computer rooms or data centres. Inevitably, new equipment has to go somewhere. Additional servers and network equipment may be slotted into existing racks. Of course, all this must be done without disturbing existing equipment or disrupting current services. The additional equipment may mean additional air-conditioning or changes to the power supplies.

So who does all this work? Well, the software applications are written by programmers. The physical infrastructure can be built by almost anyone. Many IT organisations have build departments that look like a mad professor's laboratory: cables sticking out of every drawer, CDs scattered on desks, and piles of computer equipment covering every remaining bit of floor space.

The important point is to make sure that your build activities are coordinated and controlled. This is where the ITIL change management and release and deployment management processes help – skip to the later section 'Bringing Together ITIL and Service Transition Projects' to see how.

Testing the service

Testing is a discipline in itself, one in which you can attend training courses and get qualified. But what is testing all about? What does testing mean? Testing what?

Put very simply, *testing* ensures that the thing being tested will do what it is intended to do. Testing a washing machine ensures that you can use it to wash your clothes. Test driving a car ensures that it meets your requirements. Testing the temperature of a shower ensures that you don't hurt yourself when you jump in. So testing an IT service ensures that it can be used to help the business do what the business wants to do, and that it performs the way the business expects, or rather performs in the way that has been agreed. In other words, testing an IT service ensures that it is *fit for purpose* (utility) and *fit for use* (warranty). I explain utility and warranty in Chapter 2.

Testing for utility and warranty

Here's how you test for utility and warranty:

- ✔ **Testing the utility of the service:** You ensure that the business can use the service to perform its business activities. For example, can it really use the service to record sales orders? Can the factory plan the manufacturing schedule? Can you send emails to those you want to? The functionality is usually provided by the software application. A lot of the training and qualifications that you can gain in testing are related to software testing. When it comes to testing application software, there are two main approaches:

  - Ensure that the application performs the functions it is intended to perform.

  - Ensure that the application is free from bugs – that there are no errors that will stop the application in its tracks.

  Many companies have specialist test departments whose job it is to test software as it is created to ensure that it conforms to its specification.

- ✔ **Testing the warranty of the service:** You ensure that the agreed levels of availability, capacity (and performance), security and continuity can be achieved. This cannot be achieved by testing the application alone, but by testing the entire service once it is built. Chapter 6 covers the warranty processes.

Types of testing

Testing includes the testing of the individual components and the complete service, not just testing the software application. There are many types of testing. Here are a few:

- ✔ **Component testing:** The testing of individual components or parts of a service – maybe a module of software, a server or a network router. Each part of the service should be tested individually before it is assembled into the service.

- ✔ **System testing:** Taking many parts (such as software modules), building them into a system and then testing the assembly.

- ✔ **Service testing:** Checking the entire service after it is built and assembled. This is often the only way to test the agreed service levels such as availability, capacity and performance of the service.

If the agreed transaction response time is two seconds (in other words, from the moment you press the return button on your PC, something must appear on your screen in less than two seconds) then the only way to test this is with the entire service working in the way it's intended to in a replica of the live environment, but without using the live environment.

- ✔ **Operational readiness testing:** You ensure that the operations staff can deliver and support the service. This can include service management tests, such as testing whether the service desk staff are ready and prepared for dealing with any incidents related to the new service.

- ✔ **Service acceptance testing:** Many of the tests I described here will be done in the privacy of the IT department to ensure that you have done you job properly before putting your head above the parapet. But eventually you have to talk to the customers and users to check that the service does what they expect it to, and in the way they expect. In an ideal world this should be easy. If you have agreed the requirements correctly, designed the service to meet the requirements, built what you designed and tested it to be sure that it works, then everything will be fine . . . won't it? Service acceptance testing is often the last hurdle before you decide to go ahead and implement the service into the live environment.

Planning the tests

Testing shouldn't be random. I've known occasions when a software application has been more or less thrown at an IT colleague with the words 'Here – see if you can break this.' All tests must have a purpose. So every request for a test must be accompanied by a plan describing the purpose of the test and the conditions that are to be tested.

The SAC (see the earlier section 'Getting started') are the starting point for testing. They ensure that you focus on making sure that the customer gets the service that it needs.

Don't test things in the live environment – that is, using the same systems that the users are using to their job. Instead, create a duplicate system (a *test environment*). It is not always possible exactly to replicate the live environment, so you must decide how near is near enough.

Implementing the service

Once the service has been built and tested (see the previous sections), there is only one thing left to do: make it available for use. In other words, implement the new or changed service into the live environment. *Implementation* is an all-encompassing word. To implement the service may mean as little as switching it on, or it may refer to delivering and installing equipment and software across your organisation.

Implementation is often referred to as *deployment*. Is there a difference between implementation and deployment? Well, I think that *implementation* is a broader expression that refers to the bigger piece of work, especially if you're preparing to implement a major change or a new service. It can sometimes refer to the build and test activities as well as the actual implementation into the live environment. *Deployment* refers to the individual activity of taking a piece of equipment or service and deploying it in its intended location. Deployment also refers to adding additional ones, once the implementation project is complete.

Implementation, or deployment, can involve three stages:

- **Distribution:** In the case of hardware, this may involve a white-van man transporting the equipment to each of your sites. In the case of software, automated systems are often used to distribute software automatically over your network, in the same way that your favourite software manufacturer gets you to download updates to the applications you have on your PC at home.

- **Installation:** Once the hardware and software have been distributed, they have to be installed. In the case of hardware this usually involves a technical engineer popping a new PC on a user's desk and getting it working. Software, too, can be installed by an engineer. However, the installation is often done using the same automated tools that distributed the software. The tools can automatically perform the software installation and, if necessary, prompt the user to press a few buttons at the right time.

✔ **Activation:** Sometimes hardware and software are installed, but the users are told not to touch it until the official launch date. In some cases users may not even be aware that a new version of an application has been installed on their PCs. When the launch day arrives an automated message is sent to the PC to tell it to put an icon on the desktop or a new entry in a menu – and the service is now live.

Implementation requires careful planning and can potentially involve a lot of logistics – that is, getting the right equipment and the right people in the right place at the right time.

Bringing Together ITIL and Service Transition Projects

The previous section gives you an overview of the activities that form part of a service transition project. Now I describe how the ITIL service transition processes can provide control and structure to your service transition project. There are seven processes described in the ITIL service transition book, and you find descriptions of five of these processes in Chapter 7 of this book. The processes can work together to ensure that when you introduce new services or major changes to your business, you do so with the minimum of fuss and disruption, and you end up with happy customers and users.

There are two service transition processes that I don't describe in Chapter 7, so I will describe them here.

Service validation and testing

The purpose of the service validation and testing process is to ensure that a new or changed IT service matches its design specification and will meet the needs of the business.

Testing can be triggered from both change management and release and deployment management, and provides factual evidence that the correct assets are in place, and that they are configured correctly such that the service will provide the agreed value to the customer in terms of utility and warranty. In short, you must prove that the service is fit for purpose and fit for use. (You can find out more about utility and warranty in Chapter 2.)

Testing is unlikely to consist of a single test. Even though the change may be to a single component, it's still necessary to confirm that the entire service will continue to perform as required once the change has been made. Tests must be performed in a coordinated manner from the bottom up.

Figure 13-1 shows an example of a V-model and is taken from the ITIL service transition book. The V-model is a well-known model that comes from a software development background. This version has been adapted to show how changes to components, and hence services, should be tested at various levels.

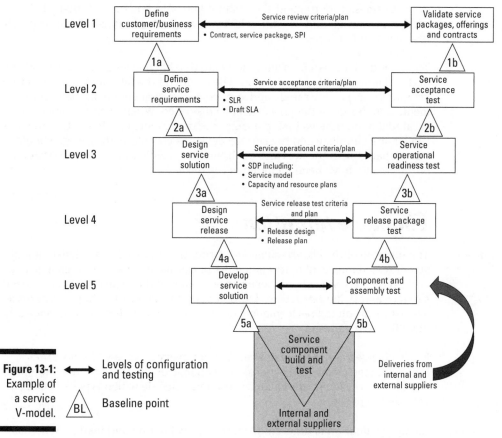

Figure 13-1: Example of a service V-model.

One of the main considerations of service validation and testing is to perform an appropriate set of tests at the appropriate level of detail. Testing should not be limited to testing the software application. While testing the software application is clearly important, once the application is tested you should test it as part of the service. In some cases this is referred to as system testing or integration testing. ITIL suggests several levels and types of testing to ensure that the entire service provides both the utility and warranty agreed with the customer. Some examples of tests are as follows:

✔ Component tests

✔ Service test

- ✔ Service management tests
- ✔ Operational readiness tests

The V-model also helps us to understand that testing starts right at the top with the business requirements, as shown at the top left in Figure 13-1. For every business requirement there should be SAC. It is the SAC that will be used in the design and transition lifecycle stages to establish the appropriate test plans and criteria.

The V-model can also be used to indicate that each level on the left-hand side of the diagram involves validation. The layers on the left-hand side reflect the activities of service strategy and service design that establish the requirements and design of the new or changed service. When each document is created it should be validated against the documents created at the previous level. For example, when the service design is complete, the design should be compared with the service requirements specification to ensure that all requirements have been included in the design.

Change evaluation

The purpose of the *change evaluation* process is to provide a consistent and standardised means of determining the performance of a service change in the context of likely impacts on business outcomes and on existing and proposed services and IT infrastructure. The actual performance of a change is assessed against its predicted performance. Risks and issues related to the change are identified and managed.

Every change should be evaluated, but not every change will follow the formal change evaluation process. The change evaluation process should be used for more significant changes. You must decide which types of change will use the process.

Change evaluation is different from service validation and testing. Whereas the latter ensures that the new or changed service meets its specification, change evaluation is comparing an actual outcome with the intended outcome and reporting on any deviations to change management. Change evaluation also ensures that risks have been managed and helps to determine whether to proceed with a proposed change.

Change evaluation is performed at many points during the change, release and deployment cycle. Here are three possible points at which you may perform a change evaluation:

- ✔ **At the assess and evaluation step in the change management process.**
  Prior to authorising the change, the change manager may send a request to the change evaluation process to trigger the evaluation of the design of the new or changed service to review the intended effects of the change.

✔ **Just prior to the deployment of the change or release, a second evaluation will be performed.** Now the results of testing can be used to represent the actual performance of the service after the change, such that the predicted and actual performance can be compared.

✔ **When the deployment or transition is complete and early life support is coming to its end, a final evaluation will be carried out.**

In some organisations, changes and releases may have been deployed using good change management and release and deployment management processes. The implementation is completed successfully and service levels are met. However, users or customers may not be satisfied. This is sometimes mystifying. In these cases, performing change evaluation may identify the unpredicted effects that influenced user satisfaction, or, in this case, dissatisfaction.

Linking the service transition processes

Figure 13-2 shows most of the service transition processes and how they link together. Hopefully, you can see from the picture that there is a logical flow of *requests for change* (RFCs) coming into the change management process and travelling from the left to the right of the picture. (I've not shown the *service asset and configuration management* (SACM) process in this figure simply because it's difficult to show in a picture, but the SACM process is present throughout the service transition project.)

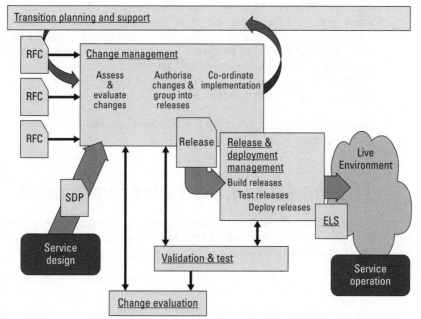

Figure 13-2:
Example of service management involvement in transition projects.

Change management is the controlling process that provides authority for all other work to start. It also makes sure that each change is a good use of your organisation's time and money. There are likely to be many RFCs involved in transitioning a new or changed service. Inevitably, there will be the RFC that is authorised for the overall change or new service. This provides the trigger for the service transition project. There will also be an SDP associated with the RFC and the project. Once the project is authorised, the transition planning and support process will take the RFC and the SDP and plan the project. The SDP will include overall details of the resources required to build, test and deploy the new service or major change, and the transition planning and support process will take this information and put flesh on the bones. The transition planning and support process can start to allocate resources to the different parts of the project. It also raises more RFCs to control the build, test and implementation of parts, or components, of the new service or major change.

As the RFCs are raised, the change management process assesses and evaluates each change. It also decides which changes should be grouped into releases. The release and deployment management process is involved in helping to make this decision. The build, test and deployment activities are ultimately controlled from change management, but where releases are used, the release and deployment management process will take delegated control of the build, test and deployment of the release.

It is normal that the coordination of build and test of some components or parts of the service will be done by the change management process. Sometimes those components that will, later, form part of a release may be built and tested as separate units under the coordination of change management. In the case where a release is used, all the parts that have been built and tested separately are now assembled as a release, and the release can now be built, tested and prepared for deployment. So testing is triggered from both change management and release and deployment management. Once all the build and test is complete, the release and deployment process prepares and deploys the release.

As each ITIL process becomes involved in the transition project, it triggers its own sequence of activities.

ITIL and build, test and implement

You can find details of the basic process flows for each of the service transition processes in Chapter 7. In the following sections I provide a little more detail about their involvement in a service transition project.

Transition planning and support

The transition planning and support process provides coordination to the whole service transition project. It's a bit like a project or a programme office – a team or individual who hands out the work instructions and tells you which bit of work to do next. Such people don't necessarily have authority, but they coordinate work that has been authorised.

Transition planning and support also ensures that the agreed policies, strategies, standards, process and procedure are used. For example, it may have been agreed that all deployments of your sales office IT service are always implemented using the big bang approach (deploying everything all at once; see Chapter 7), and this decision is documented as a policy. It is the role of the transition planning and support process to recognise when the policy is appropriate and gather together all the documentation appropriate to the big bang deployment.

The transition planning and support process often identifies and raises the necessary RFCs for the project.

Change management

This is the controlling process: everything stops and starts here. Control is a great thing. It is sometimes perceived as bureaucracy, but when you consider the number of activities that must happen in order to built, test and implement the parts of an entire service, an awful lot can go wrong. So change management provides the authority to perform the activities.

Change management also works with release and deployment management (see the later section on this process) to decide which changes to group into releases.

For each RFC, the change management process ensures that each change is assessed, evaluated and authorised before building of the change commences. Authority is often sought from change management a second time for each change after the build and test is complete and prior to deployment.

Service asset and configuration management

Service asset and configuration management (SACM) is the provider of the information about the services and their component parts. It is critical that the impact of any change is understood, and the *configuration management system* (CMS) that is maintained by SACM will provide this information.

Baselines are often used to simplify your IT infrastructure. A baseline shows the intended build of a component or service. A good example of a baseline is the standard build of a desktop PC: every PC that leaves the IT department is built in exactly the same way. Baselines will be unique and recorded as *configuration items* (CIs) in the CMS. Baselines are often used to automate the build of some components and assemblies. For example, using the same example as earlier, the standard build of a PC can be configured using an 'imaging' tool that allows the configuration of the PC to be copied easily to create many PCs with the identical build.

Release and deployment management

Release and deployment activities are triggered by authority from change management (see the earlier section on this process). Release and deployment management looks at the release policy and release units to help decide how to group changes into releases and which type of release is appropriate, and discusses this with change management.

When the release is part of a new service or major change, the release and deployment management process creates further RFCs in order to get authorisation from change management to deploy the release.

Release and deployment management is responsible for any pilots that are required. A *pilot* is a deployment of a service in advance of the formal deployment. A pilot tests:

✔ The software on real business transactions

✔ The deployment activities and mechanisms

Choose a site for the pilot where representative business activities are performed and representative technology is used.

Service validation and testing

Testing will be triggered from both change management and release and deployment management (see the earlier sections on these processes). The service validation and testing process ensures that all agreed tests are performed.

The outline of the testing should be designed at the same time as the service, as part of the service design. Testing will be driven by the SAC. The SAC will be included in the SDP. During the design of the service, a top-down approach is taken ensuring that the business requirements are clearly understood. Then service requirements are created from the business requirements: the service is broken down into parts until the requirements of each service component are established. Each component and the service are then designed to meet these requirements. As each service is built, a bottom-up approach is taken. First the components are built and each component is tested. Then systems are created from the components and the system tested. When the whole service is assembled, it will be tested again. These service tests must prove that the SAC can be met. Go to Chapters 5, 6 and 12 for more discussion on design.

Create test plans to ensure that the right tests are performed at the right time by the right people.

Change evaluation

Change evaluation is triggered from the change management process and aims to provide an independent view of what's going on so that change management can alert the customer to any unexpected effects of the change. In some cases, if an evaluation report shows that the change in performance of a service after the change has been made is unacceptable, the change manager may reject the change.

Finishing off the projects: business acceptance and sign-off

In the good old bad old days it was considered acceptable for the IT department to throw new systems 'over the wall' into live use and pop off down the pub to have the end-of-project party. Fortunately, this is no longer the case. Here are some important activities that must be performed at the end of a service transition project:

Early-life support/handover to service operation

Early-life support (ELS) is part of the release and deployment management process, but can be viewed as a mini process in its own right. It involves the activities required for service transition staff to work alongside service operation staff during the first few weeks of live operation of the service. The purpose is to make sure that service operation staff know what is considered to be normal in terms of how the service works. Also they should know what to do when something abnormal happens.

There should be criteria agreed for when ELS starts and when it finishes. ELS will end when service levels are achieved consistently and the users can use the service as intended. Hopefully, when the ELS period is over, the business will be in a position to sign off the service.

Business sign-off

The final acceptance of the new or changed service must be done by the business. The IT department must demonstrate that the SAC have been met, and that the service not only supports the business outcomes but can be delivered and supported in a way that meets the service level targets.

This is a good time to make the business aware of any unexpected variations in performance and agree any actions that should be taken to resolve them, if necessary. SLAs can be finalised and signed off, if this is not already done.

Looking at an Example of a Service Transition Project

Dummy Co. is a manufacturing organisation that sells its own products through its sales departments. Dummy Co. has implemented ITIL and allocated many of the service management roles to members of the technical teams.

The IT department is in the middle of a project to implement a new *customer relationship management* (CRM) IT service into the sales departments across four sites. The new CRM service has been chartered using the service portfolio management process (which I explain in Chapter 4). A service design project is complete and an SDP produced. The SDP has been reviewed along with an updated business case, and senior management have approved the project to go ahead into the service transition stage.

The new service consists of the following components and systems:

✔ Software application to be installed on the sales staff's PCs

✔ New server equipment to be installed in the data centres

✔ New database to be installed on the servers

Take a look at Figure 13-3, which shows an overview of the activities that take place in Dummy Co. in order to transition the service. The figure is incomplete (I can only fit so much on a page of this book), but you get the picture. (Do remember this is an example, and you need to make your own process flow for your organisation.) I've shown in italics any ITIL roles that have been assigned to people in Dummy Co.

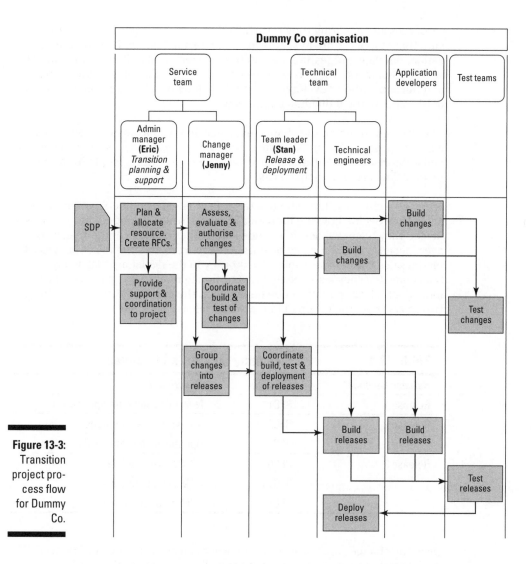

Figure 13-3:
Transition project process flow for Dummy Co.

Now I look at some of the steps of the process in more detail.

The SDP along with senior management approval has gone to Eric. Eric is the administration manager in the IT service team and has been allocated the role of transition planning and support manager. Now Eric has the SDP he can start planning the transition project. This includes allocating the resources and ensuring they are available. So, in this case, he needs to be sure that resources are available for building and testing the software application, building and testing the database system, and building and testing the server equipment. These resources come from the technical engineer teams and the application developers. The other thing that Eric does is to raise lots of RFCs for all the individual components.

The RFCs go to Jenny, the change manager. Jenny follows her change management process. She must ensure that each change is assessed, evaluated and authorised. To do this, she involves the appropriate people from the technical teams and the business.

Jenny also chats to Stan, who has the role of release and deployment manager. They decide how the individual changes will be grouped into releases. In fact, they have decided to include some other changes in the release packages, because this will make best use of resources and minimise the impact on the sales teams. The Table 13-1 shows you the decisions that Jenny and Stan come to. They also decided that although release 1 and release 2 are individual releases, they can be deployed at the same time, therefore these two releases will be grouped into a single release package.

Table 13-1		Dummy Co. Agreed Changes
Release Number	*Changes*	*Description*
Release 1	RFC1	New CRM software application
Release 2	RFC2	Anti-virus client upgrade
	RFC3	Updates to desktop build baseline
Release 3	RFC6	CRM server hardware
	RFC7	CRM server software
	RFC8	CRM database installation

Once the changes are authorised, the work can start. Jenny and Eric will work together to raise works orders and allocate them to the application development and technical staff.

The build and test of individual components will be done first. This will be done by the usual suspects: the software application programming will be done by Dummy Co.'s application developers, and the building of the servers and databases will be done by Dummy Co.'s technical engineers. Once these are complete, the release building and testing can start. The build and test of the release will include the build and test of the deployment mechanisms. So, in this case, the software application will be distributed using an automatic software distribution tool that uses the network to send the software release package to each PC. So this tool is tested as well.

Jenny and Stan also decide on the type of deployment to be used – a big bang or a phased approach. In this case they decide on a phased approach. In fact they choose as a pilot site the local sales department, which is in the same building as the IT department, and do this one first. This allows the IT department to check that the deployment mechanisms work as planned and that the sales team is happy with the new IT service. The remaining three sales offices will be deployed at one-week intervals.

I've now talked through all the activities that are shown on Figure 13-3, but this isn't the end of the story. Once the service is deployed, the early-life support process must kick in. Members of the technical and application teams will be put on standby to deal with issues as they arrive within the first few weeks after deployment.

Finally, Jenny must liaise with the sales director to ensure that the aims of implementing the new CRM system have been achieved. Hopefully this is the case and the sales director will sign off the project as a success. Yippee!

Part IV
The Part of Tens

The 5th Wave   By Rich Tennant

In this part . . .

Every *For Dummies* book has a Part of Tens: bite-sized chunks of handy, quick-reference info that enhances the contents of the book. Here I provide some condensed advice on making ITIL work for your organisation, suggest some elements of ITIL to implement first if you want quick results, and a list of the ten best places to head for when you want some ITIL-related advice.

Chapter 14

Ten Ways to Help ITIL Work for You

In This Chapter

▶ Having a clear vision

▶ Planning the changes

▶ Getting key people on board

▶ Training staff

Sometimes ITIL can seem a bit dry and theoretical. It isn't! But working out how ITIL fits into your organisation (or your customer's) takes a little bit of time and thought. Here are ten things that help your ITIL project run a little more smoothly.

Detailing Your Vision for ITIL

Just because you think ITIL is a good idea doesn't mean everyone around you magically agrees. You must understand why you think it's a good idea and be able to explain your reasoning to other people. So, don't just pile into implementing ITIL the minute you get inspired. To be successful, the project must be well thought through and well implemented. So take a few moments to consider what you're trying to achieve.

To help you to create a vision for your ITIL initiative, answer the following three questions:

▶ **What if we don't do it?** So, if you don't implement ITIL now, what will happen, or what won't happen? Will the provision of your IT services get worse? Will the cost of the services rise? Will your company fail to achieve its goals and targets? Make your responses specific and try to quantify things if you can.

✔ **What's in it for the stakeholder?** In order to get commitment for implementing ITIL, you need to persuade others that they can benefit. Who are the stakeholders – the people who have an interest in, or are affected by, what you're doing – and what do they want? Find out who'll be affected and get an understanding of their needs.

✔ **What's in it for the business as a whole?** Find out what the overall business goals and plans are, and emphasise how the implementation of ITIL helps support those goals.

Having a Plan

When you have a vision (see the previous section), you can then create a plan of how you'll achieve that vision. ITIL isn't just training or a nice-to-have. It's a framework of processes, a set of ways of doing things. And if you do things properly, you can expect to improve your effectiveness and efficiency and improve the IT services that you provide to your customers.

When organisations adopt ITIL, this means they implement the ITIL processes in their organisations, usually as a project. So ask yourself, 'Which ITIL processes do I need to achieve my vision?' Now create a high-level project plan of how you'll implement these.

Plans have a habit of not implementing themselves. You need to plan how to implement ITIL. Don't reinvent the wheel. Implement ITIL as a project, and use an established project management methodology. PRINCE2® is a well-known project management methodology that can help you. For guidance, check out *PRINCE2 For Dummies* by Nick Graham (Wiley).

PRINCE2® is a Registered Trade Mark of the Cabinet Office.

Chapter 10 has more advice about implementing ITIL in your organisation.

Doing Your Homework: Building a Good Business Case

You'll never get started with ITIL unless you get senior management to loosen the purse strings and give you the money. A good, compelling business case helps you gain support. (You need to include a description of your vision; see the earlier section 'Detailing Your Vision for ITIL').

A *business case* is a document that describes the reasons for and costs involved in a project or other initiative. Often its main purpose is to justify the expenditure on a project. The main section of a business case is a *cost–benefit analysis* – an analysis of the costs and benefits involved in the project.

Try to think of those occasions when things went wrong in the past. For example, the time the email service failed because someone had forgotten to mention the change they made before they went on holiday. Remember for how long the system was down. You should be able to calculate what this cost in terms of lost business revenue. By including this in the business case, you show both the tangible and intangible savings that can be made, and thus gain support and funding for your ITIL project.

Involving People

In my experience, some IT people have a habit of keeping things quiet – 'If I tell people what I'm doing, they may not like it, or they may want me to change it.' Also, some IT departments out there are cocooned in their own little worlds, believing that only they know best. I believe the opposite is true.

You're bound to face opposition when implementing processes, because you're telling people how to do their jobs. But if you inform and involve people from the start, you minimise the fuss.

Don't wait until people come up and ask you what this ITIL stuff is all about. People who don't feel involved are less likely to commit to your project and support it. You're more likely to succeed if everyone has a chance to have their say.

Getting the Right People Involved

Yes, you must involve people, but is everyone equal? Well yes – but some are more equal than others! You may be tempted to involve only those you think will support you. Or you may involve only those who are most affected. But you must get a good mix of people involved. You need senior management commitment as well as the involvement of those who'll be using your processes.

Just to get you started, think about the following potential stakeholder groups:

✔ **Customers and the business:** You provide IT services that help your customers do what your customers do. They know if you're doing a good job. If your organisation is a commercial provider (providing IT services in exchange for money) then you have a main customer contact who provides feedback. If you're an internal IT provider (providing IT services to other parts of the same company) then it can sometimes be more complicated. Each department manager or business unit manager is a customer, and managers may have different needs and different opinions. You also have access to the users who are on the front line.

✔ **IT management:** These are the people who will provide the money and the resources needed to implement ITIL. Find out what their aims and goals are, and see whether you can link your vision to their needs.

✔ **The rest of IT:** These are the staff who are going to adopt the ITIL processes – you hope! Skip to the previous section, 'Involving People', to see how to get staff onside.

Communicating

You may think communicating is an easy thing. It is – when you communicate properly. Just sending the odd email or popping something on the notice board isn't communicating. Communication is a two-way thing. To truly communicate with someone, you must send a message *and* receive a reply – even if it's simply a nod or a grunt.

If you don't communicate properly, you may be seen as deliberately excluding people.

Mind you, it's also very easy to overdo it. You know what it's like when your boss continually sends you emails enthusiastically telling you about something that will happen in six months, when you're struggling to cope with today's workload. So the trick here is to mix up the format and methods of communication. Try a mix of emails, Internet and social networking sites, team meetings and workshops and training. Oh, and by the way – keep it interesting.

Documenting

A process is a way of working, and in some people's minds that means you don't need to write it down – 'I know what I'm doing'. But when people follow the same procedure time and again they achieve consistency and accuracy, so sharing procedures by documenting them is critical to the success of your ITIL project.

The simple act of writing gets you thinking. Here are some advantages of documenting processes:

- ✔ It shows that you take the process seriously.
- ✔ It makes sure you really understand the process yourself.
- ✔ It ensures you understand what you are asking other people to do.
- ✔ Others can check the documentation and tell or whether you've got the process right.

Training

Surely all you have to do is read the procedure and do as it says, right? Wrong. A common mistake is assuming that you don't need to train staff to carry out a process. When you implement the ITIL processes, staff won't follow your procedures unless they're trained in how to use them. Documentation (see the last section) is great, but you can't pop a procedure in front of people and expect them to get on with it without explanation.

Don't underestimate the power of training. Staff feel valued if you bother to invest in training them. Plus, in training, you have the opportunity to tell staff why you think the new process is a good idea and what the benefits are for all concerned.

While I'm talking about training your staff to use your processes, I can't miss the opportunity to say something about ITIL training. Appendix A tells you all about the ITIL qualification scheme, and a suitable qualification exists for everyone. If you're serious about implementing ITIL in your organisation, nothing is better than getting an independent person to tell your staff about ITIL. Sending all your IT staff on an ITIL foundation course, or at least a one-day overview, gives everyone the same understanding of ITIL. It also demonstrates your commitment.

As a final point on training, do think about timing. It you train staff too long before you implement the processes, the training can seem irrelevant and people may forget their new knowledge by the time they need it. On the other hand, leaving it too late means that staff are trying to use your new processes without adequate help and support. It's a tricky balance to strike. Give it some thought.

Being Pragmatic

ITIL is guidance; it's not prescriptive. There are a few basic rules such as sticking to the basic process flows, but overall you need to use your common sense. Not every organisation can employ lots of staff, but every organisation can adopt processes to make better use of what they've got. The clever bit is making it work for you.

Do you have to implement all the ITIL processes? Well, eventually, I hope. The real power of ITIL comes from having all the processes working together. But you must be pragmatic – Rome wasn't built in a day. The best approach is to have a vision that you eventually implement all the processes, but break this into a number of projects and concentrate initially on the processes that give your organisation most benefit. ITIL has a lot of processes but they don't have to be all singing and dancing. Some are very simple and straightforward.

Adopt ITIL but adapt it to suit your organisation. So adopt the basic process flow relatively unchanged then decide how each activity is performed.

There is a danger that staff will see ITIL as needless and unnecessary bureaucracy. Decide what is fixed and what can be flexible. After you've implemented a process you mustn't believe this is it and it will never change. Tell the staff that they can change things. The best processes are the ones that are adapted and nurtured by those who use them. So be prepared to change – as long as you can still achieve your vision.

Chapter 10 has more advice about implementing ITIL in your organisation.

Persevering When Something Doesn't Go as Planned

If at first you don't succeed, try, try and try again. Unfortunately some service management projects fail. This is sometimes blamed on ITIL. You will encounter problems, and not everything will go as planned. But if you have a clear vision in mind and use your common sense, you'll achieve your aims and improve your IT services and the way you manage them.

Chapter 15

Ten Key Bits of ITIL: Some Possible Quick Wins

In This Chapter

▶ Identifying your customer's needs

▶ Getting a basic agreement in place

▶ Seeing the benefits of a service desk

▶ Knowing how to deal with incidents and problems

*1*TIL is great, but you can easily be put off by the size of it: five publications describing more than 20 processes. Whether your organisation is big or small, each ITIL implementation comes with its own difficulties. You have to start somewhere, and I'm a great believer in keeping things simple. Yes, planning is important, but you don't want to fall into the trap of analysis paralysis and end up doing nothing. One thing you can do to get your spirits up is to identify and implement some *quick wins* – things that are relatively easy to do and that get visible results, keeping stakeholders happy.

Implement the suggestions in this chapter as soon as possible. Say when you're going to do it, do it, and then publish the results.

Implementing Basic Service Level Management

If you don't know what your customers need, you can never know whether you're meeting their needs. It's like fighting in the dark. You can never be right. (On the other hand, you can never be wrong – some people find this prospect attractive, but your customers won't be impressed.)

Service level management is, pretty obviously, the process that manages service levels. The process tries to set up a proper relationship with your customers and understand their business needs. Of course first you need to know who your customers are. If you're the internal IT department that provides IT stuff to other people and departments within the same company, your customers are the business unit managers or department managers. If you're a commercial IT services company providing IT services to other companies in exchange for money, your customers are those other companies; usually there is an assigned representative who talks to you.

To implement service level management:

1. **Set up a dialogue with your customers.**

2. **Find out what they want.**

3. **Agree with them what you can provide (see the next section on service level agreements).**

4. **Monitor and report on what you've achieved.**

If you haven't done this before, you'll be surprised at the difference simply starting a dialogue with the business makes. In some cases the business will be amazed that you bothered to talk to it. If you're open and honest and state your intentions up front, your customers will be happy to talk to you.

ITIL also defines the process of business relationship management and the role of business relationship manager. The service level manager defines, agrees and reports on the service level for specific services – the business relationship manager maintains an overall relationship with the customer, keeps in contact, and looks for new opportunities to support the customer's needs. Many organisations combine these roles into one job description. When setting up some basic service level management, you consider which roles you need.

For more information about service level management, look at Chapter 5. For more information about business relationship management, look at Chapter 4.

Introducing a Service Level Agreement

After you work with your customers to identify their needs (see the previous section), start thinking about setting up a *service level agreement* (SLA) – a document that contains the targets you've agreed for your IT services, covering such things as:

- ✔ When the service is needed
- ✔ How long it should work for without failure
- ✔ How long you should take to fix it
- ✔ How fast it should work for a given number of users

You can't do everything all at once. Who knows whether you'll be able to achieve the service levels that your customers ask for? In the first instance, you can set up a single blanket SLA that just indicates your intention to control the level of service you provide. Something is better than nothing. Measurement and reporting are essential to building up an understanding about what you can achieve. So, on the assumption that you have no SLAs in place at the moment, set up a basic SLA and start measuring the actual service levels. Then set up regular meetings with each customer to report your achievements and discuss whether you're improving the services and support that you provide. Now you can improve your SLAs.

For more information about SLAs, look at Chapter 5.

Creating an Operational Level Agreement

The previous section covers SLAs, but you can't set these up in isolation without getting some commitment from the rest of the IT organisation that the service levels are achievable and the resources and willingness to meet service levels exist.

An *operational level agreement* (OLA) is an agreement between the service provider and another part of the same organisation. For example, the IT manager may have an agreement with the server team that commits it to meeting targets for the availability and performance of the server equipment in its care. Similarly, the IT manager may have an agreement with the service desk that gives it targets for picking up the phone and dealing with calls.

Make sure you involve IT staff in deciding what is needed to agree to service levels with the business, and what is achievable. Staff are more likely to agree to the targets in the OLAs if they were involved in setting them up.

For more information about OLAs, look at Chapter 5.

Setting Up a Service Desk

The main purpose of a service desk is to provide a single point of contact for users – someone for them to contact about IT issues.

In some companies the users don't know who to contact, so they just ring any phone number that gets them through to an IT person. This person is probably not the right one to deal with the query, and doesn't want to talk to the user, who is interrupting other work.

Nowadays, many organisations have set up a point of contact for IT, but if you haven't, you'll find it a very powerful thing to do. The users like it because they know who to contact. Your IT staff like it because they don't get interrupted so often. And you can be more confident that issues will be dealt with in a consistent manner.

When setting up a service desk, make sure you understand the business needs and priorities. Setting up the service desk in parallel with setting up service level management is a good idea. Through service level management, you get an understanding of which incidents need to be fixed first and how long it should take.

Head over to Chapter 3 for further discussion on the service desk.

Cataloguing Services

A *service catalogue* is a catalogue of the IT services that your IT organisation provides to its customers. In its most basic form, it's simply a list of the IT services, usually by application name or however they're known to the users and most other people.

Setting up a service catalogue is the first step to understanding your priorities. After you list the services, you can start to identify how important to the business each one is and attribute a level of criticality. This helps when you start to negotiate service levels with the business and agree response times for recovering services.

You can find more about service catalogues in Chapter 5.

Establishing Some Basic Change Control

Don't shoot yourself in the foot! Many IT service failures happen because somebody changed something and messed something else up in the process. This often happens because of a failure to sit down and think about and plan the change, giving careful thought to the repercussions.

Implementing a basic change management process can save your IT organisation a lot of embarrassment. As ever, you will get resistance from both inside and outside the IT organisation. But if you keep the process simple to start with and have a good justification for doing it, you can start to get things under control.

I explain change management in Chapter 7.

Knowing the Difference between Incidents and Problems

An *incident* is an unplanned outage, and a *problem* is the underlying cause of one or more incidents. Understanding this distinction can really help to make a difference to the way your users perceive the support they get from the IT organisation.

Users get frustrated if they have to wait around doing nothing because some techie guy is diligently trying to get to the bottom of an incident without first getting the user up and running. Equally, users become just as frustrated if an incident continues to recur on a regular basis and the IT organisation appears to be doing nothing.

The IT organisation must get the balance right. Through the incident management process, the service desk (not got one? head to the earlier section 'Setting Up a Service Desk'), possibly with the help of second-line support, deals with the symptoms of the incident and restores the service to the user. The user may well be happy for the incident to be closed. The IT organisation now has an important decision to make. Should it:

- ✔ Close the incident record and do nothing about the incident until it happens again?
- ✔ Raise a problem record and start to investigate the underlying cause before further incidents create more business impact?

These choices are part of the domain of the problem management process. The incident management process deals with the symptoms. Problem management deals with the cause. By implementing these processes, you improve your ability to organise your resources better and focus on the correct priorities.

Getting your support staff to differentiate between incidents and problems and deal with them differently is relatively simple to do and it creates results that people notice.

Chapter 8 covers incident and problem management.

Measuring Your Achievements

Measurement and reporting are essential to building up an understanding about what you can achieve. However, many organisations that have not yet adopted ITIL or service management practices don't know how well they're performing. You can easily assume that you're performing badly, or well, when the opposite is true. One of the first things to do when you want make a difference is to start to measure the level of service you currently provide.

Keep it simple to start with. For example, you can probably estimate how much time is lost due to IT failures – I'm sure you have a log of significant outages. If you add up the time and compare it with the amount of time you claim that your services are available, you can come up with a rudimentary service availability percentage. It may not be a measurement you want to share with your customers yet, but it provides some sort of benchmark.

When you start to discuss service levels with a customer, even the most rudimentary measurement gives you some idea of what you can achieve and can become a starting point for negotiations.

After you build up a history of the measurements of your service achievements, and you start to get things right and begin to meet the expectations of the customer, the time may come when you want to shout it from the rooftops.

Gathering Tools

What do I mean by tools? Well, I'm referring to IT using IT in order to deliver IT. All the IT staff who manage and deliver the services use IT. I expect you have a PC, and that PC has software installed that you use in your job. You may use a word-processing package to create a policy document, or you may use a call-logging software tool to record incidents reported to the service desk. Many different types of tool exist of varying complexity.

You hear a lot of talk about *integrated service management toolsets* – sets of software applications that support your service management processes. Such things sound very grand, and if you're in a large organisation going for service management in a big way, you will find acquiring such tools is beneficial. But you don't have to buy these straight away. Use basic tools to help you understand your needs, and then you can move up to more 'grown-up' tools as things develop. If you're just starting out to try to improve your IT services, basic tools like a spreadsheet or simple database to log service desk calls are a good start.

Make good use of what you've got. Every organisation has an email system. Many of these have extra functions that allow you to create forms that can be filled in and sent to email addresses. You can use this as a basic process flow engine for circulating incident and problem details to support engineers. Similarly, you can use forms to circulate *requests for change* (RFCs) for review.

A quick search on the Internet for service management tools, using your favourite search engine, will yield a long list of websites, white papers and general help to get you started.

Getting Your Staff ITIL Trained

Considering this book is written by a training consultant, I'm bound to recommend training. But training is the right and proper thing to do. Plus staff can receive training in so many ways. You don't have to stick to classroom training – many different computer-based training options are available.

In Chapter 14, I describe training as one of the ten ways to get ITIL to work for you, so I won't repeat myself here. But training is also a quick win. For a small amount of investment you can demonstrate your commitment to making a difference by arranging some ITIL training. The philosophy of ITIL is really quite simple but not always obvious unless time is taken to explain it to staff. Sending as many of your staff as possible on some sort of ITIL training course ensures that everyone has the same view of what you're trying to achieve. In addition, if you send them on a foundation course, they obtain an industry-standard qualification (hopefully).

Have a look at Appendix A if you'd like to find out about the ITIL qualification scheme.

Chapter 16

Ten Places to Go for Help

In This Chapter

▶ Using Cabinet Office resources

▶ Getting in touch with an examination institute

▶ Seeing how other approaches can complement ITIL

Don't bother reinventing the wheel. Many people and organisations out there have implemented ITIL or are willing to provide you with help; some are closer to home than you think. Here are ten suggestions of where to go for help.

I start this section with some general, and maybe obvious, places to go for help. Then I move on to the other organisations that can help you.

Your Colleagues

Before I bombard you with details and websites of organisations that can provide help for your ITIL implementation, I want to say a quick word or two about the blindingly obvious. I'm a great believer in keeping things simple. Help may be closer at hand than you think. You'll be surprised how many examples of service management you find in ordinary life. Each is a useful analogy to get you thinking about how to improve your services.

Whenever I turn on the TV or radio, it's not long before I say to myself 'That's a real-life example of service management.' For example, when the Government talks about the underlying reasons for unemployment, symptoms and causes relate to each other in the same way as incidents and problems do. Recently, my local news talked of the benefits of traffic officers clearing motorway accidents as soon as possible to recover the flow of traffic, just as you restore IT services when you have an incident. Of course, when I go shopping I only have to look at a queue and I go off on a diatribe about capacity management. Or is that just me?

All of these things help to exemplify and improve your understanding of service management. They also provide great examples that are easy to understand and that you can share with others.

The point of this section is that you and your colleagues represent a source of help. You have, no doubt, developed your own processes and procedures and ways of resolving issues that are just as effective as those documented in ITIL and elsewhere. The important point is to capture these and make them official. When you resolve issues and establish the best way of achieving something, you create good practice. Document it and follow it.

Don't forget, for your ITIL implementation to be successful you must involve all staff. Getting their involvement will help get support and commitment for the changes you make.

The Internet

I'm sure I don't need to tell you that the Internet is a great source of information. Online you find lots of stuff about service management and ITIL. Admittedly, if you simply search for 'ITIL', you end up with a list of training companies; however, if you dig a little further you uncover useful information.

A couple of years ago I was doing research and searched for *invitation to tender* (ITT). I found a copy of the official ITT from NASA to bid for one of the space shuttles when they retired from service. I was nearly tempted to put in a bid to have a space educational centre in my back garden. The moral of the story, of course, is that you never know what you're going to find.

Searching for terms such as *service level agreement* (SLA), *operational level agreement* (OLA) or *service portfolio* will yield many useful resources and examples.

In the following sections I list many websites that can help you. Here are some others that don't fit in those sections:

- ✔ MOF (Microsoft Operations Framework) is closely related to ITIL. It provides a framework of practices intended to help you manage your IT systems. It describes similar processes to ITIL. This guidance is now available free to download at the following website:

  `http://technet.microsoft.com/en-us/solutionaccelerators/dd320379.aspx`

> ✔ The IT Skeptic. The name of this website may sound like a joke – but it isn't. You'll find some interesting stuff here. Yes, occasionally you may find some challenging comments made about ITIL, but there is no harm in this. If you fancy a look go to:
>
> www.itskeptic.org

Cabinet Office

The Office of Government Commerce (OGC) was the custodian of ITIL and the UK Government department that sponsored best practice. In 2011 these duties transferred to the UK Government Cabinet Office. The Cabinet Office now sponsors many best practices and other relevant guidance, including ITIL and others such as:

> ✔ M_o_R® (Management of Risk)
>
> ✔ MSP® (Managing Successful Projects)
>
> ✔ PRINCE2 – project management methodology

M_o_R® and MSP® are Registered Trade Marks of the Cabinet Office.

The Cabinet Office licenses the day-to-day running of ITIL to the APM Group (see the following section).

The best sources of news updates and basic information about ITIL and the qualifications are these websites:

> ✔ www.best-management-practice.com
>
> ✔ www.itil-officialsite.com
>
> ✔ www.cabinetoffice.gov.uk

All three websites are run by a combination of the Cabinet Office, TSO (originally The Stationery Office) and the APM Group. You will find information about all of the Government best-practice guidance mentioned above, along with ITIL information regarding exams, accreditation and much more.

APM Group

The APM Group is the accreditor of all examination institutes for ITIL qualifications (see the following section). This means that it accredits examination institutes worldwide. The examination institutes then accredit other organisations that deliver training. Any ITIL training course that leads to an exam must be an accredited course run by an accredited trainer, using accredited material.

You can find more information at www.apmgroupltd.com.

Examination Institutes

The examination institutes accredit training organisations around the world. If you go to these websites you'll find information about training companies near you that are accredited to provide ITIL training.

Here's a list of the current examination institutes:

- **APMG-International:** Global organisation based in the UK (see the previous section).

- **BCS:** UK-based British Computer Society, provider of BCS Professional Certifications

- **Cert-IT:** Based in Germany.

- **CSME:** Based in the USA.

- **DANSK IT:** Based in Denmark.

- **DF Certifiering AB:** Wholly owned subsidiary of the Swedish Computer Society.

- **EXIN:** Global certification company based in The Netherlands.

- **Loyalist Certification Services:** Based in Canada and provides ITIL exams around the world.

- **PEOPLECERT Group:** Global exam institute.

- **TÜV SÜD Akademie:** Germany-based organisation.

You can see an up-to-date list at www.itil-officialsite.com/ExaminationInstitutes.

ITIL Live

ITIL Live is the online portal for advice and guidance for using ITIL, and has heaps more stuff. You can find process flow diagrams, role descriptions, white papers and much more there. You have to pay a subscription to get access to all this.

The ITIL Live website is www.bestpracticelive.com.

IT Service Management Forum (ITSMF)

The IT Service Management Forum (ITSMF) is the equivalent to a user group for IT service management and is a great source of information for anyone interested in ITIL-based service management. You can join the ITSMF and get discounts on books, and access to discussion forums.

The ITSMF has chapters in many countries. Each chapter organises events to give the opportunity for members to get together, attend seminars and discuss service management topics.

There are two main websites for the ITSMF:

- ✔ www.itsmfi.org is the website for the international ITSMF, where you will find details of the many worldwide chapters of the ITSMF.
- ✔ www.itsmf.co.uk is the website for the UK chapter of the ITSMF.

ISO/IEC 20000

ISO/IEC 20000 is the international standard for IT service management. The standard allows companies to demonstrate excellence and prove best practice in IT management. As a standard, ISO/IEC 20000 simply tells you what your organisation must achieve in order to be accredited to the standard. ITIL describes the same processes but gives much more advice on how to implement the processes in your organisation. So the two complement each other.

If your organisation wants to take ITIL to the highest level, then it may want to become accredited to the standard ISO/IEC 20000. This will indicate that your organisation has adopted the ITIL service management processes and achieved a certified level of maturity.

You can find more information about the accreditation scheme at www.isoiec20000certification.com.

Complementary Approaches

Many approaches, methodologies and guidance can help you improve the way you manage and provide IT services. Occasionally, people make the mistake of believing they can adopt only one set of guidance or one standard at a time. This isn't true. Many approaches are complementary to ITIL. Depending on your needs, you may find that these can be used to help your ITIL implementation project. Here are a few:

- **Control Objectives for Information and related Technology (COBIT):** Covers similar areas to ITIL but is more of an auditing tool: a controls-based, value and risk management framework that can support overall IT governance. Get the low-down at www.isaca.org/Knowledge-Center/cobit/Pages/Overview.aspx.

- **Capability Maturity Model Integration (CMMI):** A process improvement approach that provides models you can use to assess the maturity of a process. ITIL is a framework of processes, so the approach is invaluable in setting baselines for improvement of your service management processes. Visit www.sei.cmu.edu/cmmi to find out more.

- **Six Sigma:** A process improvement approach you can use to analyse and improve processes, including the ITIL service management processes. There are many websites for Six Sigma, and the best approach is to launch your favourite search engine and have a look. However, a good starting place is www.asq.org, which is the site for the American Society for Quality.

SFIA

SFIA is the Skills Framework for the Information Age. It is an approach to defining IT skills. It defines and clarifies the skills and levels of responsibility required to perform many common IT roles. Lots of the roles align easily with the ITIL roles. You can use a combination of the ITIL role descriptions and the SFIA framework to create role or job descriptions for your ITIL implementation.

You can view and download the skills framework at www.sfia.org.uk.

Part V
Appendixes

"ITIL sounds interesting. We've been using the UNTIL service strategy. We don't worry about customers UNTIL we hear from them."

In this part . . .

This part contains some additional information. First I talk about the ITIL qualification structure, in case you're thinking of adding ITIL to your CV. Then I offer a glossary of key ITIL terms that I use in the book, and a quick reference guide to the service lifecycle processes.

Appendix A

Getting Qualified in ITIL

• •

*I*TIL qualifications are becoming quite a commodity, and no doubt such qualifications look impressive on your CV. But so many qualifications exist; how do you choose? In this appendix, I describe the various ITIL qualifications that are available, how you qualify and who they best suit.

Looking at the ITIL Qualification Structure

The qualification structure (see Figure A-1) is relatively straightforward. ITIL has four levels:

- ✔ Foundation
- ✔ Intermediate
- ✔ Expert
- ✔ Master

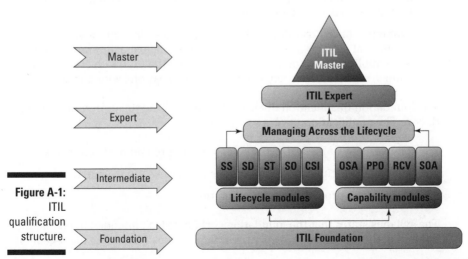

Figure A-1: ITIL qualification structure.

Source: The APM Group Ltd 2008

The ITIL qualification scheme has something for everyone. Although the shape of the diagram gives the impression of aiming for the top level, this couldn't be further from the truth. The ITIL scheme was developed in 2007 to allow candidates to obtain qualifications in their skill areas. Each certificate is a qualification in its own right and demonstrates the acquisition of skills and knowledge in this area. However, in addition to collecting these skills you can, over time, obtain an overall qualification demonstrating knowledge and skills across the service lifecycle.

The following sections look at each level of the ITIL qualification scheme in turn.

Foundation

You gain the foundation qualification by taking the foundation exam. The foundation qualification is the only one where attendance on a course isn't a requirement. So you have a choice of three ways to prepare for the exam:

✔ **Do-it-yourself approach:** If you're brave enough, you could read a book, and maybe get hold of some sample questions and other study material, then, when you're ready, take the exam.

I wrote the first two parts of this book with the foundation examination in mind. This book isn't an examination guide or replacement for a training course. However, the first two parts cover the foundation syllabus. In fact, I probably include more information than you need in these parts.

✔ **Classroom-based training course:** A foundation training course usually lasts for three days with the exam on the afternoon of the final day. As a trainer I'm duty bound to uphold the honour of all trainers everywhere and tell you that the *best* way to get a good understanding of the foundation material is to attend a course.

✔ **Computer-based training (CBT) course:** You sit in front of your PC at home or at work and study the course material using interactive software applications. You sometimes combine the CBT with attendance at a much shorter classroom event, or online sessions with a trainer.

The foundation qualification does what it says on the tin: it provides a foundation. The qualification covers

✔ An overview of the ITIL terminology, structure and basic concepts

✔ The core principles of ITIL practices for service management

✔ Many of the processes and the functions

The syllabus states that the foundation certificate isn't intended to enable the holders of the certificate to apply the ITIL practices for service management without further guidance. This further help and guidance is provided by the intermediate level qualifications. These are described in the forthcoming sections.

Intermediate

The intermediate level encompasses nine qualifications, which are split into two streams: lifecycle and capability. These certificates are qualification in their own right. Once you obtain one you can refer to yourself as having achieved intermediate level in that subject e.g. Intermediate certificate in service operation. You can also use these certificates to contribute towards attaining the ITIL expert qualification – more details coming up in a forthcoming section.

For all the intermediate qualifications, course attendance is mandatory and the exam is usually on the final day of the course. Courses can be classroom based or include virtual study. In all cases the foundation certificate is a prerequisite.

Lifecycle

The five lifecycle courses, unsurprisingly, are based on the service lifecycle; one course for each lifecycle stage.

The lifecycle courses provide the *management* view of the ITIL material: the aspects required to understand each process and its interfaces, oversee the implementation of each process, and judge the effectiveness and efficiency of each process.

In each case the syllabus covers most of the content of the ITIL book relevant to the lifecycle stage, so it includes learning units on

- Principles of the lifecycle stage
- The processes
- Any special activities associated with the lifecycle stage
- Organisational matters
- Technology

Classroom courses usually last for three days with the exam on the last day. The syllabus suggests a minimum number of 21 contact hours and a further 21 hours of personal study.

Capability

The four capability courses provide the *practice*, or practical, view of ITIL, and cover the skills and knowledge needed to execute the process activities on a daily basis. The courses logically group processes and focus on the details of the processes, along with associated methods and techniques.

The majority of the syllabus focuses on a detailed view of the processes covered in each qualification. Additional sections look at the roles, technology and implementation considerations associated with the processes.

Classroom courses usually last for five days with the exam on the last day. The syllabus suggests a minimum number of 30 contact hours and a further 12 hours of personal study.

The four capability courses are:

- ✔ **SOA:** Service offerings and agreements
- ✔ **PPO:** Planning, protection and optimisation
- ✔ **RCV:** Release control and validation
- ✔ **OSA:** Operational support and analysis

Table A-1 shows the processes covered on each course.

Table A-1	Processes Covered on the Capability Courses		
SOA	**PPO**	**RCV**	**OSA**
Service portfolio management	Capacity management	Change management	Event management
Financial management for IT services	Availability management	Service asset and configuration management	Incident management
Demand management	IT service continuity management	Service validation and testing	Request fulfilment
Business relationship management	Information security management	Release and deployment management	Problem management
Service level management	Demand management	Request fulfilment	Access management
Service catalogue management		Change evaluation	
Supplier management		Knowledge management	

Expert

The intermediate qualifications allow candidates to obtain recognition of their skills and knowledge of their chosen parts of the service lifecycle. However, many people want to study all areas of the lifecycle and obtain a higher level qualification in recognition of this achievement. The ITIL expert certificate is this qualification.

You can only obtain the ITIL expert certificate after taking a number of intermediate courses. In doing so, you collect credits. The credits you can obtain from each certificate are as follows.

- Foundation certificate: 2 credits
- Each intermediate lifecycle certificate: 3 credits
- Each intermediate capability certificate: 4 credits
- Managing across the Lifecycle certificate: 5 credits

To obtain the ITIL expert certificate you must have 22 credits, 2 which come from the foundation certificate and 5 from Managing across the Lifecycle. This leaves you with 15 credits from your choice of intermediate courses. You can mix and match from lifecycle and capability courses.

Some overlap exists between the lifecycle and capability courses, so you must ensure that your chosen combination gives you sufficient coverage of the entire service lifecycle before attempting the Managing across the Lifecycle course.

The Managing across the Lifecycle course has a similar structure to the intermediate courses and usually lasts for five days with the exam on the final day. The purpose of the course is to demonstrate that you've gained sufficient knowledge and skill of the entire service lifecycle. This course presents the end-to-end view of management and brings together all the lifecycle and capabilities activities related to

- Key concepts of the service lifecycle
- Communication and stakeholder management
- Integrating service management processes across the service lifecycle
- Managing services across the service lifecycle
- Governance and organisation
- Measurement
- Implementing and improving service management capability

The qualification covers material from all five core ITIL publications.

Master

Many people are extremely proud to achieve ITIL expert level (see the previous section) and are content to leave things there. However, the ITIL master qualification exists for those who still have fuel in their tank.

This qualification doesn't involve any training courses or further exams. To obtain the master qualification you submit a report describing a real-life experience that demonstrates your ability to use ITIL in the workplace. First you submit an outline of your suggested report for approval. Then, if accepted, you write the full report.

The ITIL Master Qualification Certificate shows that you have the capability to apply the principles, methods and techniques from ITIL in the workplace. To achieve the qualification you must be able to explain and justify how you selected and individually applied a range of knowledge, principles, methods and techniques from ITIL and supporting management techniques, to achieve desired business outcomes in one or more practical assignments.

To be eligible for the ITIL Master Qualification you must already have reached ITIL Expert Level and must have worked in IT service management for at least five years in leadership, managerial or higher management advisory levels.

Examining the Exams

The exams are all multiple choice, but some are more complicated than others.

Foundations exam

The format of the foundation exam is as follows:

- ✔ 1 hour, closed book exam
- ✔ 40 multiple choice questions
- ✔ You must score 26 out of 40 (65 per cent) in order to pass

Intermediate exams

The format of all the intermediate exams is as follows.

- ✔ 90 minute, closed book exam
- ✔ 8 complex, gradient scenario multiple choice questions
- ✔ You must score 28 out of 40 (70 per cent) in order to pass

What on earth is a *complex, gradient scenario multiple choice question*? Each question of the exam paper consists of scenario, usually not more than half a side of A4 paper. It describes a situation at some mythical organisation. The question consists of four possible answers, each of which could be a paragraph of text or a series of bullets. Candidates must select the one answer that they feel is correct. The answer options are graded as follows.

- Best answer – 5 marks
- Second best answer – 3 marks
- Third best answer – 1 marks
- Distracter answer – 0 marks

Distracter here refers to any answer that is completely wrong.

The intermediate exams test your ability to analyse a situation and apply ITIL to that situation. The scenarios provide the opportunity for you to apply what you have learnt about ITIL to a given situation.

Managing across the Lifecycle

At the time of writing (end of 2011), the format of the Managing across the Lifecycle exam is the same as the intermediate exams described in the previous section. However, this will change during 2012. The new format of the Managing across the Lifecycle exam will be as follows.

- 120 minute, closed book exam
- 10 complex, gradient scenario multiple choice questions (this is the same format as described in the previous section)
- The exam uses a single case study on which at least 8 of the questions will be based. The case study is available in advance of the exam.
- You must score 35 out of 50 (70 per cent) in order to pass

Knowing Where to Attend Courses and Sit Exams

Chapter 16 helps you track down course and exam providers. Also try an internet search. You're sure to discover several companies in your area that can provide training and the exams.

All training courses must be accredited. This means that they are approved by an Examination Institute (EI). These bodies review training material and accredit trainers. This allows the training organisation to use the Examination Institute's logo. When looking for a training course make sure you find a training organisation that can prove their course is accredited. Chapter 16 tells you how to find your nearest Examination Institute.

Appendix B

Glossary

The following are just some ITIL terms I use in this book. The official ITIL glossary, from which these definitions are taken, is about 70 pages long, so if you need further definitions, you know where to go.

Quoted ITIL text is from *The Official Introduction to the ITIL Service Lifecycle* © Crown copyright 2011. Reproduced under licence from the Cabinet Office.

Alert. A notification that a threshold has been reached, something has changed, or a failure has occurred. Alerts are often created and managed by system management tools and are managed by the event management process.

Application. Software that provides functions which are required by an IT service. Each application may be part of more than one IT service. An application runs on one or more servers or clients.

Application management. The function responsible for managing applications throughout their lifecycle.

Asset. Any resource or capability. The assets of a service provider include anything that could contribute to the delivery of a service. Assets can be one of the following types: management, organisation, process, knowledge, people, information, applications, infrastructure or financial capital.

Audit. Formal inspection and verification to check whether a standard or set of guidelines is being followed, that records are accurate, or that efficiency and effectiveness targets are being met. An audit may be carried out by internal or external groups.

Availability. Ability of an IT service or other configuration item to perform its agreed function when required. Availability is determined by reliability, maintainability, serviceability, performance and security. Availability is usually calculated as a percentage. This calculation is often based on agreed service time and downtime. It is best practice to calculate availability of an IT service using measurements of the business output.

Baseline. A snapshot that is used as a reference point.

Business case. Justification for a significant item of expenditure. The business case includes information about costs, benefits, options, issues, risks and possible problems.

Business continuity management (BCM). The business process responsible for managing risks that could seriously affect the business. Business continuity management safeguards the interests of key stakeholders, reputation, brand and value-creating activities. The process involves reducing risks to an acceptable level and planning for the recovery of business processes should a disruption to the business occur. Business continuity management sets the objectives, scope and requirements for IT service continuity management.

Business impact analysis (BIA). Business impact analysis is the activity in business continuity management that identifies vital business functions and their dependencies. These dependencies may include suppliers, people, other business processes, IT services etc. Business impact analysis defines the recovery requirements for IT services. These requirements include recovery time objectives, recovery point objectives and minimum service level targets for each IT service.

Business relationship manager (BRM). A role responsible for maintaining the relationship with one or more customers. This role is often combined with the service level manager role.

Capability. The ability of an organisation, person, process, application, IT service or other configuration item to carry out an activity. Capabilities are intangible assets of an organisation.

Change. The addition, modification or removal of anything that could have an effect on IT services. The scope should include changes to all architectures, processes, tools, metrics and documentation, as well as changes to IT services and other configuration items.

Change advisory board (CAB). A group of people that support the assessment, prioritisation, authorisation and scheduling of changes. A change advisory board is usually made up of representatives from: all areas within the IT service provider; the business; and third parties such as suppliers.

Change model. A repeatable way of dealing with a particular category of change. A change model defines specific agreed steps that will be followed for a change of this category. Change models may be very complex with many steps that require authorisation (e.g. major software release) or may be very simple with no requirement for authorisation (e.g. password reset).

Change proposal. A document that includes a high level description of a potential service introduction or significant change, along with a corresponding business case and an expected implementation schedule. Change proposals are normally created by the service portfolio management process and are passed to change management for authorisation. Change management will review the potential impact on other services, on shared resources, and on the overall change schedule. Once the change proposal has been authorised, service portfolio management will charter the service.

Change record. A record containing the details of a change. Each change record documents the lifecycle of a single change. A change record is created for every request for change that is received, even those that are subsequently rejected. Change records should reference the configuration items that are affected by the change. Change records may be stored in the configuration management system, or elsewhere in the service knowledge management system.

Change schedule. A document that lists all authorised changes and their planned implementation dates, as well as the estimated dates of longer-term changes. A change schedule is sometimes called a forward schedule of change, even though it also contains information about changes that have already been implemented.

Charter. A document that contains details of a new service, a significant change or other significant project. Charters are typically authorised by service portfolio management or by a project management office. The term charter is also used to describe the act of authorising the work required to complete the service change or project.

Configuration. A generic term used to describe a group of configuration items that work together to deliver an IT service, or a recognisable part of an IT service. Configuration is also used to describe the parameter settings for one or more configuration items.

Configuration baseline. The baseline of a configuration that has been formally agreed and is managed through the change management process. A configuration baseline is used as a basis for future builds, releases and changes.

Configuration item (CI). Any component or other service asset that needs to be managed in order to deliver an IT service. Information about each configuration item is recorded in a configuration record within the configuration management system and is maintained throughout its lifecycle by service asset and configuration management. Configuration items are under the control of change management. They typically include IT services, hardware, software, buildings, people and formal documentation such as process documentation and service level agreements.

Configuration management database (CMDB). A database used to store configuration records throughout their lifecycle. The configuration management system maintains one or more configuration management databases, and each database stores attributes of configuration items, and relationships with other configuration items.

Configuration management system (CMS). A set of tools, data and information that is used to support service asset and configuration management. The CMS is part of an overall service knowledge management system and includes tools for collecting, storing, managing, updating, analysing and presenting data about all configuration items and their relationships. The CMS may also include information about incidents, problems, known errors, changes and releases. The CMS is maintained by service asset and configuration management and is used by all IT service management processes.

Configuration record. A record containing the details of a configuration item. Each configuration record documents the lifecycle of a single configuration item. Configuration records are stored in a configuration management database and maintained as part of a configuration management system.

Configuration structure. The hierarchy and other relationships between all the configuration items that comprise a configuration.

Contract. A legally binding agreement between two or more parties.

Critical success factor (CSF). Something that must happen if an IT service, process, plan, project or other activity is to succeed. Key performance indicators are used to measure the achievement of each critical success factor. For example, a critical success factor of 'protect IT services when making changes' could be measured by key performance indicators such as 'percentage reduction of unsuccessful changes', 'percentage reduction in changes causing incidents' etc.

Customer. Someone who buys goods or services. The customer of an IT service provider is the person or group who defines and agrees the service level targets. The term is also sometimes used informally to mean user – for example, 'This is a customer-focused organisation.'

Customer agreement portfolio. A database or structured document used to manage service contracts or agreements between an IT service provider and its customers. Each IT service delivered to a customer should have a contract or other agreement that is listed in the customer agreement portfolio.

Customer portfolio. A database or structured document used to record all customers of the IT service provider. The customer portfolio is the business relationship manager's view of the customers who receive services from the IT service provider.

Data-to-Information-to-Knowledge-to-Wisdom (DIKW). A way of understanding the relationships between data, information, knowledge and wisdom. DIKW shows how each of these builds on the others.

Definitive media library (DML). One or more locations in which the definitive and authorised versions of all software configuration items are securely stored. The definitive media library may also contain associated configuration items such as licences and documentation. It is a single logical storage area even if there are multiple locations. The definitive media library is controlled by service asset and configuration management and is recorded in the configuration management system.

Deployment. The activity responsible for movement of new or changed hardware, software, documentation, process etc. to the live environment. Deployment is part of the release and deployment management process.

Effectiveness. A measure of whether the objectives of a process, service or activity have been achieved. An effective process or activity is one that achieves its agreed objectives.

Efficiency. A measure of whether the right amount of resource has been used to deliver a process, service or activity. An efficient process achieves its objectives with the minimum amount of time, money, people or other resources.

Emergency change. A change that must be introduced as soon as possible – for example, to resolve a major incident or implement a security patch. The change management process will normally have a specific procedure for handling emergency changes.

Emergency change advisory board (ECAB). A subgroup of the change advisory board that makes decisions about emergency changes. Membership may be decided at the time a meeting is called, and depends on the nature of the emergency change.

Environment. A subset of the IT infrastructure that is used for a particular purpose – for example, live environment, test environment, build environment. Also used in the term 'physical environment' to mean the accommodation, air conditioning, power system etc. Environment is used as a generic term to mean the external conditions that influence or affect something.

Escalation. An activity that obtains additional resources when these are needed to meet service level targets or customer expectations. Escalation may be needed within any IT service management process, but is most commonly associated with incident management, problem management and the management of customer complaints. There are two types of escalation: functional escalation and hierarchic escalation.

Event. A change of state that has significance for the management of an IT service or other configuration item. The term is also used to mean an alert or notification created by any IT service, configuration item or monitoring tool. Events typically require IT operations personnel to take actions, and often lead to incidents being logged.

Facilities management. The function responsible for managing the physical environment where the IT infrastructure is located. Facilities management includes all aspects of managing the physical environment – for example, power and cooling, building access management, and environmental monitoring.

First-line support. The first level in a hierarchy of support groups involved in the resolution of incidents. Each level contains more specialist skills, or has more time or other resources.

Function. A team or group of people and the tools or other resources they use to carry out one or more processes or activities – for example, the service desk.

Functional escalation. Transferring an incident, problem or change to a technical team with a higher level of expertise to assist in an escalation.

Governance. Ensures that policies and strategy are actually implemented, and that required processes are correctly followed. Governance includes defining roles and responsibilities, measuring and reporting, and taking actions to resolve any issues identified.

Hierarchic escalation. Informing or involving more senior levels of management to assist in an escalation.

Impact. A measure of the effect of an incident, problem or change on business processes. Impact is often based on how service levels will be affected. Impact and urgency are used to assign priority.

Incident. An unplanned interruption to an IT service or reduction in the quality of an IT service. Failure of a configuration item that has not yet affected service is also an incident – for example, failure of one disk from a mirror set.

Incident record. A record containing the details of an incident. Each incident record documents the lifecycle of a single incident.

Information security policy. The policy that governs the organisation's approach to information security management.

IT infrastructure. All of the hardware, software, networks, facilities etc. that are required to develop, test, deliver, monitor, control or support applications and IT services. The term includes all of the information technology but not the associated people, processes and documentation.

IT operations. Activities carried out by IT operations control, including console management, job scheduling, backup and restore, and print and output management. IT operations is also used as a synonym for service operation.

IT operations control. The function responsible for monitoring and control of the IT services and IT infrastructure.

IT operations management. The function within an IT service provider that performs the daily activities needed to manage IT services and the supporting IT infrastructure. IT operations management includes IT operations control and facilities management.

IT service. A service provided by an IT service provider. An IT service is made up of a combination of information technology, people and processes. A customer-facing IT service directly supports the business processes of one or more customers and its service level targets should be defined in a service level agreement. Other IT services, called supporting services, are not directly used by the business but are required by the service provider to deliver customer-facing services.

IT service continuity plan. A plan defining the steps required to recover one or more IT services. The plan also identifies the triggers for invocation, people to be involved, communications etc. The IT service continuity plan should be part of a business continuity plan.

IT service management (ITSM). The implementation and management of quality IT services that meet the needs of the business. IT service management is performed by IT service providers through an appropriate mix of people, process and information technology.

IT service provider. A service provider that provides IT services to internal or external customers.

Key performance indicator (KPI). A metric that is used to help manage an IT service, process, plan, project or other activity. Key performance indicators are used to measure the achievement of critical success factors. Many metrics may be measured, but only the most important of these are defined as key performance indicators and used to actively manage and report on the process, IT service or activity. They should be selected to ensure that efficiency, effectiveness and cost effectiveness are all managed.

Known error. A problem that has a documented root cause and a workaround. Known errors are created and managed throughout their lifecycle by problem management. Known errors may also be identified by development or suppliers.

Known error database (KEDB). A database containing all known error records. This database is created by problem management and used by incident and problem management. The known error database may be part of the configuration management system, or may be stored elsewhere in the service knowledge management system.

Known error record. A record containing the details of a known error. Each known error record documents the lifecycle of a known error, including the status, root cause and workaround. In some implementations, a known error is documented using additional fields in a problem record.

Major incident. The highest category of impact for an incident. A major incident results in significant disruption to the business.

Mean time between failures (MTBF). A metric for measuring and reporting reliability. MTBF is the average time that an IT service or other configuration item can perform its agreed function without interruption. This is measured from when the configuration item starts working, until it next fails.

Mean time between service incidents (MTBSI). A metric used for measuring and reporting reliability. It is the mean time from when a system or IT service fails, until it next fails. MTBSI is equal to MTBF plus MTRS.

Mean time to repair (MTTR). The average time taken to repair an IT service or other configuration item after a failure. MTTR is measured from when the configuration item fails until it is repaired. MTTR does not include the time required to recover or restore. It is sometimes incorrectly used instead of mean time to restore service.

Mean time to restore service (MTRS). The average time taken to restore an IT service or other configuration item after a failure. MTRS is measured from when the configuration item fails until it is fully restored and delivering its normal functionality.

Metric. Something that is measured and reported to help manage a process, IT service or activity.

Operational level agreement (OLA). An agreement between an IT service provider and another part of the same organisation. It supports the IT service provider's delivery of IT services to customers and defines the goods or services to be provided and the responsibilities of both parties.

Operations bridge. A physical location where IT services and IT infrastructure are monitored and managed.

Outsourcing. Using an external service provider to manage IT services.

Pattern of business activity (PBA). A workload profile of one or more business activities. Patterns of business activity are used to help the IT service provider understand and plan for different levels of business activity.

Priority. A category used to identify the relative importance of an incident, problem or change. Priority is based on impact and urgency, and is used to identify required times for actions to be taken. For example, the service level agreement may state that Priority 2 incidents must be resolved within 12 hours.

Proactive problem management. Part of the problem management process. The objective of proactive problem management is to identify problems that might otherwise be missed. Proactive problem management analyses incident records, and uses data collected by other IT service management processes to identify trends or significant problems.

Problem. A cause of one or more incidents. The cause is not usually known at the time a problem record is created, and the problem management process is responsible for further investigation.

Problem record. A record containing the details of a problem. Each problem record documents the lifecycle of a single problem.

Procedure. A document containing steps that specify how to achieve an activity. Procedures are defined as part of processes.

Process. A structured set of activities designed to accomplish a specific objective. A process takes one or more defined inputs and turns them into defined outputs. It may include any of the roles, responsibilities, tools and management controls required to reliably deliver the outputs. A process may define policies, standards, guidelines, activities and work instructions if they are needed.

Projected service outage (PSO). A document that identifies the effect of planned changes, maintenance activities and test plans on agreed service levels.

RACI. A model used to help define roles and responsibilities. RACI stands for responsible, accountable, consulted and informed.

Release. One or more changes to an IT service that are built, tested and deployed together. A single release may include changes to hardware, software, documentation, processes and other components.

Release package. A set of configuration items that will be built, tested and deployed together as a single release. Each release package will usually include one or more release units.

Release record. A record that defines the content of a release. A release record has relationships with all configuration items that are affected by the release. Release records may be in the configuration management system or elsewhere in the service knowledge management system.

Release unit. Components of an IT service that are normally released together. A release unit typically includes sufficient components to perform a useful function. For example, one release unit could be a desktop PC, including hardware, software, licences, documentation etc. A different release unit may be the complete payroll application, including IT operations procedures and user training.

Reliability. Measure of how long an IT service or other configuration item can perform its agreed function without interruption. Usually measured as MTBF or MTBSI. The term can also be used to state how likely it is that a process, function etc. will deliver its required outputs.

Remediation. Actions taken to recover after a failed change or release. Remediation may include back-out, invocation of service continuity plans, or other actions designed to enable the business process to continue.

Request for change (RFC). A formal proposal for a change to be made. It includes details of the proposed change, and may be recorded on paper or electronically. The term is often misused to mean a change record, or the change itself.

Request model. A repeatable way of dealing with a particular category of service request. A request model defines specific agreed steps that will be followed for a service request of this category. Request models may be very simple, with no requirement for authorisation (e.g. password reset), or may be more complex with many steps that require authorisation (e.g. provision of an existing IT service).

Resilience. The ability of an IT service or other configuration item to resist failure or to recover in a timely manner following a failure. For example, an armoured cable will resist failure when put under stress.

Resource. A generic term that includes IT infrastructure, people, money or anything else that might help to deliver an IT service. Resources are considered to be assets of an organisation.

Response time. A measure of the time taken to complete an operation or transaction. Used in capacity management as a measure of IT infrastructure performance, and in incident management as a measure of the time taken to answer the phone, or to start diagnosis.

Return on investment (ROI). A measurement of the expected benefit of an investment. In the simplest sense, it is the net profit of an investment divided by the net worth of the assets invested.

Risk. A possible event that could cause harm or loss, or affect the ability to achieve objectives. A risk is measured by the probability of a threat, the vulnerability of the asset to that threat, and the impact it would have if it occurred. Risk can also be defined as uncertainty of outcome, and can be used in the context of measuring the probability of positive outcomes as well as negative outcomes.

Role. A set of responsibilities, activities and authorities assigned to a person or team. A role is defined in a process or function. One person or team may have multiple roles – for example, the roles of configuration manager and change manager may be carried out by a single person. Role is also used to describe the purpose of something or what it is used for.

Root cause. The underlying or original cause of an incident or problem.

Second line support. The second level in a hierarchy of support groups involved in the resolution of incidents and investigation of problems. Each level contains more specialist skills, or has more time or other resources.

Service. A means of delivering value to customers by facilitating outcomes customers want to achieve without the ownership of specific costs and risks. The term 'service' is sometimes used as a synonym for core service, IT service or service package.

Service acceptance criteria (SAC). A set of criteria used to ensure that an IT service meets its functionality and quality requirements and that the IT service provider is ready to operate the new IT service when it has been deployed.

Service catalogue. A database or structured document with information about all live IT services, including those available for deployment. The service catalogue is part of the service portfolio and contains information about two types of IT service: customer-facing services that are visible to the business; and supporting services required by the service provider to deliver customer-facing services.

Service charter. A document that contains details of a new or changed service. New service introductions and significant service changes are documented in a charter and authorised by service portfolio management. Service charters are passed to the service design lifecycle stage where a new or modified service design package will be created. The term charter is also used to describe the act of authorising the work required by each stage of the service lifecycle with respect to the new or changed service.

Service contract. A contract to deliver one or more IT services. The term is also used to mean any agreement to deliver IT services, whether this is a legal contract or a service level agreement.

Service design package (SDP). Document(s) defining all aspects of an IT service and its requirements through each stage of its lifecycle. A service design package is produced for each new IT service, major change or IT service retirement.

Service desk. The single point of contact between the service provider and the users. A typical service desk manages incidents and service requests, and also handles communication with the users.

Service improvement plan (SIP). A formal plan to implement improvements to a process or IT service.

Service knowledge management system (SKMS). A set of tools and databases that is used to manage knowledge, information and data. The service knowledge management system includes the configuration management system, as well as other databases and information systems. The service knowledge management system includes tools for collecting, storing, managing, updating, analysing and presenting all the knowledge, information and data that an IT service provider will need to manage the full lifecycle of IT services.

Service level agreement (SLA). An agreement between an IT service provider and a customer. A service level agreement describes the IT service, documents service level targets, and specifies the responsibilities of the IT service provider and the customer. A single agreement may cover multiple IT services or multiple customers.

Service level requirement (SLR). A customer requirement for an aspect of an IT service. Service level requirements are based on business objectives and used to negotiate agreed service level targets.

Service level target. A commitment that is documented in a service level agreement. Service level targets are based on service level requirements, and are needed to ensure that the IT service is able to meet business objectives.

Service management. A set of specialised organisational capabilities for providing value to customers in the form of services.

Service owner. A role responsible for managing one or more services throughout their entire lifecycle. Service owners are instrumental in the development of service strategy and are responsible for the content of the service portfolio.

Service pipeline. A database or structured document listing all IT services that are under consideration or development, but are not yet available to customers. The service pipeline provides a business view of possible future IT services and is part of the service portfolio that is not normally published to customers.

Service portfolio. The complete set of services that is managed by a service provider. The service portfolio is used to manage the entire lifecycle of all services, and includes three categories: service pipeline (proposed or in development), service catalogue (live or available for deployment), and retired services.

Service provider. An organisation supplying services to one or more internal customers or external customers. Service provider is often used as an abbreviation for IT service provider.

Service request. A formal request from a user for something to be provided – for example, a request for information or advice; to reset a password; or to install a workstation for a new user. Service requests are managed by the request fulfilment process, usually in conjunction with the service desk. Service requests may be linked to a request for change as part of fulfilling the request.

Serviceability. The ability of a third-party supplier to meet the terms of its contract. This contract will include agreed levels of reliability, maintainability and availability for a configuration item.

Single point of contact (SPOC). Providing a single consistent way to communicate with an organisation or business unit. For example, a single point of contact for an IT service provider is usually called a service desk.

Single point of failure (SPOF). Any configuration item that can cause an incident when it fails, and for which a countermeasure has not been implemented. A single point of failure may be a person or a step in a process or activity, as well as a component of the IT infrastructure.

Snapshot. The current state of a configuration item, process or any other set of data recorded at a specific point in time. Snapshots can be captured by discovery tools or by manual techniques such as an assessment.

Stakeholder. A person who has an interest in an organisation, project, IT service etc. Stakeholders may be interested in the activities, targets, resources or deliverables. Stakeholders may include customers, partners, employees, shareholders, owners etc.

Standard change. A pre-authorised change that is low risk, relatively common and follows a procedure or work instruction – for example, a password reset or provision of standard equipment to a new employee. Requests for change are not required to implement a standard change, and they are logged and tracked using a different mechanism, such as a service request.

Strategy. A strategic plan designed to achieve defined objectives.

Super user. A user who helps other users, and assists in communication with the service desk or other parts of the IT service provider. Super users are often experts in the business processes supported by an IT service and will provide support for minor incidents and training.

Supplier. A third party responsible for supplying goods or services that are required to deliver IT services. Examples of suppliers include commodity hardware and software vendors, network and telecom providers, and outsourcing organisations.

Technical management. The function responsible for providing technical skills in support of IT services and management of the IT infrastructure. Technical management defines the roles of support groups, as well as the tools, processes and procedures required.

Third party. A person, organisation or other entity that is not part of the service provider's own organisation and is not a customer – for example, a software supplier or a hardware maintenance company. Requirements for third parties are typically specified in contracts that underpin service level agreements.

Third-line support. The third level in a hierarchy of support groups involved in the resolution of incidents and investigation of problems. Each level contains more specialist skills, or has more time or other resources.

Type I service provider. An internal service provider that is embedded within a business unit. There may be several Type I service providers within an organisation.

Type II service provider. An internal service provider that provides shared IT services to more than one business unit. Type II service providers are also known as shared service units.

Type III service provider. A service provider that provides IT services to external customers.

Underpinning contract (UC). A contract between an IT service provider and a third party. The third party provides goods or services that support delivery of an IT service to a customer. The underpinning contract defines targets and responsibilities that are required to meet agreed service level targets in one or more service level agreements.

Urgency. A measure of how long it will be until an incident, problem or change has a significant impact on the business. For example, a high-impact incident may have low urgency if the impact will not affect the business until the end of the financial year. Impact and urgency are used to assign priority.

User. A person who uses the IT service on a day-to-day basis. Users are distinct from customers, as some customers do not use the IT service directly.

Utility. The functionality offered by a product or service to meet a particular need. Utility can be summarised as 'what the service does', and can be used to determine whether a service is able to meet its required outcomes, or is 'fit for purpose'. The business value of an IT service is created by the combination of utility and warranty.

Vital business function (VBF). Part of a business process that is critical to the success of the business. Vital business functions are an important consideration of business continuity management, IT service continuity management and availability management.

Warranty. Assurance that a product or service will meet agreed requirements. This may be a formal agreement such as a service level agreement or contract, or it may be a marketing message or brand image. Warranty refers to the ability of a service to be available when needed, to provide the required capacity, and to provide the required reliability in terms of continuity and security. Warranty can be summarised as 'how the service is delivered', and can be used to determine whether a service is 'fit for use'. The business value of an IT service is created by the combination of utility and warranty.

Work instruction. A document containing detailed instructions that specify exactly what steps to follow to carry out an activity. A work instruction contains much more detail than a procedure and is only created if very detailed instructions are needed.

Work order. A formal request to carry out a defined activity. Work orders are often used by change management and by release and deployment management to pass requests to technical management and application management functions.

Workaround. Reducing or eliminating the impact of an incident or problem for which a full resolution is not yet available – for example, by restarting a failed configuration item. Workarounds for problems are documented in known error records. Workarounds for incidents that do not have associated problem records are documented in the incident record.

Appendix C

Cross Referencing Processes

• •

*D*ue to the nature of this book, some of the processes are scattered across the chapters. The aim of this appendix is to give you an easy means of locating the processes you wish to read about. Table C-1 provides this reference.

Table C-1	Process cross-reference		
Process	*Description*	*Service lifecycle stage most closely associated with*	*Chapter*
Strategy management for IT services	Identifies and manages the strategy for your IT services	Service strategy	Chapter 11
Service portfolio management	Manages a provider's set of services throughout the lifecycle. Approves business cases for investment in IT services.	Service strategy	Chapter 4
Financial management for IT services	Manages budgeting, accounting and charging for IT services. Identifies the cost of providing the IT services.	Service strategy	Chapter 4
Demand management	Understands the patterns of business activity and how these relate to the usage of the IT services.	Service strategy	Chapter 4 and Chapter 11

(continued)

Table C-1 *(continued)*

Process	Description	Service lifecycle stage most closely associated with	Chapter
Business relationship management	Maintains a relationship with the customer and identifies opportunities to fulfil customer needs.	Service strategy	Chapter 4
Design coordination	Provides a single point of coordination and control for all activities and processes of the service design stage.	Service design	Chapter 5
Service level management	Ensures that a defined level of service is agreed and delivered.	Service design	Chapter 5
Service catalogue management	Ensures that a service catalogue exists and is a reliable source of information about live services.	Service design	Chapter 5
Supplier management	Manages third party suppliers and the products and services that they supply.	Service design	Chapter 5
Availability management	Manages that availability of the services to ensure that they are available for use by the users as agreed.	Service design	Chapter 6

Process	Description	Service lifecycle stage most closely associated with	Chapter
Capacity management	Manages the capacity and performance of the services to ensure that there is enough of it and that it works fast enough.	Service design	Chapter 6
IT service continuity management	Manages the recovery of the services when effected by a disaster or event of large impact upon the business.	Service design	Chapter 6
Information security management	Ensures that the integrity of the information and data that is contained and used by the IT service is maintained at the appropriate level to meet the business needs.	Service design	Chapter 6
Change Management	Manages and controls changes from request through to closure.	Service transition	Chapter 7
Service asset and configuration management	Maintains a source of information about the services, their component parts and the other assets required to deliver the services and the relationships between them.	Service transition	Chapter 7

(continued)

Table C-1 *(continued)*

Process	Description	Service lifecycle stage most closely associated with	Chapter
Release and deployment management	Manages the physical introduction of new or changed services and their equipment into the live environment.	Service transition	Chapter 7
Knowledge management	A lifecycle wide process that improves the quality of management decision making by ensuring that the right information and data are available throughout the service lifecycle.	Service transition	Chapter 7
Transition planning and support	Provides coordination of all service transition activities.	Service transition	Chapter 7
Service validation and testing	Ensures that components and services are tested and will provide the value in terms of utility and warranty that has been agreed with the business.	Service transition	Chapter 13
Change evaluation	The activities required to ensure that an independent view of any unexpected effects of a change has been evaluated, and ensures that the customer's expectations are set.	Service transition	Chapter 13

Process	Description	Service lifecycle stage most closely associated with	Chapter
Event management	Identifies electronic notifications that come from the IT equipment and uses them to ensure that the services are operating normally or respond appropriately if services are behaving abnormally.	Service operation	Chapter 8
Incident management	Manages interruptions or reductions in the quality of the services and ensures that the service is restored within agreed timescales.	Service operation	Chapter 8
Request fulfilment	Manages requests that come from the user. These could range from simple questions about how to use an application or could be requests for new equipment or software.	Service operation	Chapter 8
Access management	Makes sure that users have usernames and passwords for services that they are allowed to use.	Service operation	Chapter 8
Problem management	Investigates and identifies the cause of incidents when considered necessary, and recommends permanent solutions.	Service operation	Chapter 8

(continued)

Table C-1 *(continued)*

Process	Description	Service lifecycle stage most closely associated with	Chapter
Seven step process	An approach to measuring a service or service management process and acting on the results of analysing information and data about the service or process	Continual service improvement	Chapter 9

Some of the processes have activities that are performed in many stages of the service lifecycle. Figure C-1 gives you a guide to which processes are used in which service cycle stage.

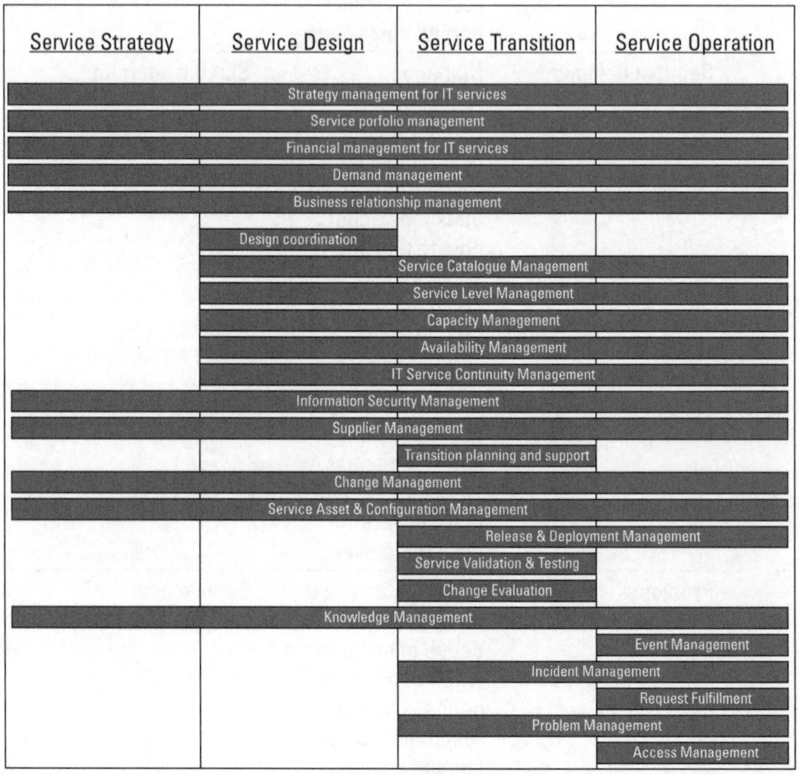

Service Strategy	Service Design	Service Transition	Service Operation

Strategy management for IT services

Service porfolio management

Financial management for IT services

Demand management

Business relationship management

Design coordination

Service Catalogue Management

Service Level Management

Capacity Management

Availability Management

IT Service Continuity Management

Information Security Management

Supplier Management

Transition planning and support

Change Management

Service Asset & Configuration Management

Release & Deployment Management

Service Validation & Testing

Change Evaluation

Knowledge Management

Event Management

Incident Management

Request Fulfillment

Problem Management

Access Management

© Crown copyright 2011. Reproduced under licence from the Cabinet Office.

Figure C-1: Processes across the lifecycle

Index

• A •

access, defined, 184
access management, 44, 50, 183–185, 193
access request, 183, 185
accreditation, 321, 332
activation stage of deployment, 288
activities. *See also specific service processes*
  application management, 59–60
  CSI, 44
  functions, relationship to, 46–49
  process function of, 30–31
  in projects, 45–46
  service lifecycle function, 38
  service operation, 43–44, 55–56
  service strategy, 40
  service transition, 42
  technology management, 57–58
activity-based demand management, 87
adopting compared to adapting ITIL
    processes, 228
advocacy function of business relationship
    management, 91
agile methods for application
    development, 270
alert, operational, 172, 333
analyse activities of service portfolio
    management, 77
APM Group (website), 319
application, defined, 333
application development, 58, 270, 284–285
application management, 47–48, 58–60,
    314–315, 333
application portfolio, 72
application sizing, 276
approve activities of service portfolio
    management, 77
asset, defined, 333
asset management, defined, 148
assets, IT. *See also* performance
  capacity management, 124, 126
  cost model, 79–81

defined, 343
  ITSM as strategic asset, 246
  prioritising for security purposes, 132
  process benefits, 30
  retirement of, 159
  SACM, 42, 222–223, 293–294
  service strategy, 40
  transfer of, 159
  value of, 27–29, 66–67
attributes of CIs, 149
audit, defined, 333
audit and verification, CMS, 153–154
authorisation of user requests, 182
automatic deployment option, 157
automation for service management, 93
availability, defined, 120, 333
availability aspect of warranty, 26
availability management, 41, 118–123, 133,
    223, 275

• B •

back-out plan for change build and test, 146
backup and restore of data, 55
baseline, 150, 200–201, 293–294, 334, 335
BCM (business capacity management), 126
BCM (business continuity management), 334
BIA (business impact analysis), ITSCM,
    129, 276, 334
big bang deployment option, 157
build phase
  authorising, 146
  coordinating, 146
  elements of, 283–285
  implementation function, 219–220
  overview, 46
  in release and deployment
      management, 158
  transition project, 292–295
bureaucracy, equating ITIL with added, 17
business acceptance and sign-off, 98, 283,
    286, 295–296

business capacity management (BCM), 126
business case
  building, 304–305
  for CSI, 199–200
  defined, 81–82, 334
  project initiation, relationship to, 45, 266
  in service portfolio management, 76, 260
business continuity management (BCM), 334
business impact analysis (BIA), ITSCM, 129, 276, 334
business outcomes, 20, 252–253, 254
business relationship management, 40, 76, 88–92, 310
business relationship manager (BRM), 334
business service catalogue, 109

• *C* •

CAB (change advisory board), 143, 334
Cabinet Office (websites), 319
capabilities, IT service, 22, 28–29, 66–67
capability, defined, 334
capability courses in ITIL qualification training, 327–328
Capability Maturity Model Integration (CMMI) (website), 322
capability review, 279
capacity aspect of warranty, 26
capacity management
  demand management, relationship to, 87, 125
  grouping options for implementation, 223
  overview, 41
  service design stage, 87, 123–127, 276
capacity plan, 126
capital costs, 80
categorising
  incidents, 177
  problems, 190
  suppliers, 115
  user requests, 182
CCM (component capacity management), 127
Central Computer and Telecommunications Agency (CCTA), 18
centralised service desk, 51, 52
change, defined, 142, 334
change advisory board (CAB), 143, 334
change authority, 146
change evaluation, 43, 145, 290–291, 295

change management. *See also* request for change (RFC)
  basic level for maximum control, 313
  change evaluation in, 145, 290
  configuration items, 149
  grouping options for implementation, 222
  implementation of ITIL project, 218, 219–220
  service transition function, 42, 141–147, 158, 293
change model, 143, 334
change proposal, 77–78, 143, 335
change record, 144, 147, 189, 335
change schedule, 145, 335
charter, defined, 78, 335
chartered services, 70
CI (configuration item), 149, 152–153, 335–336
classifying services, 253–254
closure
  change record, 147
  deployment, 159–160
  incident, 179
  problem, 191
  user requests, 183
cloud computing, 257, 269
CMDB (configuration management database), 149, 336
CMMI (Capability Maturity Model Integration) (website), 322
CMS (configuration management system)
  audit and verification, 153–154
  configuration items, relationship to, 152–153
  defined, 149, 194, 336
  example view, 150
  grouping ITIL processes, 222–223
  RFC recording, 144
  transition projects, 293–294
commodity supplier category, 115
communication, 170, 243–244, 306
complaints and compliments from customers, 91, 106–107, 181
component capacity management (CCM), 127
component testing, 286
confidentiality in security management, 133
configuration, defined, 335
configuration baseline, 150, 335

configuration control, 153

configuration identification in SACM, 151–153

configuration item (CI), 149, 152–153, 335–336

configuration management, defined, 148–149

configuration management database (CMDB), 149, 336

configuration management system (CMS)
  audit and verification, 153–154
  configuration items, relationship to, 152–153
  defined, 149, 194, 336
  example view, 150
  grouping ITIL processes, 222–223
  RFC recording, 144
  transition projects, 293–294

configuration record, 149, 153, 336

configuration structure, 336

console management, 55

continual service improvement (CSI)
  availability management, 123
  business relationship management, 92
  CSI approach, 202–204, 221
  Deming Cycle, 201–202
  governance link to, 210
  identifying roles, 212–213
  implementation function, 220
  introduction, 195
  measuring improvement, 204–209, 314
  overview, 44
  principles, 197–201
  purpose, 196–197
  risk analysis and management, 210–212
  service lifecycle function, 38, 44, 46, 198
  service portfolio, relationship to, 76
  technology support, 213

continuity aspect of warranty, 26, 27

continuity management, 41

contract, defined, 336

Control Objectives for Information and related Technology (COBIT) (website), 322

controls, security, 134, 135, 136

coordination of design, 115–116

corporate level SLA, 102

cost model, creating for service portfolio, 79–81

cost-benefit analysis, 81–82

costs
  assigning to service provider, 20
  quality of service compared to, 169
  resources compared to, 124

critical success factor (CSF), 205, 253, 336

CRM (customer relationship management), 81, 296

CSI (continual service improvement)
  availability management, 123
  business relationship management, 92
  CSI approach, 202–204, 221
  Deming Cycle, 201–202
  governance link to, 210
  identifying roles, 212–213
  implementation function, 220
  introduction, 195
  measuring improvement, 204–209, 314
  overview, 44
  principles, 197–201
  purpose, 196–197
  risk analysis and management, 210–212
  service lifecycle function, 38, 44, 46, 198
  service portfolio, relationship to, 76
  technology support, 213

CSI register, defined, 201

customer agreement portfolio, 89, 336

customer level multi-level SLA, 102

customer portfolio, 89, 337

customer relationship management (CRM), 81, 296

customer satisfaction, 102–103, 106

customer service, 11–13, 17, 22, 199.
    See also service desk

customer-based SLA, 102

customer-facing IT services, defined, 21

customers. *See also* users; value
    for customers
  basic SLM implementation, 309–310
  business relationship management, 40, 76, 88–92, 310
  complaints and compliments, 91, 106–107, 181
  CSI role of, 197
  defining, 24, 336
  demand management, 83–87
  identifying and understanding in defining services, 251–252

customers *(continued)*
  importance of service operation for,
      167–168
  outcomes of service changes for,
      20, 252–253, 254
  service performance monitoring and
      reporting, 104–106
  signing off on IT changes, 98, 283, 286,
      295–296

• *D* •

data
  backup and restore, 55
  in build during transition, 284
  CMDB, 149, 336
  defined, 161
  KEDB, 179, 187, 340
data protection, 132–133. *See also*
      information security management (ISM)
Data-to-Information-to-Knowledge-to-
      Wisdom (DIKW) model, 161–162, 337
define activities in service portfolio
      management, 76
defined process maturity (Level 3), 226
definitive media library (DML), 151, 337
delivery and support function in service
      lifecycle, 46
demand compared to supply in capacity
      management, 124
demand for service aspects of service
      portfolio management, 73
demand management
  capacity management, relationship to,
      87, 125
  overview, 40
  service design stage, 86
  service portfolio management, 260
  service strategy stage, 83–87, 260–264
  technology support, 93
Deming Cycle, 136, 201–202
deployment
  activities of, 158–160
  change evaluations during, 291
  defined, 155, 156, 337
  grouping options, 222
  implementation role, 220
  overview, 43, 147
  purpose, 154

terminology, 155–158
  transition projects, 287–288, 294
depreciation, defined, 80
design
  availability management, 118–123
  business relationship management, 92
  capacity management, 87, 123–127, 276
  coordination of design, 41, 115–116
  coordination of processes, 270–277
  demand management, 86
  identifying roles, 116, 137
  for implementation, 219, 227–232, 234–241
  information security management, 131–136
  introduction, 95–96, 117–118
  ITSCM, 128–131, 223, 276
  overview, 41–42
  principles, 96–98
  production of, 46
  project application, 265–270, 277–280
  purpose, 96
  service catalogue management, 107–110
  service level management, 98–107
  supplier management, 41, 110–115, 120, 274
  technology support, 137
  testing outline, 294–295
diagnostic tools, 194
differentiated offering development, 87
DIKW (Data-to-Information-to-Knowledge-
      to-Wisdom) model, 161–162, 337
direct costs, 80
directory services, defined, 184
disaster recovery (ITSCM), 128–131, 223, 276
discovery/deployment/licensing
      technology, 194
distribution stage of deployment, 287
DML (definitive media library), 151, 337
documenting
  change record, 144, 147, 189, 335
  configuration record, 149, 153, 336
  incident record, 177, 339
  for ITIL adoption, 306–307
  known error record, 191, 340
  problem record, 341
  process implementation, 240–241
  release record, 342
  requirements, 266
  RFC, 144
downtime, decreasing for availability, 121

• E •

early-life support (ELS), 159, 295
ECAB (emergency change advisory board), 143, 337
effectiveness, defined, 337
efficiency, defined, 337
Eight Steps to Transforming Your Organization, 242
ELS (early-life support), 159, 295
emergency change, 142–143, 337
emergency change advisory board (ECAB), 143, 337
end-to-end IT service, 21
environment, defined, 337
escalation, incident, 179, 338
event, defined, 171–172, 338
event correlation, 173
event detection, 173
event filtering, 173
event logging, 173
event management, 43, 170–174, 193
event notification, 172–173
examination institutes (website), 320, 332
examinations for ITIL qualifications, 320, 330–331, 332
exception event, 172
exception report, 105
expert level, ITIL qualification, 329
external business view compared to internal IT view, 169
external compared to internal customer, 24
external IT environment, strategic assessment, 247
external service provider (Type III), 23, 67, 257–258, 347

• F •

facilities management, 56, 338
financial aspects of service portfolio management, 73
financial asset management, 148
financial benefit, analysing for CSI, 200
financial management
  grouping options for implementation, 223, 224
  overview, 40

service strategy stage, 78–83, 260
technology support, 93
first-line support, 192, 338
fit for purpose, making a service, 25–26, 66
fit for use, making a service, 26–27, 66
fixed asset management, defined, 148
follow-the-sun service desk, 51, 53
forecasting of demand, identifying sources of, 86
foundation level, ITIL qualification, 18, 326–327, 330
functional escalation of an incident, 179, 338
functional requirements, 267
functions. *See also* service lifecycle
  application management, 58–60
  defined, 338
  operations management, 54–56
  outline of, 46–49
  overview, 31–32, 33
  service desk, 49–54
  technical management, 56–58

• G •

Gantt chart, 235
governance, 35, 210, 338
Graham, Nick (author)
  PRINCE2 For Dummies, 304
grouping ITIL processes for implementation, 222–224

• H •

hierarchical escalation of an incident, 179, 338

• I •

identity, user, 184, 185
impact, defined, 338
implementation. *See also* deployment; service transition
  designing processes, 227–232
  example project, 232–241
  function in service lifecycle, 46, 219–220, 224–225
  introduction, 217
  planning, 218–226, 233–234, 304

implementation *(continued)*
   of service strategy, 219, 249–250
   staff buy-in considerations, 241–244
   transition project, 292–295
improvement process, 207–209. *See also*
      continual service improvement (CSI)
incident, defined, 175, 338, 340
incident management
   decreasing downtime, 120, 121
   escalation types, 179, 338
   grouping options, 223
   overview, 43
   problem management, relationship to,
      174–175, 188–189, 313–314
   roles for, 192
   as service desk responsibility, 50
   service operation stage, 56, 174–179
incident model, 176
incident record, 177, 339
indirect costs, 80
information, defined, 161
information requests from users, 181
information security management (ISM),
      41, 131–136, 276–277
information security management system
      (ISMS), 135–136
information security policy, 134–135, 136,
      184, 339
informational event type, 171
infrastructure in build during transition, 284
initial process maturity (Level 1), 225
initiate process activities of service
      portfolio management, 76
installation stage of deployment, 287
integrated IT service management toolsets,
      177, 314–315
integrity in security management, 133
intermediate level, ITIL qualification,
      327–328, 330–331
internal compared to external customer, 24
internal IT environment, strategic
      assessment, 247
internal IT view compared to external
      business view, 169
internal service provider (Type I), 23, 67,
      255–257, 347
Internet as resource for IT improvement,
      318–319

Internet provider, 10
investigation and diagnosis of a problem, 190
investigation and diagnosis of an
      incident, 179
invitation to tender (ITT) process, 113
ISM (information security management),
      41, 131–136, 276–277
ISMS (information security management
      system), 135–136
ISO/IEC 20000 (international standard)
      (website), 321
IT infrastructure, defined, 339
IT operations, defined, 339. *See also*
      service operation
IT operations control, 55, 339
IT operations management, defined, 339
IT outsourcer, 10
IT service, defined, 10, 21, 49, 339. *See also*
      service lifecycle
IT service continuity management (ITSCM),
      128–131, 276
IT service continuity plan, defined, 339
IT service management (ITSM)
   as customer service, 11–13, 22
   defined, 10, 19–20, 21–22, 339, 345
   design projects, 270–272
   as strategic asset, 246
   strategy's role in, 65
IT Service Management Forum (ITSMF)
      (website), 321
IT service provider
   assigning costs to, 20
   defined, 10, 339, 345, 347
   types, 22–23, 67, 255–258
IT Skeptic (website), 319
ITIL® (Information Technology
      Infrastructure Library®). *See also*
      specific topics
   adopting compared to adapting
      processes, 228
   best practices overview, 13–14
   complementary approaches for IT, 321–322
   content overview, 15
   as guidance rather than prescription, 308
   help resources, 317–322
   history, 18
   introduction, 1–5
   misconceptions, 16–17

processes cross-reference, 349–354
qualifications, 14, 18, 325–332
service management as customer service, 11–13, 22
structure
  application management, 47–48, 58–60, 314–315, 333
  functions outline, 46–49
  introduction, 37
  operations management, 43–44, 54–56
  service desk, 49–54
  service lifecycle, 37–46
  technical management, 47, 56–58, 346
terminology definitions, 10
ITIL Continual Service Improvement, 220
ITIL Live (website), 320
ITSM (IT service management)
  as customer service, 11–13, 22
  defined, 10, 19–20, 21–22, 339, 345
  design projects, 270–272
  as strategic asset, 246
  strategy's role in, 65
ITSMF (IT Service Management Forum) (website), 321
ITT (invitation to tender) process, 113

• J •

job scheduling operations function, 56

• K •

KEDB (known error database), 179, 187, 340
key performance indicators (KPIs), 34, 205, 236, 339–340
knock down dominoes in known error management, 189
knowledge, defined, 161
knowledge management, 43, 160–163, 337, 344
knowledge transfer, 162
known error, defined, 187, 340
known error database (KEDB), 179, 187, 340
known error record, 191, 340
Kotter, John P. (researcher), 242
KPIs (key performance indicators), 34, 205, 236, 339–340

• L •

Level 1 - initial process maturity, 225
Level 2 - repeatable process maturity, 226
Level 3 - defined process maturity, 226
Level 4 - managed process maturity, 226
Level 5 - optimising process maturity, 226
licensing technology, 194
lifecycle, service. *See also individual stages*
  application management function, 47–48, 58–60, 314–315, 333
  applying to IT projects, 45–46
  availability management function, 41, 119
  business relationship management, 92
  CSI function, 38, 44, 46, 198
  defined, 37–38
  demand management, 86
  as implementation tool, 46, 219–220, 224–225
  overview, 37–39
  risk management's function, 211–212
  service design stage, 41–42
  service operation stage, 43–44
  service strategy stage, 39–41, 69–70
  service transition stage, 42–43, 140
  technical management function, 57–58
live environment, 167, 320. *See also* service operation
local service desk, 51, 52
logging
  access, 185
  event, 173
  problem, 189–190
  user requests, 182
logical configuration model, 149

• M •

maintainability, defined, 120
major incident, 176, 340
managed process maturity (Level 4), 226
management requirements, 267
Managing across the Lifecycle course, 329, 331
manual deployment option, 157
market space definition, 247–248, 251–252, 254

master level, ITIL qualification, 330
maturity of service management
  processes, 225–226, 233–234, 322
mean time between failures (MTBF), 120, 340
mean time between service incidents
  (MTBSI), 120, 340
mean time to repair (MTTR), 340
mean time to restore service (MTRS),
  120, 340
measurement systems aspect of design, 97
measuring improvement, 204–209, 314
metrics for processes, 204, 205, 206, 236, 341
modelling during design project, 276
MOF (Microsoft Operations Framework)
  (website), 318
MTBF (mean time between failures), 120, 340
MTBSI (mean time between service
  incidents), 120, 340
MTRS (mean time to restore service),
  120, 340
MTTR (mean time to repair), 340
multi-level SLAs, 102

• *N* •

network administration, 185
network operations centre (NOC), 56
new suppliers, dealing with, 113–114

• *O* •

objectives of process, 235, 248, 256
Office of Government Commerce (OGC),
  18, 319
OLA (operational level agreement), 99, 104,
  274, 311, 341
operation, service
  access management, 183–185
  business relationship management, 92
  demand management, 86
  event management, 43, 170–174, 193
  identifying roles, 191–193
  implementation function, 220
  incident management, 56, 174–179
  introduction, 167–168
  overview, 43–44, 54–56
  principles, 169–170
  problem management, 56, 186–191

purpose, 168–169
  request fulfilment, 179–183, 185
  technology support, 194
operational alert, 172, 333
operational costs, 80
operational demand management, 87
operational environment, 167. *See also*
  service operation
operational level agreement (OLA), 99, 104,
  274, 311, 341
operational readiness testing, 286
operational requirements, 267
operational supplier category, 115
operations bridge, 56, 341
optimising process maturity (Level 5), 226
OSA (operational support and analysis)
  course, 328
outcome of process, defined, 235
outcomes, business, 20, 252–253, 254
outsourcing IT services, 10, 111, 341

• *P* •

pattern of business activity (PBA), 85–86,
  261–263, 341
patterns of action, adopting, strategy
  assessment, 249, 257, 258
people involvement for ITIL adoption. *See*
  staff and staffing; stakeholders
performance
  capacity management, 126
  KPIs, 34, 205, 236, 339–340
  monitoring and reporting, 104–106
  supplier, 114
perspective, determining, in strategy
  creation, 248, 256, 258
phased approach deployment option, 157
physical environment in build during
  transition, 284
pilot deployment, 158, 294
pipeline, service, 69–70, 345
planning
  for adopting and adapting ITIL, 304
  implementation, 218–226, 233–234, 304
  involving people in, 242
  strategic, 249, 257, 258
  tests, 286–287
  transition, 42, 163–164, 293

planning, protection and optimisation (PPO) course, 328
policies
  governance, relationship to, 35
  information security, 134–135, 136, 184, 339
  release, 157–158, 294
  writing, 236
portfolio, defined, 70. *See also* service portfolio management
position, forming, in strategy creation, 248–249, 257, 258
post implementation review, 147
PPO (planning, protection and optimisation) course, 328
PRINCE2 For Dummies (Graham), 304
print and output operations function, 56
prioritising
  assets for security purposes, 132
  incidents, 177–178
  problems, 190
  user requests, 182
priority, defined, 341
priority codes for incidents, 178
privileges or rights, managing, 184, 185
proactive availability management, 121–123
proactive compared to reactive operations, 170
proactive problem management, 187, 341
problem, defined, 186, 341
problem management
  decreasing downtime, 121
  grouping options for implementation, 223
  incident management, balancing with, 174–175, 188–189, 313–314
  overview, 44
  proactive, 187, 341
  roles for, 193
  service operation stage, 56, 186–191
problem models, 187
problem record, 341
procedures, 35, 228–232, 238, 239, 341
process flow diagram, 230, 238, 240
process manager, 34
process maturity framework, 225–226
process metrics, 204

process model, 227
process owner, 34, 212
process practitioner, 35
processes. *See also* implementation; *specific processes*
  as aspect of design, 97
  defined, 13, 30, 341
  flexibility from, 15
  overview, 30–31, 32, 33
procurement, 113
production environment, 167. *See also* service operation
professional peers as IT improvement resources, 317–318
project management
  activities overview, 45–46
  business case, 45, 266
  change management, 218, 219–220
  implementation example, 232–241
  service design
    availability management, 275
    capacity management, 276
    coordinating processes, 272
    example project, 277–280
    information security, 276–277
    introduction, 265
    ITSCM, 276
    process overview, 270–272
    requirements, 266–267, 273–275
    solution design, 267–270
    supplier management, 274
  service transition
    build, test and implement phase, 292–295
    business acceptance and sign-off, 295–296
    change evaluation, 290–291
    example, 296–299
    introduction, 281–282
    linking of processes, 291–292
    overview, 283–288
    service validation and testing, 288–290, 294–295
project portfolio, 72
projected service outage (PSO), 342
push compared to pull deployment options, 157

• Q •

qualifications, ITIL, 14, 18, 325–332
quality management methods, 199,
     201–204. *See also* continual service
     improvement (CSI)
quality of service compared to cost, 169

• R •

RACI matrix, 229–230, 237, 342
RAG chart, 105
rapid application development (RAD), 270
rationalising a service decision, 77
RCV (release control and validation)
     course, 328
reactive availability management, 123
reactive compared to proactive
     operations, 170
reactive problem management, 187, 341
recovering from service failure, 121
re-factoring a service decision, 77
release, defined, 155, 156, 342
release and deployment management
   activities of, 158–160
   grouping options, 222
   overview, 43, 147
   purpose, 154
   terminology, 155–158
   transition projects, 294
release control and validation (RCV)
     course, 328
release package, 156–157, 342
release policy, 157–158, 294
release record, 342
release unit, 156
reliability, defined, 120, 342
remediation, 146, 342
remote control, 194
renewal or termination of supplier
     contracts, 114
renewing a service decision, 77
repeatable process maturity (Level 2), 226
replacing a service decision, 77
reporting
   dashboards for service operation, 194
   service performance, 104–106
   service portfolio status, 74

status accounting for CIs, 153
supplier performance, 114
request for change (RFC)
   business relationship management, 91
   change management process, 78, 292
   creating and recording, 144
   defined, 143, 342
   reviewing, 145
request fulfilment
   grouping options for implementation, 223
   overview, 44
   roles for, 193
   as service desk responsibility, 50
   service operation stage, 179–183, 185
request model, 181, 342–343
requirements gathering and analysis
   documenting, 266
   overview, 46
   service level management, 273–274
   SLRs, 101, 103–104, 119, 345
   SOR, 274
   supplier management, 274
   types of requirements, 267
resilience, 120, 121, 343
resolution, problem, 191
resolution and recovery of an incident, 179
resources, IT, 343. *See also* assets, IT
response selection for events, 173
response time, 343
responsiveness compared to stability, 169
retail customer view, service catalogue, 109
retaining a service decision, 77
retired services in service portfolio
     management, 70, 77
retirement of assets, deployment phase, 159
return on investment (ROI), 73, 200, 343
reviews
   capability, 279
   change process, 145, 147
   event, 174
   major problem, 191
   release and deployment, 159–160
   service, 104–105
   user request, 182
RFC (request for change)
   business relationship management, 91
   change management process, 78, 292
   creating and recording, 144

defined, 143, 342
reviewing, 145
rights or privileges, managing, 184, 185
risk, defined, 210, 343
risk analysis and management
CSI stage, 210–212
information security, 132, 134, 136
ITSCM, 129–130, 276
ROI (return on investment), 73, 200, 343
role, defined, 343
roles and responsibilities
CSI, 212–213
implementation design, 237–238, 239
overview, 32–35
processes, compared to, 90
service design, 116, 137
service operation, 191–193
service transition, 164
root cause, 343

• **S** •

SaaS (software as a service), 253
SAC (service acceptance criteria),
283, 343–344
SACM (service asset and configuration
management), 42, 222–223, 293–294
Sarbanes-Oxley Act (2002), 210
SCM (service capacity management), 127
SCMIS (supplier and contract management
information system), 112, 114–115
scope of change management process, 144
SDP (service design package)
defined, 97–98, 344
design process function, 272
SAC and testing, 282
service transition function, 140, 163
second line support, 343
security aspect of warranty, 26
security management, 41, 131–136, 184,
276–277, 339
self-help technology, 181, 194
service, defined, 10, 19–21, 343
service acceptance criteria (SAC),
283, 343–344
service acceptance testing, 286

service asset and configuration management
(SACM), 42, 222–223, 293–294
service capacity management (SCM), 127
service catalogue
defined, 344
overview, 41
as quick win, 312
service design stage, 107–110
service portfolio management, 70, 259
service charter, defined, 344
service contract, defined, 344
service design
availability management, 118–123
business relationship management, 92
capacity management, 87, 123–127, 276
coordination of design, 41, 115–116
coordination of processes, 270–277
demand management, 86
identifying roles, 116, 137
for implementation, 219, 227–232, 234–241
information security management, 131–136
introduction, 95–96, 117–118
ITSCM, 128–131, 223, 276
overview, 41–42
principles, 96–98
production of, 46
project application, 265–270, 277–280
purpose, 96
service catalogue management, 107–110
service level management, 98–107
supplier management, 41, 110–115, 120, 274
technology support, 137
testing outline, 294–295
service design package (SDP)
defined, 97–98, 344
design process function, 272
SAC and testing, 282
service transition function, 140, 163
service desk, 49–54, 176, 223, 312, 344
service improvement, 13. *See also*
continual service improvement (CSI)
service improvement plan (SIP),
103, 199, 344
service knowledge management
system (SKMS), 162, 163, 344.
See also configuration management
system (CMS)

service level agreement (SLA)
  creating, 104
  customer satisfaction, relationship to,
    102–103
  customer's role, 24
  defined, 21, 99, 100–101, 344–345
  frameworks, 101–102
  incident definition, 175
  introducing as quick win, 310–311
  measurement definitions, 208
  reviewing, 104
  revising, 104
  sample, 100
  service desk, relationship to, 50
  SLRs, 101
  UCs, 99, 101, 104, 274, 347
service level management (SLM)
  business relationship management
    compared to, 89
  CSI, relationship to, 198–199
  grouping options for implementation, 224
  implementing basic, 309–310
  overview, 41
  service design stage, 98–107, 273–274
  supplier management, relationship to, 112
service level requirements (SLRs), 101,
    103–104, 119, 345
service level SLA, 102
service level target, 24, 87, 198–199, 345
service lifecycle. *See also individual stages*
  application management function, 47–48,
    58–60, 314–315, 333
  applying to IT projects, 45–46
  availability management function, 41, 119
  business relationship management, 92
  CSI function, 38, 44, 46, 198
  defined, 37–38
  demand management, 86
  as implementation tool, 46, 219–220,
    224–225
  overview, 37–39
  risk management's function, 211–212
  service design stage, 41–42
  service operation stage, 43–44
  service strategy stage, 39–41, 69–70
  service transition stage, 42–43, 140
  technical management function, 57–58

service management. *See* IT service
    management (ITSM)
service metrics, 204
service model, 254
service offerings and agreements (SOA)
    course, 328
service operation
  access management, 183–185
  business relationship management, 92
  demand management, 86
  event management, 43, 170–174, 193
  identifying roles, 191–193
  implementation function, 220
  incident management, 56, 174–179
  introduction, 167–168
  overview, 43–44, 54–56
  principles, 169–170
  problem management, 56, 186–191
  purpose, 168–169
  request fulfilment, 179–183, 185
  technology support, 194
service oriented architecture, 269–270
service owner, 33, 212, 345
service pipeline, 69–70, 345
service portfolio, defined, 69–70, 345.
    See also service catalogue
service portfolio management
  activities, 75–78
  applicability of, 75
  cost model, 79–81
  financial management, relationship to, 82
  overview, 40
  service catalogue, 70, 259
  service strategy function, 65, 259–260
  technology support, 92
  terminology, 69–74
service provider, defined, 345. *See also* IT
    service provider
service request, 181, 345
service reviews, 105
service solutions aspect of design, 97
service strategy
  asset defining, 246
  business relationship management, 88–92
  creating, 246–250
  defining, 64
  demand management, 83–87, 260–264

examples, 255–258
financial management, 78–83, 260
implementation function, 219, 249–250
introduction, 63–64
overview, 39–41
principles, 66
process overview, 68–69
purpose, 65–66
service defining, 251–255
service portfolio management, 65, 69–78, 259–260
supplier management, 113, 115
technology support, 92–93
value for customers, 66–67, 252–253
service testing. *See* testing
service transition
  business relationship management, 92
  change management, 42, 141–147, 158, 293
  demand management, 86
  identifying roles, 164
  implementation function, 219–220
  introduction, 139
  knowledge management, 43, 160–163, 337, 344
  overview, 42–43
  planning and support for, 42, 163–164, 293
  processes overview, 140–141
  projects
    build, test and implement phase, 292–295
    business acceptance and sign-off, 295–296
    change evaluation, 290–291
    example, 296–299
    introduction, 281–282
    linking of processes, 291–292
    overview, 283–288
    service validation and testing, 288–290, 294–295
  purpose, 139–140
  release and deployment management, 154–160, 287–288
  SACM, 148–154
  supplier management, 114
  technology support, 165
service validation and testing, 43, 288–290, 294–295
serviceability, defined, 120, 345
service-based SLA, 102

services or service groups, defined, 184
seven-step improvement process, 207–209
SFIA (Skills Framework for the Information Age) (website), 322
shared costs, 80
shared services provider (Type II), 23, 67, 347
single point of contact (SPOC), 49, 346
single point of failure (SPOF), 121, 346
SIP (service improvement plan), 103, 199, 344
Six Sigma (website), 322
Skills Framework for the Information Age (SFIA) (website), 322
SKMS (service knowledge management system), 162, 163, 344. *See also* configuration management system (CMS)
SLA (service level agreement)
  creating, 104
  customer satisfaction, relationship to, 102–103
  customer's role, 24
  defined, 21, 99, 100–101, 344–345
  frameworks, 101–102
  incident definition, 175
  introducing as quick win, 310–311
  measurement definitions, 208
  reviewing, 104
  revising, 104
  sample, 100
  service desk, relationship to, 50
  SLRs, 101
  UCs, 99, 101, 104, 274, 347
SLAM chart, 105
SLM (service level management)
  business relationship management compared to, 89
  CSI, relationship to, 198–199
  grouping options for implementation, 224
  implementing basic, 309–310
  overview, 41
  service design stage, 98–107, 273–274
  supplier management, relationship to, 112
SLR (service level requirements), 101, 103–104, 119, 345
snapshot, configuration, defined, 150, 346

SOA (service offerings and agreements) course, 328
software as a service (SaaS), 253
software development, 58, 270, 284–285
software management, 47–48, 58–60, 314–315, 333
solution design for service management, 268–270
SOR (statement of requirements), 274
SPOC (single point of contact), 49, 346
SPOF (single point of failure), 121, 346
stability compared to responsiveness, 169
staff and staffing
  allocating roles and responsibilities, 228–232
  application management, 59
  implementation considerations, 241–244
  service desk, 53–54
  technical management, 56–57
  training, importance in adopting ITIL, 307, 315
stakeholders. *See also* customers; users
  business acceptance and sign-off, 98, 283, 286, 295–296
  business requirements engineering, 266
  defined, 346
  involving in ITIL adoption, 305–306
  process implementation buy-in, 243
  suppliers, 24–25, 112, 346
  types, 23–24
  vision, detailing for ITIL use, 304
standard change type, 142, 181, 346
statement of requirements (SOR), 274
status accounting for CIs, 153
status report, service portfolio, 74
strategic assessment, 247–249, 255, 257, 258
strategic objectives, establishing, 248, 256
strategy, defined, 64, 346. *See also* service strategy
structure of ITIL
  application management, 47–48, 58–60, 314–315, 333
  functions outline, 46–49
  introduction, 37
  operations management, 43–44, 54–56
  service desk, 49–54
  service lifecycle, 37–46
  technical management, 47, 56–58, 346

super user, 346
supplier, defined, 24, 112, 346
supplier and contract management information system (SCMIS), 112, 114–115
supplier management, 41, 110–115, 120, 274
supply compared to demand in capacity management, 124
supporting services, 21, 46, 109, 284
surveys of customer satisfaction, 106
swimline diagram, 230–231
SWOT analysis, 255–256, 258
synergy, defined, 222
system administration, 185
system architecture considerations, 269–270
system testing, 286

• *T* •

tactical supplier category, 115
target market definition, 251–252
technical management, 47, 56–58, 346
technical service catalogue, 109
technology architecture systems aspect of design, 97
technology metrics, 204
technology support
  activities overview, 57–58
  automating implementation of processes, 241
  CSI stage, 213
  event management, 170–174
  service design stage, 137
  service operation stage, 181, 194
  service strategy stage, 92–93
  service transitions stage, 165
termination or renewal of supplier contracts, 114
terminology definitions, 10
testing
  authorising, 146
  coordinating, 146
  implementation function, 219–220
  overview, 46
  release and deployment management, 158
  in service validation, 43, 288–290, 294–295
  in transition project, 285–287, 292–295

third party, defined, 346
third-line support, 347
third-party supplier management, 41,
 110–115, 120, 274
three-view service catalogue, 109
tools, operational, defined, 172
traffic chart, 105
training
 examinations, 320, 330–331, 332
 importance in adopting ITIL, 307, 315
 ITIL as, 16
 qualification, 14, 18, 325–332
 service desk, 53–54
transfer of assets, deployment phase, 159
transition, service
 business relationship management, 92
 change management, 42, 141–147, 158, 293
 demand management, 86
 identifying roles, 164
 implementation function, 219–220
 introduction, 139
 knowledge management, 43, 160–163, 163,
  337, 344
 overview, 42–43
 planning and support for, 42, 163–164, 293
 processes overview, 140–141
 projects
  build, test and implement phase, 292–295
  business acceptance and sign-off, 295–296
  change evaluation, 290–291
  example, 296–299
  introduction, 281–282
  linking of processes, 291–292
  overview, 283–288
  service validation and testing, 288–290,
   294–295
 purpose, 139–140
 release and deployment management,
  154–160, 287–288
 SACM, 148–154
 supplier management, 114
 technology support, 165
triggers for processes, 76, 91, 236
troubleshooting. *See* problem management
two-view service catalogue, 109
Type I, internal service provider, 23, 67,
 255–257, 347

Type II, shared services provider, 23, 67, 347
Type III, external service provider, 23, 67,
 257–258, 347

• U •

UK Government Cabinet Office
 (websites), 319
underpinning contracts (UCs), 99, 101, 104,
 274, 347
unique selling point (USP), 248–249
uptime, increasing for availability, 121
urgency, defined, 347
usability requirements, 267
user profile, 85
users. *See also* request fulfilment
 access management, 44, 50, 183–185, 193
 complaints or compliments from, 181
 defined, 23–24, 347
 incident resolution role of, 179
 service desk, 49–54, 176, 223, 312, 344
 super user, 346
USP (unique selling point), 248–249
utility factor, 25–26, 66, 253, 285, 347

• V •

validation and testing, 43, 288–290, 294–295
validation of user requests, 182
value for customers
 creating, 25–27
 IT resources, 27–28, 66–67
 operations management function, 54
 service definition, 20
 service desk function, 49
 service management purpose, 22
 service strategy stage, 66–67, 252–253
value of investment (VOI), 200
value of IT service assets, 27–29
value proposition, defined, 25–27, 66
VBF (vital business function), 347
verification
 CMS, 153–154
 user identity, 185
views, service catalogue, 109
virtual service desk, 51, 53
vision, detailing for ITIL use, 303–304

vital business function (VBF), 347
V-model, 289, 290
VOI (value of investment), 200

• *W* •

warning event type, 172
warranty
    availability management, 118–123
    capacity management, 87, 123–127, 276
    defined, 347–348
    in design project, 274–275
    grouping options for implementation, 224
    identifying service design roles, 137

information security management, 131–136
introduction, 117–118
ITSCM, 128–131, 223, 276
testing for, 285
in value for customer, 26–27, 66, 253
websites. *See specific websites*
wholesale customer view, service
    catalogue, 109
wisdom, defined, 161
work instruction, defined, 348
work order, defined, 348
workaround, defined, 187, 348
workflow or process engine technology, 194

Notes

Notes

FOR DUMMIES®

Making Everything Easier! ™

UK editions

BUSINESS

978-0-470-97626-5

978-0-470-97211-3

978-1-119-97527-4

REFERENCE

978-0-470-68637-9

978-0-470-97450-6

978-0-470-74535-9

HOBBIES

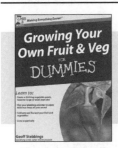

978-0-470-69960-7

978-0-470-68641-6

978-0-470-68178-7

Asperger's Syndrome For Dummies
978-0-470-66087-4

Basic Maths For Dummies
978-1-119-97452-9

Boosting Self-Esteem For Dummies
978-0-470-74193-1

British Sign Language
For Dummies
978-0-470-69477-0

Cricket For Dummies
978-0-470-03454-5

Diabetes For Dummies, 3rd Edition
978-0-470-97711-8

English Grammar For Dummies
978-0-470-05752-0

Flirting For Dummies
978-0-470-74259-4

IBS For Dummies
978-0-470-51737-6

Improving Your Relationship
For Dummies
978-0-470-68472-6

Keeping Chickens For Dummies
978-1-119-99417-6

Lean Six Sigma For Dummies
978-0-470-75626-3

Management For Dummies,
2nd Edition
978-0-470-97769-9

Neuro-linguistic Programming
For Dummies, 2nd Edition
978-0-470-66543-5

Nutrition For Dummies, 2nd Edition
978-0-470-97276-2

A world of resources to help you grow

UK editions

SELF–HELP

978-0-470-66541-1

978-1-119-99264-6

Mindfulness

978-0-470-66086-7

STUDENTS

978-0-470-68820-5

978-0-470-74711-7

978-1-119-99134-2

HISTORY

978-0-470-**68792**-5

978-0-470-74783-4

978-0-470-97819-1

Origami Kit For Dummies
978-0-470-75857-1

Overcoming Depression For Dummies
978-0-470-69430-5

Positive Psychology For Dummies
978-0-470-72136-0

PRINCE2 For Dummies, 2009 Edition
978-0-470-71025-8

Project Management For Dummies
978-0-470-71119-4

Psychometric Tests For Dummies
978-0-470-75366-8

Reading the Financial Pages
For Dummies
978-0-470-71432-4

Rugby Union For Dummies, 3rd Edition
978-1-119-99092-5

Sage 50 Accounts For Dummies
978-0-470-71558-1

Self-Hypnosis For Dummies
978-0-470-66073-7

Study Skills For Dummies
978-0-470-74047-7

Teaching English as a Foreign Language
For Dummies
978-0-470-74576-2

Time Management For Dummies
978-0-470-77765-7

Training Your Brain For Dummies
978-0-470-97449-0

Work-Life Balance For Dummies
978-0-470-71380-8

Writing a Dissertation For Dummies
978-0-470-74270-9

FOR DUMMIES®

The easy way to get more done and have more fun

LANGUAGES

978-0-470-68815-1
UK Edition

978-1-118-00464-7

978-0-470-90101-4

MUSIC

978-0-470-97799-6
UK Edition

978-0-470-66603-6
Lay-flat, UK Edition

978-0-470-66372-1
UK Edition

SCIENCE & MATHS

978-0-470-59875-7

978-0-470-55964-2

978-0-470-55174-5

Art For Dummies
978-0-7645-5104-8

Bass Guitar For Dummies, 2nd Edition
978-0-470-53961-3

Criminology For Dummies
978-0-470-39696-4

Currency Trading For Dummies,
2nd Edition
978-1-118-01851-4

Drawing For Dummies, 2nd Edition
978-0-470-61842-4

Forensics For Dummies
978-0-7645-5580-0

Guitar For Dummies, 2nd Edition
978-0-7645-9904-0

Hinduism For Dummies
978-0-470-87858-3

Index Investing For Dummies
978-0-470-29406-2

Knitting For Dummies, 2nd Edition
978-0-470-28747-7

Music Theory For Dummies, 2nd Edition
978-1-118-09550-8

Piano For Dummies, 2nd Edition
978-0-470-49644-2

Physics For Dummies, 2nd Edition
978-0-470-90324-7

Schizophrenia For Dummies
978-0-470-25927-6

Sex For Dummies, 3rd Edition
978-0-470-04523-7

Sherlock Holmes For Dummies
978-0-470-48444-9

Solar Power Your Home
For Dummies, 2nd Edition
978-0-470-59678-4

Available wherever books are sold. For more information or to order direct go to www.wiley.com or call +44 (0) 1243 843291

32812 (p3)

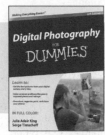

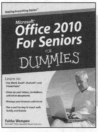
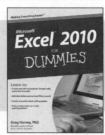